Advance Praise for

Staying the Course with Professional Development Schools

"This second volume of Towson University's three-part series on professional development schools conceptualizes the growth of school and university partnerships across state and national levels. *Staying the Course with Professional Development Schools* illustrates the growth of the professional development school movement from each partnership addressing individual needs to providing information for partnerships across the country as the movement continues to grow and mature."

Sally Yahnke, Associate Professor,
Secondary Education, Kansas State University

Staying the Course with Professional Development Schools

PETER LANG
New York • Washington, D.C./Baltimore • Bern
Frankfurt am Main • Berlin • Brussels • Vienna • Oxford

Staying the Course with Professional Development Schools

EDITED BY
Jane E. Neapolitan
Terry R. Berkeley

PETER LANG
New York • Washington, D.C./Baltimore • Bern
Frankfurt am Main • Berlin • Brussels • Vienna • Oxford

Library of Congress Cataloging-in-Publication Data

Staying the course with professional development schools /
edited by Jane E. Neapolitan and Terry R. Berkeley.
p. cm.
Includes bibliographical references and index.
1. Laboratory schools—United States. 2. Teachers—Training of—
United States. I. Neapolitan, Jane E.
LB2154.A3S72   370'.71'1—dc22   2004018797
ISBN 0-8204-7601-3

Bibliographic information published by **Die Deutsche Bibliothek**.
Die Deutsche Bibliothek lists this publication in the "Deutsche
Nationalbibliografie"; detailed bibliographic data is available
on the Internet at http://dnb.ddb.de/.

Cover design by Lisa Barfield

© 2005 Peter Lang Publishing, Inc., New York
275 Seventh Avenue, 28th Floor, New York, NY 10001
www.peterlangusa.com

All rights reserved.
Reprint or reproduction, even partially, in all forms such as microfilm,
xerography, microfiche, microcard, and offset strictly prohibited.

Contents

Acknowledgments.. ix

Foreword... xi
Lee Teitel

PART ONE
BUILDING AND NURTURING THE PROFESSIONAL DEVELOPMENT SCHOOL

1 Addressing an Emergency in Teacher Education: The Evolution of a Professional Development School for Emerging Professionals 3
James S. Cantor & Sue A. Schaar

2 Collaborating to Renew and Reform K–16 Education 21
Sally Yahnke, Gail Shroyer, Lisa Bietau, Melisa Hancock, & Andrew Bennett

3 PDS First Steps: Baby Steps and Giant Steps 37
Jennifer E. Aldrich

PART TWO
MAINTAINING, SUSTAINING, AND SUPPORTING THE PROFESSIONAL DEVELOPMENT SCHOOL

4 Cross-Currents of Change: PDS Maintenance 47
Martha M. Mobley & Nancy Norris-Bauer

5   PDS Collaboration: Providing Opportunities for Systemic Change...... 55
Clare Kruft

6   Sound Ways of Learning: Anchoring Music Education to the
PDS P–16 Reform Movement 67
Carol Frierson-Campbell

7   Using Literature Circles to Research Instructional Strategies 79
Teena R. Gorrow & John R. Bing

8   Empowering Interns as Partners in Mentoring..................... 83
Frank Sweeney, Roberta Strosnider, & Jo Ellen Smallwood

PART THREE:
SHAPING THE PROFESSIONAL DEVELOPMENT
SCHOOL THROUGH STANDARDS

9   Co-Constructing an Accountability System for Professional
Development Schools.. 97
Marsha Levine & Roberta Trachtman

10   Systematic Evaluation in PDS-Centered Educator Preparation:
Turning State and National Accreditation Standards
to Program Advantage 127
Mary Gendernalik Cooper

11   Teacher Candidates Document Professional Growth by Connecting
Theory to Practice in a Rural Clinical Setting 143
Dennis R. King & Cherie L. Roy

PART FOUR:
DETERMINING THE IMPACTS OF PROFESSIONAL
DEVELOPMENT SCHOOLS THROUGH RESEARCH

12   Service Learning: Where the Action Is!.......................... 153
Diane Davis, RaeAnn T. Wuestman, Betty Kansler, & Linda Williams

13   Measuring the Perceived Competency of Physical Education Interns:
A Two-Year Analysis of the Physical Education Professional
Development School 165
Marybeth P. Miller, Patricia Rawson, & Carl Holmes

14 Inquiry in Professional Development Schools:
The "Misunderstood" Component............................ 179
Jane E. Neapolitan & Terry R. Berkeley

List of Contributors 191

Index.. 197

Acknowledgments

In the first volume of this three-volume series on Professional Development Schools (PDS), we recognized the important contributions of Dennis Hinkle, the late dean of Towson University's College of Education, for his dedication in the establishment of Towson's PDS Network. This network presently includes more than 70 partnerships, encompassing more than 100 schools, in 13 Maryland counties and the city of Baltimore. In addition, we recognized the contributions of the Maryland State Department of Education (MSDE) and its superintendent, Dr. Nancy Grasmick. Their influence and leadership continues to be profound and important. The MSDE assisted by providing sponsorship and resources to the Second National PDS Conference held at Towson during Spring 2003. This volume is, in great measure, the result of that conference.

In order for a PDS network as extensive as Towson's to thrive, and to thrive to the extent that we do, many people must contribute their talents and skills. We appreciate that the contributors to this volume brought their views about their PDS efforts from across the nation to Towson and Baltimore. Lee Teitel's Foreword also recognizes this work. Significantly, the conference was an exciting and provocative experience, with participants sharing their dedication to the PDS and their care for the learning and achievement of children in the nation's public schools.

The PDS Network at Towson is now 10 years old. Throughout this time, there has been a guiding force—a person who provides shepherding and professional oversight—to the many creative directions that Towson partnerships take, as teachers, staff, and school administrators come together with university faculty and administrators, to be the best that we can be. This beacon for national PDS efforts is Tom Proffitt, our co-editor of the first volume in this series, the Associate Dean of Towson's

College of Education. From January 2003 through June 2004, as the College's Acting Dean, he has been that source of inspiration and drive for the Network. With profound respect, we dedicate this book to him. We are proud and privileged to be his colleagues, as well as to have him for a friend, because we have learned much from him about "doing good, and doing good well!"

Every book requires patient dedication to the task of producing the manuscript to be submitted to the publisher. The deadlines are too short, and the detailed list of guidelines is long, painstakingly detailed, and sometimes difficult to figure out. We thank Phyllis Korper, our acquisitions editor at Peter Lang Publishing, for her assistance and care in taking all that was given to her and making sense of our comments and thoughts. She should know that the contributors to this book are most appreciative of her professionalism and expertise.

Also, we thank Lisa Dillon, our production/creative director at Peter Lang for her constant support in pushing us to work much more rapidly and thoroughly than we ever thought possible. Also, the reviewers of the first book, *Traditions, Standards & Transformations: A Model for Professional Development School Networks*, and this book have hit the mark in their understanding of what we do and what our contributors have said. Thank you!

Personally, we are appreciative of our colleagues in the College of Education for their support of our efforts as they continue to lend us kind words of encouragement even as they hope that we will stop editing their work. We are especially grateful to our project assistant, Scott Iskow, whose expertise in both computer science and professional writing has been a true gift. Finally, we are most appreciative of those in our personal lives who listen to us kvetch about one thing or another, back us in what we do, and wonder if the very lengthy project of our writing about the PDS (now into the fifth year of collaboration) will ever end. In the spirit of caring, we thank the following:

JEN: My longtime friend and former classmate, Lorraine C. Smith, who "knew me when." I have learned the most about publishing from you. Your success as an author continues to encourage me. And none of this, of course, would have been possible without the love and support of my dear Michael, Chris, Andy, Tony, and Olinda.

TRB: First and foremost, a wonderful co-author, co-editor, colleague, and friend, Jane Neapolitan, who contends with details (and me) with patience and grace. And second, but no less important, to those who are always so supportive: Suzanne, Anna and Jason, Kris and Wes; Lori and Bish, and Bill and Karen.

Foreword

In his Foreword to the first volume in this three-part series on Professional Development Schools, Terry Berkeley framed its central questions around what Towson University and its partner schools have done in the design and development of the PDS, and how this has led to a "deep cultural change between and among partners, the 'state,' the public schools, and the University, whose past efforts often were unappreciated by one another" (p. viii).

The first volume did an excellent job of focusing on those questions, providing a variety of powerful personal and institutional stories of growth and transformation as the Towson partnerships grew from one to more than 80. This meteoritic local growth was in parallel to the growth of the Professional Development School movement and the development of standards at the national and state level. While contributing to the growth, Towson and its partners were shaped by the changes and growth in the external environment. At the same time, the Towson-based partnerships have been a dramatic scale-up story—proof that with conviction, hard work, and a collaborative spirit, school and university partners can bring high-quality Professional Development Schools to scale, even in a large teacher-producing university.

This second volume continues and expands this story in several important ways. First, it takes the story nationally, and draws on PDS stories, data, and analyses from around the country. With chapters drawn from Maine to California, with stops in New Jersey, Kansas, Maryland, Missouri, and elsewhere, the second volume, appropriately, broadens to look at the Professional Development School movement nationally.

Furthermore, this volume goes deeper on approaches, conceptual frameworks, data use, and analysis. For example, it includes chapters that look more closely at the possibilities of PDS networks helping to bring about systemic change (Chapter 5, by Kruft) and at the preparation and use of mentors in Professional Development Schools (Chapter 8, by Sweeney, Strosnider & Smallwood). Other chapters focus on PDS and early-childhood education (Chapter 3, by Aldrich), music (Chapter 6, by Frierson-Campbell), and physical education (Chapter 13, by Miller, Rawson & Holmes); and the use of portfolios to document pre-service teacher growth (Chapter 11, by King & Roy).

Two of the chapters provide important depth in conceptualizing PDSs, their standards, and their impacts. In Chapter 9, Marsha Levine and Roberta Trachtman describe the history of the PDS Standards Project of the National Council for the Accreditation of Teacher Education (NCATE). They outline how the "co-constructed" nature of the process laid the basis for the use of standards for accountability in education as well as for the development and improvement of PDSs. In Chapter 10, Mary Gendernalik Cooper details a comprehensive data-collection system that draws on a variety of different information sources to increase the accountability and monitor the short- and long-term impacts of PDS on pre-service teachers, and on the institutions and partnerships that prepare them.

Several chapters provide depth on the use of data and the impacts of Professional Development Schools on students, pre-service teachers, and experienced educators. In the first chapter, James Cantor and Sue Schaar describe how their PDS-modeled school, developed for emergency credentialed teachers, has drawn upon external evaluations of teaching performance and student test scores to document its impact on teachers and their students. In Chapter 2, Sally Yahnke and her colleagues in Kansas also take a close look at student data, making strong connections between the gains made by students and the innovations supported by their PDSs. In an unusual and important contribution, they also make strong connections between the NCATE PDS Standards, the use of action research in their PDSs, and the strength of the outcomes for student learning.

Other forms of action research are cited in other chapters—the use of literature circles to research instructional strategies (Chapter 7, by Gorrow & Bing), or as a powerful professional development tool for experienced teachers (Chapter 4, by Mobley & Norris-Bauer). In Chapter 12, Diane Davis and her colleagues describe how the power of action research is amplified many-fold when the efforts of interns and teachers are carefully focused on the goals outlined by the school improvement team. In Chapter 14, Neapolitan and Berkeley round out the volume by focusing on the use of inquiry as the driver in Professional Development Schools. In telling the "front-stage" and "backstage" stories, the authors address the challenges of conducting inquiry, how it stretches the limits of the partnerships, and how critical it is for the success of the partnerships.

In expanding its focus to the national scene, even as it maintains important depth and detail, this volume makes a powerful contribution to the increasing volume of literature on the expanding PDS movement and its growing impacts.

Lee Teitel
Brookline, Massachusetts
April 30, 2004

PART I

Building and Nurturing the Professional Development School

CHAPTER 1   *James S. Cantor & Sue A. Schaar*

Addressing an Emergency in Teacher Education
The Evolution of a Professional Development School for Emerging Professionals

Introduction

In this chapter, the experiences and understanding gained from the implementation of a unique and innovative approach to Professional Development Schools (PDSs) are discussed. The Professional Development School in Local District G was designed to certify full-time working, non-credentialed teachers in one year. The project was initially funded by grants from the Stuart Foundation and the U.S. Department of Education. It is the collaborative initiative of three entities: the Los Angeles Unified School District (LAUSD); California State University Dominguez Hills (CSUDH); and the Los Angeles Educational Partnership (LAEP), a non-profit school-reform agency.

While most Professional Development Schools are designed to improve the quality of preparation for pre-service student teachers, this PDS is unique because it is centered on the professional development of minimally trained, non-credentialed, beginning teachers,[1] who are working full time in elementary classrooms thanks to Emergency Permits. Leaders from the three agencies agreed that the old ways were not working. Out-of-the-box thinking was needed in order to attract, train to teach, and successfully retain teachers in urban schools in which low-income, language-minority populations were the norm. This PDS exemplifies a model of urban teacher preparation that understands the challenges of reforming such school districts. It is a complex response to a multi-dimensional crisis. This chapter examines the first year of implementation and the modifications followed in order to improve the PDS.

The Problem: How to Apply PDS Precepts to Support Non-Credentialed Teachers

There is a teacher-shortage crisis in California public schools. Population growth, the accelerating retirements of veteran teachers, and class-size reduction contribute to the shortage. Never before have there been so many minimally trained teachers teaching without certification, especially in inner cities. Retaining high-quality teachers in urban schools with low-income, language-minority populations is so problematic and worrisome that current school-reform legislation stipulates public listing of each classroom teacher's credential qualifications, and parents are informed if their child's teacher is not credentialed. Because many school districts have labor agreements allowing classroom selection by seniority, teachers without full certification generally are hired to teach the difficult classes nobody else wants. These classes are often filled with children who are the hardest to teach. The California Commission on Teacher Credentialing reports that many non-credentialed teachers feel so inadequate that they quit before the end of their first year, and more than half of them leave the profession within five years. Academic success, then, in these urban schools is typically low.

The more academically successful schools, generally located in the suburbs, keep good teachers and have few non-credentialed teachers on their staffs. There are general differences in the way these schools function, and this affects stability in staffing. There is research that shows that, in the most ineffective schools, teachers maintain individualistic practices and keep to themselves rather than promote a school-wide culture of teacher dialogue and support (Bullough & Gitlin, 1991). The best schools are places where teachers meet on a regular basis to look at student work and discuss their teaching practices (Louis, Kruse & Marks, 1996; McLaughlin & Talbert, 1993; Nave, 2000). Schools that are doing well are characterized by teams of teachers collaboratively focusing on assessment and pedagogy. They are commonly developing action plans for student improvement in these schools (Newmann & Wehlage, 1995). New ways are being sought to help teachers create collaborative educational communities (Oakes, Quartz, Ryan & Lipton, 2000; Gutierrez & Meyer, 1995; Oakes & Quartz, 1995; Rogoff, Goodman Turkanis & Bartlett, 2001). By helping teachers create supportive learning communities, educators will become more successful in training and inducting beginning teachers into the profession in ways that can contribute to long-term commitment and successful teaching in these difficult-to-staff schools.

New efforts are being made to effectively connect learning theories with teaching practices, to break down isolation, and to provide support for beginning teachers by designing supervised clinical experiences and curricula related to real-life classroom situations. Communication and collaboration between school practitioners and university educators are essential. The Professional Development School/School-

University Partnership model (PDS/SUP) articulated by the Holmes Group, Goodlad, and others (Book, 1996; Darling-Hammond, 1994; Goodlad, 1990; Holmes, 1990; Valli, Cooper, Frankes & Zeichner, 1997) has the potential to be useful for attaining these goals.

The Los Angeles Unified School District, Local District G

In Academic Year 2000–2001, the school board divided LAUSD into 11 mini- or local districts. In the Local District G there are 20 elementary schools, located in South Central Los Angeles, that are participating in the PDS. These culturally and linguistically diverse schools have student populations that are approximately 70 percent Latino and 30 percent African American. Virtually all of the students qualify for free and reduced meals, and most score poorly on standardized norm-referenced tests. When the partners designed this PDS, approximately half of the teachers in Local District G schools did not have permanent status. Non-credentialed teachers held Emergency Permits[2] that allow them to teach while completing professional training through after-school university coursework. Several of the schools in this partnership had 50 percent or more of their faculty work on entry-level teaching credentials.

The Local District G Professional Development School

Several years ago, leaders from each of the partnering agencies began to collaborate on a program to infuse the best practices of the Urban Learning Centers (Johnson & McDonald, 1996) into an alternative certification program at CSUDH. The model has three guiding principles: teachers must know their students well; the curriculum must be connected to students' lives for relevant learning; and, strategies are based on research. Strategies to accomplish these include Levin's hypothesis of acceleration (Levin, 1988), multi-age teaching, interdisciplinary curriculum, thematic curriculum, social-services support, data-based decision-making, and technology that supports instruction.

Committed to changing the nature of the way universities and their schools of education do business, the leaders adopted four core PDS principles. First, full teacher-preparation programs are held at local school sites to give context to the nature of schooling for preparing teachers. Second, school site experts and university faculty engage in teaching the program's university courses. Third, the programs are directed by steering and advisory committees composed of appropriate membership from the district office of the participating school district, the university, and the school sites. Fourth, elements of reform are accomplished by all participating partners—the school district, the university, and the reform agency (Blair, 2001). The group agreed to use the PDS model for credentialing emergency-permit, full-time working teachers in hard-to-staff urban schools (Blair & Colbert, 2001). They established several goals: (a) strengthen education teacher programs (b) increase teaching proficiency of beginning teachers (c) increase technology skills of beginning teachers (d) retain proficient teachers in inner-city schools and increase leadership capacity of all teachers, and (e) increase K-5 student achievement and technology use.

It was recognized that too many non-credentialed teachers did not complete the two-year university or district intern programs. Believing that an enriched, accelerated program would improve credential candidates' focus, as well as the quality of their experience, they designed the PDS to compress into one year the amount of time it takes to earn a California Preliminary Multiple Subject Teaching Credential. The initial program design released credential candidates from their teaching responsibilities one day a week for professional development to observe accomplished standards-based teaching, to discuss strategies for school reform, and to use technology to strengthen teaching and learning. The plan called for university courses to be taught on the release day; however, they were to be field based, rather than conducted at the university campus, thus linking theory to practice in urban schools. Teacher-coaches from within the PDS schools were to provide demonstration lessons for observation and participation, on-site coaching, and curricular planning. PDS faculty facilitated Inquiry Seminars supporting the credential candidates as they examined student work and teacher practices. Advanced technological resources and training was expected to teach CCs how to use the Internet for communication, research, and enhancing classroom instruction.

The planning group hoped the cumulative effect of these innovations would result in a significantly increased retention rate of accomplished new teachers within these schools. The goal was to build a learning community of new teachers, experienced and exemplary teachers, and university faculty who would provide a smooth continuum of professional development from teacher preparation, through induction into the profession, to the development of teacher leadership.

Roles and Responsibilities

Although each of the partners has, and continues to have, specific areas of focus in the common goal, much of the work overlaps. LAUSD manages school relations for the PDS. This includes recruiting and selecting the teacher-coaches, and organizing the substitute-teacher system to ensure coverage for professional development activities. CSUDH's primary focus is credential preparation. The university provides teacher-education classes and manages the process that leads to the Preliminary Multiple Subjects Teaching Credential. LAEP is focused on providing resources for the PDS, as well as providing professional development for the teacher-coaches. LAEP also manages the inquiry process and provides advanced technology training for all participants. During Year 1, university classes were held in a classroom at one of the PDS elementary schools. Now they are housed in the new Professional Development Center.

The Participants

The ethnic breakdown of the credential candidates is diverse, thereby addressing the need to provide teachers that better match the student population. The table below represents the combined numbers of the participants in the first four years of the PDS. At the present time, the faculty who are teaching the classes are mostly Caucasian. However, it is anticipated that outstanding PDS graduates will evolve into teacher-leaders and contribute toward appropriate diversity as coaches and co-instructors later in their careers.

As in any new project, the proof comes with implementation. Although this PDS is successful, it had a difficult start and significant changes had to be made in order for the goals to be met.

Stumbling Blocks, Year 1

Coverage for Professional Development

The original design called for a full day of release, each Wednesday, for all of the credential candidates. Theoretically, it makes sense for CCs, beginning teachers, to have 20 percent of their workload to be released for professional development. In fact, Japan supports its beginning teachers in this way (Stigler & Stevenson, 1991). The key to making this work is to have qualified and reliable coverage so there is no loss of instruction. The intention was to gather a cohort of "Guest Teachers" rather than substitute teachers. The concept of the Guest Teacher visualizes a stronger connection to the CC. In this case, the Guest Teacher would provide once-a-week coverage for the same teacher, every Wednesday, and become a regular part of the teaching staff in that classroom and school. The Guest Teacher would collaborate with the CC in planning, in order to incorporate special skills or interests so the weekly professional development

TABLE 1.1. **Ethnic Breakdown of the PDS**

	Latino	African American	Asian	Caucasian	Native American
Credential Candidates, N=74	26%	45%	12%	15%	2%
Teacher-Coaches, N=61	23%	49%	7%	21%	0%
University Instructors, N=20	20%	20%	20%	40%	0%

days would become "value-added" rather than cause the usual struggle—recovering from the days teachers are absent. The children would know the Guest Teacher well and the Guest Teacher would be trained and skilled in the district's curriculum, assuring there would not be compromise regarding implementation, especially in literacy instruction. PDS staff were most interested in finding Guest Teachers who trained in Open Court, the reading curriculum adopted by the district. However, Guest Teachers were sought who had special talents such as art or music so the Guest Teachers could add their particular background to complement the curriculum. The hope was to recruit newly retired teachers whose experiences in teaching could supplement the mentoring that CCs receive from their teacher-coach.

It did not work out that way. One of the many unintended outcomes of class-size reduction was the profound shortage of qualified teachers, which resulted in a depleted pool of substitute teachers. In general, as soon as substitute teachers demonstrated adequate competence, they would be offered full-time classroom teaching positions in the school district. It was very difficult to receive a commitment from qualified and reliable individuals to substitute on a long-term basis. There were far too many days during the first year of the PDS when there were no substitute teachers available to provide coverage for the credential candidates on their professional development days. When this happened, students were dispersed in small groups to spend their day in neighboring classrooms. This diminished the quality of instruction and upset the teachers who received these groups of dispersed children, as well as the students and their parents. The principals at the school sites bore the brunt of the burden. They found themselves mediating difficulties with their staffs, students, and the parents of the children. Rather than supporting beginning teachers, the system made the CCs' jobs harder. Eventually principals withdrew their support, especially when faced with pressures to raise test scores and implement Open Court.

Coordination between Project Components

While support for the Guest Teachers was eroding, the CCs were not receiving the intended benefits from their weekly professional development days. Besides having to deal with the resulting resentment from faculty, administration, students, and parents, it became difficult for beginning teachers to regroup from leaving their classrooms with poor coverage. Compounding this difficulty was the fact the Inquiry Seminar was scheduled for every Thursday immediately after school. This meant credential candidates would be absent all day every Wednesday with inadequate coverage and then have to leave classrooms immediately after school the following day to attend and participate in the Inquiry Seminar. Frequently, tensions caused by the pullout day were left unresolved.

The University PDS Coordinator and the LAUSD PDS Coordinator indicated they needed to improve the PDS program design to complement the realities of school; thus, they focused on enrolling the support of the principals. They would not be successful in recruiting a cohort of CCs for the following year if the principals were opposed to having their new hires participate in the PDS. At the same time, the Year 1 Evaluation Report indicated the program was not working well—there was a misalignment between intended accomplishments and what was happening. In early spring, the coordinators from the partnering agencies met with a volunteer group of principals to discuss improving the PDS. They took proposed modifications to their respective agencies for review, and in late spring, bolstered by recommendations from the Year 1 evaluation, the Steering Committee and Advisory Board members met to map out roles, program strengths, and remedy weaknesses. Changes for improvement were agreed upon.

Changes Implemented in Year 2

Roles and Responsibilities

A structure was developed that was aimed at assuring effective, on-going, collaborative management of the PDS. Starting in Year 2, a four-member Operations Team met once a week to assure collaborative implementation of the PDS model. Its members include the directors of PDSs (LAEP), two university coordinators (CSUDH), and the Local District GPDS coordinator (LAUSD) working together to recruit credential candidates and teacher-coaches. They supervise the process of aligning the observation and participation guidelines, the work of coaches and inquiry-group facilitators, and the sequence and content of the credential courses. The Operations Team members monitor the process to assure that each partner's priorities are integrated and implemented. The organizational structure also includes a monthly Steering Committee meeting and a PDS Advisory Board, which holds quarterly meetings to review and oversee PDS progress.

Admissions

The PDS members were resolved that one of the requirements for admission would be a letter of recommendation from the principal that stated that the principal would support the applicant's participation in the PDS and would allocate a portion of the school's professional development budget to support the training. This made a positive impact on the quality of applicants because the principals did not recommend marginal hires or beginning teachers whom they felt could not handle the rigors of full-time teaching and participation in the credentialing program. The teachers who were not recommended for the PDS were advised to participate in alternative credentialing programs through the district or university, which were spread over two or three years. The principals' involvement in this area was deemed so important that they were asked to recommend teacher-coaches. In this way, PDS participants, teacher-coaches, and credential candidates were chosen and supported by their principals to participate in this program.

Professional Development Days

Engaging the principals in admissions and recruitment helped to improve the quality of the cohort. However, the principals expressed that they were most concerned with the way the weekly professional development days had a negative impact on teaching and learning at their school sites. Although there was no significant argument against the *concept* of structuring 20 percent of beginning-teachers' workload for professional development, it was understood that reliable substitute coverage could not be provided on a weekly basis. As a result, professional days were scaled back to two per month.

Strategies were developed to relieve the pressure on the substitute pool. The professional development days were spread out so that no more than one-third of the cohort was out on any day, but substitutes could be available for all of those days. It became a more attractive situation for substitutes to commit to, because they could be offered a long-term schedule for the full year or parts of it. Efforts were focused on gaining the commitment of off-track teachers to substitute for the credential candidates. It also helped that off-track CCs and PDS alumni often served as substitutes for the PDS. This change also diluted the impact of professional development days on the school site, since their CCs were no longer all absent on the same day, as was the case in Year 1.

Although the number of professional development days was reduced, better coordination between PDS components ensured that the quality of experience on those days made up for the time lost. An essential innovation of the program was the pairing of CCs with seasoned teacher-coaches. When the experiences from Year 1 were analyzed, it was determined that some changes would have to be made to improve this relationship. In Year 1, there was not a one-on-one relationship between CCs and coaches. CCs observed a number of classrooms. Although veteran teachers taught them, many of the demonstration teachers were not teacher-coaches, and all the CCs merely observed the same teacher and did not participate in the classroom at all. With the current changes, the observation and participation have become more focused and supportive of the mentoring relationship between novice and expert. The teacher-coach now supervises all of the observation and participation for a given CC. Sometimes credential candidates work in the teacher-coach's room, and sometimes the substitute covers for the teacher-coach and the mentoring occurs in the CC's classroom. Occasionally, the CC observes another teacher.

The second half of the professional development day consists of focused inquiry. CCs participated in reflection on their progress in applying the concepts and methods they learned in the university courses to their own classrooms. In Year 1, the Inquiry

Seminar was modeled on an action research approach and facilitated by teacher-coaches. CCs were expected to develop a research question connected to the focus of each phase. After collecting observation data or implementing changes in classroom practice, groups would report their findings. This was too much to expect in too short a time. CCs were struggling to keep up with their professional responsibilities and their coursework. Even though efforts were made to connect the action research to coursework, the beginning teachers perceived this as extra work.

It was hoped that beginning teachers would enjoy inquiry groups and see them as something they would continue to participate in throughout their careers. The design of the Inquiry Seminar was modified in Year 2, so credential candidates can have more control over their own agenda. Building community and developing reflective practices became emphasized goals. The Critical Friends Group Model (Nave, 2000) was selected and the Operations Committee members became trained facilitators. As a result, leaders from the PDS, rather than teacher-coaches, have facilitated the Inquiry Seminars, which support the credential candidates as they examine student work and teacher practices. Interaction at the Inquiry Seminars was guided by protocols that support collaborative conversations aimed at improving teaching and learning.

During Year 1, an agreement was forged to allow university courses to occur during the school day—the morning and afternoon hours of the professional development days. The intent was to design a complete day of observation and participation, followed by instruction. Although the CCs were alert and responsive, it became necessary to change this structure. Combining observation and participation with university instruction on professional development days did not provide enough time for either, and it was learned there was a requirement that teachers not participate in courses for university credit during their working hours. University coursework is now scheduled after school, two evenings per week. This allows more time in the professional development day for credential candidates to work with their teacher-coaches in observation and participation, followed by Critical Friends Groups.

In summary, steps were taken to regain support for the PDS from the principals, and to improve the quality of applicants and the assistance they would receive. The number and format of the professional development days were restructured in ways that resulted in a tighter, more effective relationship between the CCs and the teacher-coaches with a closer articulation with university coursework. The Critical Friends Group model enabled CCs to examine and discuss teaching practices and student work in a safe and collaborative setting.

Research and Evaluation

The data from the independent evaluator (Vital Research, 2002) provides evidence, from multiple sources, that the program is successful in meeting its goals, even though things did not look very promising in the early stages of the PDS. At the retreat at the end of Year 1, University faculty and administrators, LAEP representatives, LAUSD District G officials, and elementary-school principals worked together to restructure and monitor the program in the following ways:

1. Engaging in midyear and end-of-year assessments, to be conducted by the "external evaluators."
2. Providing a more efficient and effective organizing structure for monitoring and problem solving. An Advisory Board composed of officials from each of the partnering agencies would meet quarterly to hear reports and make decisions concerning important changes or additions.
3. Monitoring day-to-day issues and problems solved by an Operations Team (OT) at weekly meetings.

The value of these changes to the success of the program in Years 2 and 3 cannot be underestimated. These groups became a research mechanism by which the functioning of the PDS could be formatively assessed and evaluated throughout the year, so that necessary changes could be made immediately. The Operations Team has been important in the process because of the frequency of its meetings, and its discussions by those who were "in the trenches" with CCs on a daily basis. As Years 2, 3, and 4 have progressed, modification of past procedures has increased the integrity of the collaboration into what external evaluators called a "near seamless integration and alignment of program components to support non-credentialed teachers in the classroom and in the completion of the credential requirements," noting that this had, for the most part, been achieved by the end of Year 2 (Vital Research, 2002, p. 12).

Examples of innovations guided by the research of the external evaluators and research of the Operations Team are listed in Tables 1.2 and 1.3.

TABLE 1.2. **Innovations Guided by Formal Research**

Year 1	Changes in Year 2
• Weekly morning pullout for classroom observation in one classroom	• Alternate week whole-day pullout for coaching and inquiry group
• University classes 1 day/week late mornings through early evenings	• University classes 2 times/week 3:30–8:30 PM
• Technology training for CCs only	• Technology training for CCs and coaches
• Monthly problem-solving sessions	• Weekly monitoring of issues and CCs by OT, reporting of OT to quarterly meetings by Advisory Board; problem solving by both groups

TABLE 1.3. Example of Change Guided by Research of Operations Team: Coaching Process

Original	Change
• Informal feedback from coaches	• Monthly Coach Logs specifying accomplishments and action steps for next cycle
• Minimal written guidelines provided to coaches	• Coach Handbook with more specific goals and objectives for each phase
• CC reflective journals focused on observations in the classroom	• CC reflective journals concerning professional development with coach
• Stipend paid in beginning and at the end of the semester	• Modification of coaching stipend schedule to allow for more frequent monitoring of coachwork
• Action research model of inquiry	• Change to Critical Friends Inquiry format—CCs discuss the activities involving coach

Goal 1: Strengthen Teacher-Education Program

The Local District G PDS has been a laboratory for learning about the teacher-education process, especially since it deals with teachers on emergency permit who are responsible for the academic progress of their students. CCs continued to report that they have been surprised at how much they could learn in one year, and principals report their schools have become better places because of the program. The external evaluators report, "At the conclusion of this three-year grant, the PDS model has gained recognition as a valuable and viable field-based teacher training model to prepare new teachers" (Vital Research, 2002, p. 21). The Local District G PDS model has been disseminated through various articles and national conferences, and awards have been received for innovation at the national, state, and local levels. The model has been replicated in four local LAUSD districts; a secondary version began in the 2003–2004 school year for CCs teaching grades 6–12 in English, math, science, social studies, and physical education.

Goal 2: Increase Instructional Proficiency of New Teachers

The 13 areas measured to determine the instructional proficiency of the CCs are taken directly from the *California Standards for the Teaching Profession* [CSTP] (CCTC & CDE, 1997). These areas are the most critical for new teachers and include classroom management, student engagement, creating effective learning environments, planning instruction, and assessing students' learning. Baseline information on each CC's teaching proficiency is gathered near the beginning of the school year, midyear, and at the end of the year. In the Year 3 evaluation, it was found that "Year 2 and Year 3 Programs yielded similar results. Overall, Cohort 3 CCs showed a significant increase in instructional proficiency and technology skills" (see Figure 1.1).

14 • Building and Nurturing the Professional Development School

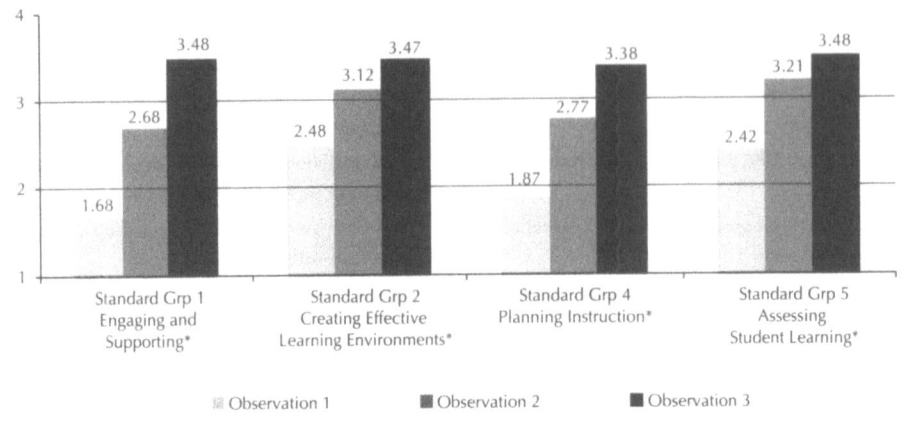

Possible ratings range from 1 = lowest to 4 = highest.
* Significant differences across the three observations, ($p < .001$)

FIGURE 1.1. Average Rating of Standard Groups from Three Observations

Goal 3: Increase Technology Skills of New Teachers

Pre- and post-test scores were calculated on each of the following technology scales: Basic Computer Use, Internet Use, and Advanced Computer Use. A two-way repeated-measures ANOVA was conducted to compare proficiency in pre- and post-basic-computer and Internet use across Cohorts I, II, and III. All Cohorts increased in skills in both areas. Although increases differed (see Table 1.4), there were no significant differences in the increases among the three Cohorts for either of these proficiencies.

Whereas about the same proportion of Cohorts I, II, and III felt that technology had changed the way they teach at baseline (61.1 percent, 68.4 percent, and 57.1 percent, respectively), by the end of the year, 86.7 percent in Cohort 1, 100 percent in Cohort II, and 91.7 percent in Cohort III felt this way.

Goal 4: Retain Proficient Teachers and Increase Leadership Capacity in Inner-City Schools

Retention of teachers has been extremely high. Of the 113 CCs who participated in the first three years of the Local District G PDS, 100 are still teaching in Local District G.

TABLE 1.4. **Average Increase in Basic Computer and Internet Proficiency across Cohorts I, II, and III**

	Cohort I	Cohort II	Cohort III
Basic Computer Use	.60	.85	.55
Internet Use	.70	.88	.57

Goal 5: Increase K–5 Student Achievement

Student achievement in reading, mathematics, and language has been measured for each of the CCs classes during their year as a student at the PDS and in succeeding years. Data have been compared with a control group of teachers matched by school, grade, and status (non-credentialed teacher). Student achievement data are significant with more than 1,200 students' progress being tracked in Years 1–3. In many cases, CCs were assigned to classrooms with significantly lower-achieving students than were control-group teachers. This may be because, overall, control-group teachers had longer tenure than did CCs. Figures 1.2 and 1.3 provide examples of student achievement for CCs during their PDS experience, and for one and two years out from it.

The external evaluators note at the end of Year 3:

> Year 2 and Year 3 programs yielded similar results. Overall, Cohort III CCs showed a significant increase in instructional proficiency and technology skills. Their students, while starting with significantly lower pretest (2001) reading and math scores, held their own in reading and math achievement as the Control Group students' scores decreased significantly. (Vital Research, 2002, p. 56)

Qualitative data have been collected to ascertain program success. Lucy, a credential candidate in the second year's cohort, describes the effect of the PDS on her teaching and learning:

> Education is a complex field. Teachers are dealing with school districts, administrators, policy, parents, public accountability, and most importantly, the students themselves.

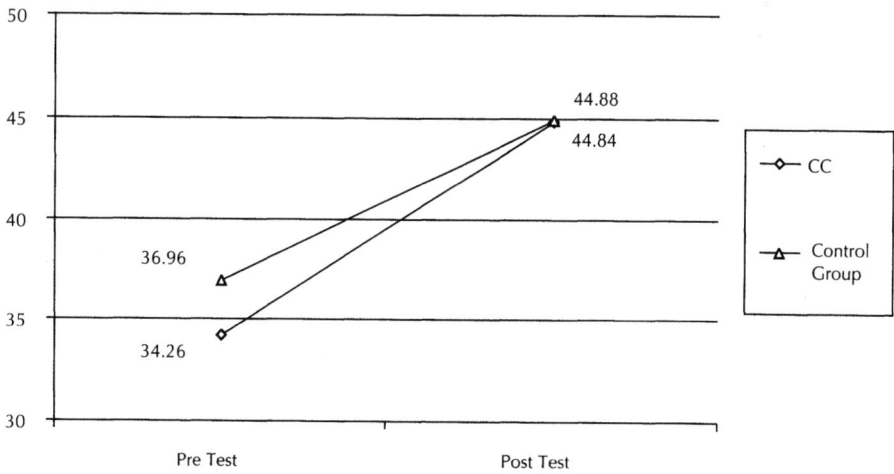

FIGURE 1.2. Cohort 1, Year 3, SAT 9 NCE Adjusted Means for Math

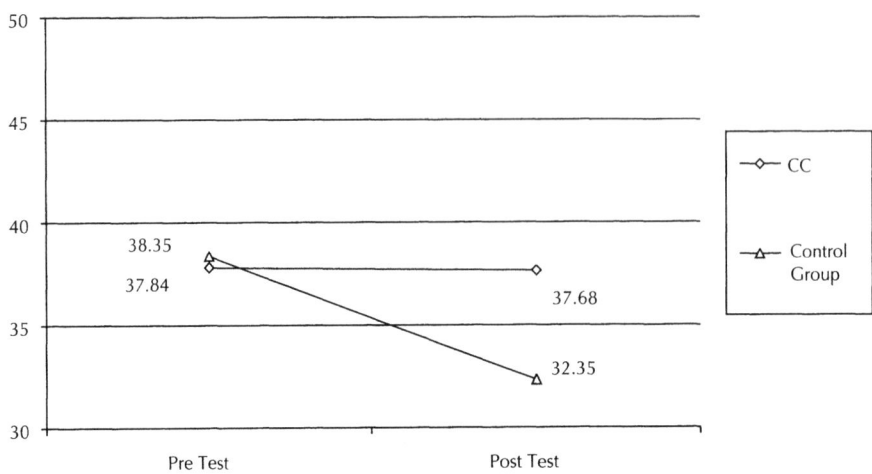

FIGURE 1.3. Cohort III, Year 1, SAT NCE Adjusted Means for Reading

There are many issues in education, particularly in our district, such as raising test scores, making sure students can read, teaching skills necessary to success, dealing with English Language Learners, poverty, child abuse, and working with children who have not-so-ideal home environments (due to drugs, poverty, immigrant issues, etc.). As new teachers we are constantly forced to make decisions based on what's good for the students, what the school district requires of us, what administration expects of us, and public accountability.

The PDS helps us deal with the cognitive dissonance that arises from all of this. Because the PDS is made up of the three different organizations we are exposed to the various views on education. This coalition makes our experience valuable because we are given information from these various perspectives, but ultimately, we are the ones responsible for effective teaching. The PDS helps mitigate the issues that arise and offers guidance as we teachers are faced with the current educational issues and trends.

Discussion

The Local District G PDS effectively provides professional development and support so that beginning teachers are successful and valued in improving schools. As the effort continues, it is useful to reflect on how those gains were made in three areas that contribute toward progress: human resources, operational structure that connects theory and practice, and inclusive collaborative relationships.

Human Resources

Any school-reform effort in low-income urban areas with culturally and linguistically diverse schools is extremely challenging. The success stories are few and far between. A project as complicated and demanding as a three-way partnership, supporting a multi-school Professional Development School for non-credentialed teachers in South Central Los Angeles, requires leaders whose professional responsibilities are focused on this project. It cannot work if all of the leaders have important non-PDS professional responsibilities. The PDS got started during Year 1 before all the pieces were in place and the problems were confounded when LAUSD reconfigured its organizational structure.

In Year 1, the most active participant from LAUSD worked out of the District Office and had many other professional responsibilities. This person's supervisor cautioned frequently about letting the PDS consume too much time and effort. Before this was resolved, LAUSD's superintendent resigned and an interim superintendent began a restructuring process. The district-wide reorganization was a distraction. Virtually all of the personnel changed, and the district's attention to the PDS went on hold until things settled down in the fall of Year 2. When the PDS held its retreat at the end of Year 1, there was little knowledge about who would be the new administrative leaders in the new mini-district and who would be actively involved in the PDS. Once those personnel were named and in place, it took time for them to settle in and focus attention on this project.

During Year 1, LAEP assigned several people to participate in varying roles in the PDS; however, they each had many other responsibilities. When things did come together in the fall of Year 2, a director was hired by LAEP to focus attention on the PDS. LAEP also assigned its academic program director to participate in the project. The restructured LAUSD Local District G began operations, and the PDS became a high priority of the PDS coordinator. This team joined the university coordinator (who remained the same from Year 1), and the Operations Team began to function. In Year 3, the university deepened its commitment by assigning a second faculty member to participate in the Operations Team.

Operational Structure

The PDS benefits from the trusting, effective relationships that members of the Operations Team have developed. The group is small and comprised of representatives from each partnering agency whose responsibilities are focused on the PDS. This group participates in the larger Steering Committee, whose responsibilities include professional development for all teachers in Local District G. They also report on a quarterly basis to the PDS Advisory Board, assuring continued support for the PDS. This structure works well because the representatives from each partnering institution contribute most of their professional attention on the PDS.

A significant turning point occurred when the PDS worked with a group of principals who offered ideas and suggestions for improvement that contributed toward changes made in Year 2. The Operations Team needed to determine effective ways of communicating with the principals and ensuring their continued support. Regular principals' meetings were not the proper venue because of their filled agendas, and the principals were too busy to add any more meetings to their schedules. Instead, the University coordinator and the LAUSD PDS coordinator went to each principal for individual conversations, explaining changes and asking them to recommend and support credential candidates and teacher-coaches for Year 2. In subsequent years, these visits were no longer necessary, as the Local District G PDS became the recommended accelerated alternative-credentialing program in the district.

In conclusion, the PDS improves each year because it is provided with focused human resources—people whose professional lives are attuned to this project. An organizational structure has been developed to promote collaboration from all involved in the partnership. Word of the improvements continues to spread, and the PDS has been featured on several local television news reports. It has also won a national award for best practices in promoting diversity, a state award for an outstanding partnership, and a commendation from the City Council of Los Angeles. During fall 2003, the partnership added three new elementary PDSs, three new secondary PDSs, and several that lead to the Special Education credential, all based on the Local District G PDS Model. However, the challenges of school reform continue to confound educators. Although teachers, administrators, and teacher educators are hard working and committed to success, they need better ways to teach. Participants in the Local District G PDS hope this project represents a better way to improve teaching and learning.

Notes

1. Throughout this paper, teacher-education students are referred to as either "credential candidates" (CCs) or " beginning teachers."
2. The California Commission on Teacher Credentialing is phasing out the Emergency Permit designation and replacing it with Pre-Interns and University Interns. This new structure is designed to assure that all non-credentialed teachers be enrolled in professional programs that will result in timely completion of requirements for the teaching credential. By 2005, Emergency Permits and the Pre-Intern Credential will be phased out as school districts throughout the nation change staffing policies to meet the federal requirements for "highly qualified" teachers.

References

Blair, B. (2001). *School of Education brochure.* Carson, CA: California State University, Dominguez Hills.

Blair, B. & Colbert, J.A. (2001). *A professional development school model for non-credentialed, full-time teachers: Manual arts PDS.* Paper presented at the American Association of Colleges for Teacher Education Annual Meeting, Dallas, TX.

Book, C.L. (1996). Professional development schools. In J. Sikula, T.J. Buttery & E. Guyton (Eds.), *Handbook of research on teacher education: A project of the Association of Teacher Educators* (Second Edition ed., pp. 194-210). New York, NY: Macmillan.

Bullough, R.V.J. & Gitlin, A.D. (1991). Educative communities and the development of the reflective practitioner. In B.R. Tabachnich & K. Zeichner (Eds.), *Issues and practices in inquiry-oriented teacher education* (pp. 35-55). London: Falmer Press.

California Commission on Teacher Credentialing and California Department of Education (1997). *California standards for the teaching profession.* Sacramento, CA: CCTC & CDE.

Darling-Hammond, L. (1994). *Professional development schools: Schools for developing a profession.* New York: Teachers College Press.

Goodlad, J.I. (1990). *Teachers for our nation's schools.* San Francisco: Jossey-Bass.

Gutierrez, K.D. & Meyer, B. (1995). Creating communities of effective practice: Building literacy for language minority students. In J. Oakes & K.H. Quartz (Eds.), *Creating new educational communities* (pp. 32-52). Chicago, IL: University of Chicago Press.

Holmes, T.G. (1990). *Tomorrow's schools: Principles for the design of professional development schools.* East Lansing, MI: The Holmes Group, Inc.

Johnson, J. & McDonald, J. (1996). Los Angeles learning centers: An initiative of Los Angeles Unified School District, United Teachers Los Angeles, and Los Angeles Educational Partnership. In S. Ross & L. Smith (Eds.), *Bold plans for school restructuring: The new American schools designs by Stringfield* (pp. 261-288). Upper Saddle River, NJ: Lawrence Erlbaum Associates, Inc.

Levin, H.M. (1988). *Accelerated schools for at-risk students.* Center for Policy Research in Education, Eagleton Institute of Politics, Rutgers, State University of New Jersey, New Brunswick, NJ.

Louis, K.S., Kruse, S.D., & Marks, H.M. (1996). Schoolwide professional community. In F.W. Newmann (Ed.), *Authentic achievement* (pp. 179-203). San Francisco, CA: Jossey-Bass Inc.

McLaughlin, M.W. & Talbert, J.E. (1993). *Contexts that matter for teaching and learning: Strategic opportunities for meeting the nation's education goals.* Palo Alto, CA: Center for Research on the Context of Secondary School Teaching, Stanford University.

Nave, B. (2000). *What are the results of two years of CFG work? Second-year report to NSRF schools* (National School Reform Faculty Evaluation). Providence, RI: Annenberg Institute for School Reform.

Newmann, F. & Wehlage, G. (1995). *Successful school restructuring.* Madison, WI: Center on Organization and Restructuring of Schools, University of Wisconsin.

Oakes, J., Quartz, K.H., Ryan, S., & Lipton, M. (2000). *Becoming good American schools: The struggle for civic virtue in education reform.* San Francisco: Jossey-Bass.

Oakes, J. & Quartz, K.H. (Eds.). (1995). *Creating new educational communities* (Vol. 94). Chicago, IL: University of Chicago Press.

Rogoff, B., Goodman Turkanis, C., & Bartlett, L. (2001). *Learning together: Children and adults in a school community.* New York: Oxford University Press.

Stigler, J.W. & Stevenson, H.W. (1991). How Asian teachers polish each lesson to perfection. *American Educator* (Spring), 12-47.

Valli, L., Cooper, D., Frankes, L., & Zeichner, K.C.E. (1997). Professional development schools and equity. In M.W. Apple (Ed.), *Review of research in education* (Vol. 22, pp. 251-304). Washington, DC: American Educational Research Association.

Vital Research (2002). *Teacher preparation and professional development (PDS) + Preparing tomorrow's teachers to use technology (PT3).* Outcome Evaluation, Year 3. Los Angeles, CA: Vital Research, LLC.

CHAPTER 2   *Sally Yahnke, Gail Shroyer, Lisa Bietau,
Melisa Hancock, & Andrew Bennett*

Collaborating to Renew and Reform K–16 Education

Vision, Values, and Beliefs of Our Collaborative Partnership

In *Tomorrow's Schools of Education,* the Holmes Group (1995) "describes our hopes and expectations for greatly improved schools of education" (p. 1). This report challenges colleges of education to raise their standards and to make important changes in their curriculum, faculty, location of their work, and in their student body. The Holmes Group also suggests "education students for too long have been learning too little of the right things in the wrong places at the wrong time" (p. 2). According to this document: "The Universities that develop education knowledge, influence education policy, and prepare teachers and other leaders for our nations' schools and education schools must overcome 'business as usual' to meet the challenge of these truly unusual times in education. The indisputable link between the quality of elementary and secondary schools and the quality of the education schools must be acknowledged—and we must respond" (p. 3). This educational crisis is based on a complex web of social, economic, political, and educational factors. According to Richardson (1994), "Educators often find themselves ensnared in a social system that is ravaging our children and youth, a political system that regulates more than it facilitates learning and an education system that is often centralized, bureaucratic and inflexible. . . . If schools and universities do not demonstrate aggressive leadership in addressing the needs of students, teachers and administrators, it is highly probable that society will continue to lose confidence in both sets of institutions. Worse than the loss of trust in these institutions is the tragedy of losing thousands of children and youth to ways of life that are unproductive or destructive" (p. 2). In addition, the push toward standards-based programs—to provide accountability for P–12 education and university programs for teacher education—also demands change in teacher-education programs to more effectively provide the career-long, standards-based preparation needed to meet the demands of educating children (Holmes Group, 1996). "Thus, colleges of education will have to reinvent themselves to prepare candidates to attain the proficiencies described in professional and state teacher performance standards, and they will have to document their candidates' attainment through clear assessments, including results on performance-oriented measures and mentoring year assessments" (Wise & Leibbrand, 2001, p. 246).

This need for enhanced professional development, combined with the need to restructure K–12 schools and teacher preparation programs, has "created a unique opportunity for collaborative systemic reform, where the many components of reform are addressed and their interdependencies and interrelationships are recognized" (National Research Council, 2001, p. 75). Such systemic reform initiatives have "created unprecedented opportunities for all players in the educational community . . . to design and implement new collaborative approaches to teacher education" (National Research Council, 2001, p. 5). Many colleges of education have responded to this call for reform and are in the process of restructuring their teacher preparation programs to prepare teachers for the challenges of preparing all students for success in the 21st century (Holmes Group, 1995). During the fall of 1989, this reform initiative provided the incentive for the creation of the Kansas State University Professional Development School Partnership. The vision of this partnership was to collaboratively restructure our teacher preparation program while simultaneously reforming K–12 education to enhance the quality of teaching and learning at all levels of schooling for all students and educators.

In 1989 Kansas State University began a collaborative teacher-education model to reform teacher education and K–12 teaching and learning. As part of this initiative, KSU has entered into a partnership with five diverse school districts across Kansas to establish 25 PDS. These five districts represent inner-city, small-town, and rural learning environments and include 15 elementary, six middle, and four high-school PDSs. Each PDS has been established progressively over a 15-year period and represents different stages in the development of quality PDS. The KSU PDS Partnership includes content faculty, education faculty, K–12 teachers, and administrators who are committed to the simultaneous and collaborative improvement of the KSU teacher preparation program and K–12 teaching and learning. All PDS partners believe that education must be viewed as a continuum that ranges from kindergarten through college. Improvements at any one of these levels cannot succeed without improvements at the other levels. Our ultimate vision is to create and sustain a community of learners dedicated to continuous learning and systemic reforms in K–12 schools. More specifically, we are committed to preparing all educators to meet the changing needs of all diverse learners, particularly those learners with the greatest educational needs.

The established PDS Partnership goals focus on the promotion of the intellectual engagement and development of all stakeholders (NCATE, 2001). In order for this to happen, we believe that partnering institutions share responsibility for:

- the clinical preparation of new teachers
- continuing professional development of all educators
- support of children's learning
- support of practice-based inquiry directed toward the improvement of teaching and learning

New Teachers

Teacher preparation is an extremely complex process that must be viewed as a continuum of career-long experiences that mold and shape the ever-changing behaviors of the classroom teacher. Where reform efforts could have been disjointed and incremental, our PDSs have permitted us to restructure our teacher preparation from this complex, holistic perspective. The PDSs facilitate systematic field experiences within realistically complex environments. These experiences have become a unifying feature of our students' education by integrating content and pedagogy and providing a sense of relevancy for their studies.

Continuing Professional Development

In the PDS, pre-service and in-service education is viewed as an inseparable continuum. The aim is to learn and to grow together as a community of learners. Professional development opportunities offered within PDS provide novice and experienced educators with the knowledge, skills, attitudes, and resources to empower them to create teaching and learning environments that will meet the needs of an increasingly diverse student population. School-based student-teaching seminars, mentor-teacher meetings, faculty meetings, and professional development offered through special projects allow novice and experienced teachers to reflect on their teaching and learning with peers, administrators, and university faculty.

Support of Children's Learning

PDS symbolizes a commitment to improving career-long teacher preparation while improving K–12 instruction. The large number of KSU students and faculty working within each PDS provides extra resources, people, and support to help all children reach high levels of academic excellence. In addition, many enrichment activities have been provided to children and their parents through family math and science programs; math, science, and technology after-school clubs; summer magnet schools; and tutoring programs. Student-teaching seminars and mentor-teacher meetings provide opportunities for PDS participants to enhance their understanding of teaching and learning.

Practice-Based Inquiry

Ultimately, PDS should exemplify the most current and best practices education has to offer. Practice-based inquiry has included action research projects and classroom innovations. This collaborative inquiry has involved pilot testing and field testing new curriculum, technology, innovative teaching, and assessment techniques. Action research projects have been conducted to examine student learning, effective instruction, teacher preparation, educational equity, parental attitudes, and school change. Examples of classroom innovations include: developing non-routine mathematical problem-solving curricula; thematic teaching; peer coaching; team teaching; multi-age classrooms; and alternative assessment strategies including authentic assessment, portfolios, non-graded report cards, and student-led parent conferences. Our intention is to explore how children learn, how teachers learn, and how schools improve.

The Simultaneous Improvement Process

Each PDS has a clinical instructor who has been identified by the school as a teacher-leader to facilitate all PDS efforts at that school. These clinical instructors are partially released, using KSU funds, to support PDS initiatives. The clinical instructor, building principal, and faculty liaison oversee all school-based PDS activities. Since 1999, funding from the U.S. Department of Education and the National Science Foundation has provided additional support for the KSU PDS Partnership. As part of these federally funded projects, the overall K–16 PDS Partnership has been directed by two faculty from the College of Education (the PDS coordinators), two faculty from Arts and Sciences (a biologist and a mathematician), district administrators, and clinical instructors who meet regularly to coordinate initiatives, monitor progress, and assess the impact of the PDS Partnership.

Federal funds have been used to support a wide variety of PDS partnership projects to develop our community of learners. Approximately 30 faculty from the College of Education, 30 faculty from the College of Arts and Sciences, and 70 practicing teachers and administrators have been meeting for more than three years in planning teams. These teams examine and improve teaching and learning in the KSU teacher-education program and the K–12 PDS. We have identified nine planning teams (math, science, language arts, humanities, social studies, foundations, special education, English-language learners, and mentoring) to collaboratively design projects to address the continuum of teacher education from pre-service preparation, through mentoring of new teachers, to professional development programs for faculty and experienced teachers, including action research projects and a network to support teachers through the National Board for Professional Teaching Standards (NBPTS) certification process.

The planning teams have created new K–12 teacher-education standards that are performance based, while simultaneously implementing standards-based curriculum and instructional strategies in their own K–16 classrooms. While implementing course improvements, team members have participated in a Peer Consultation process (Bernstein, 1996) that involves: visits to team members' classes, examinations of team members' curricula, instructional strategies, assessment approaches, and discourse concerning effective ways to enhance teaching and learning in K–16 classrooms.

Our federally funded simultaneous reform project was strengthened in 1999 by the federal funds from the U.S. Department of Education and the National Science Foundation by focusing on improvements in individual classrooms. The planning teams met monthly for professional development activities and planning sessions and during two-week Summer Institutes. Faculty and teachers were introduced to state and national content standards for teachers and K–12 students (National Council of Teachers of Mathematics, 2000; National Research Council, 1996; National Council for Social Studies, 1998; National Council of Teachers of English & International Reading Association, 1996). Teams also examined standards for beginning teachers (Interstate New Teacher Assessment and Support Consortium, 1995; National Council for Accreditation of Teacher Education, 2001) and experienced teachers (National Board for Professional Teaching Standards, 1998). In addition, teams had the opportunity to read and discuss reform documents (Darling-Hammond, 1999; National Commission on Teaching and America's Future, 1996, 1998; NRC, 2000; U.S. Department of Education, 2000, 1999, 1998).

After examining the standards and the reform documents, the first task for each team was to align an individual course or grade level curriculum to the content standards. We began with a focus on individual classrooms and courses in order to personalize the improvement process and develop ownership. The following academic year, team members were asked to implement any changes in their courses that were needed to better align with the standards. We used Peer Consultation to facilitate and support the classroom improvement process. During 2001 and 2002, we expanded individual course reform to initiate program improvements. Teams were asked to begin to develop performance-based standards for our teacher preparation program. The standards were categorized as: professional standards for all K–12 teachers, general education content standards for all teachers, and elementary, middle-school, and high-school subject-specific standards. Teams were asked to articulate the desired standard and to identify the content courses, methods courses, and field experiences where the standard would be taught and assessed. They also were asked to identify evidence that would be collected in the courses and field experiences to demonstrate that each standard had been met, and to design methods and criteria to assess this evidence (e.g., rubrics).

Since 2001 each PDS school has been asked to complete a school-improvement action plan. In this plan, each school uses student assessment data to identify school-wide strengths and weaknesses. Each school then identifies at least one school-improvement goal to become a focus for partnership improvement efforts. This information has been used each year to plan professional development opportunities during the school year and during annual summer institutes. Planning team members have been asked to identify ways in which the entire team could help the school realize its school-improvement goals.

Research Framework

In what ways do broad-based collaborations foster simultaneous renewal of teacher education and K–12 schools? "Although still tentative, there is definitely a growing collection of evaluation data that points to the positive impact of professional development school partnerships. . . . There is also the growing recognition of the importance of documenting PDS outcomes in credible ways, and the increasing use of multiple measures and conceptual frameworks that link outcomes with processes" (Teitel, 2001, p. 13). To address this concern and to construct a more meaningful understanding of reform in our teacher education program and our five partner school districts, we initiated a multifaceted, longitudinal study to examine the process and the impact of change on all our partner organizations. In addition to the organizational change literature (Fullan, 1991), we used the PDS Standards from the National Council for Accreditation of Teacher Education (NCATE, 2001) to design our research to more thoroughly examine organizational changes in relation to each PDS setting and the presence or absence of critical PDS attributes.

Since 1989, we have gathered a wide variety of quantitative and qualitative data from all stakeholders using a case-study approach. In addition, since 1998 our PDSs have been involved in self-studies based on the NCATE PDS Standards. Data sources include: multiple surveys and interviews of PDS teachers, administrators, K–12 students, parents, KSU faculty, and KSU students; numerous institutional documents; and student achievement data. We have analyzed the impact of our simultaneous reform efforts by examining institutional changes in the KSU teacher-education program and in the K–12 PDS. In addition, we have documented the impact of these reform efforts on K–12 learning in mathematics since this is the area targeted for improvement by most of our PDSs. The student achievement data used for this analysis include the State of Kansas student achievement measures in Mathematics at grades 4, 8, and 11. We have tracked achievement gains in our PDSs in comparison to statewide achievement gains. As a final step, student achievement and organizational impact have been compared to PDS stages of development, based on the NCATE PDS Standards, to identify PDS attributes critical to the simultaneous reform process. This is a continuous analysis that guides our reform efforts.

Organizational Impact

Program outcomes documented since 1993 suggest that the partnership between KSU and our PDS partners has enhanced our pre-service and in-service teacher preparation program, improved the teaching of participating teachers and faculty, enriched learning opportunities for children, and strengthened collaborative relationships between Kansas State University and PDS practitioners (Bolick, 1996; Cooper, 1995; Daisey & Shroyer, 1995; Govindarajan, 1993; Ramey-Gassert, 1996; Shroyer, Ramey-Gassert, Hancock, Moore & Walker, 1995; Shroyer & Wright, 1995; Shroyer, Wright & Ramey-Gassert, 1996; Stalheim-Smith & Scharmann, 1994; Wilhite, 1995; Wilson, 1993; Zollman, 1994). Our multi-site PDS self study indicated that we are between "At Standard" and "Leading" on the NCATE PDS Developmental Guidelines (NCATE, 2001). We are strongest in Standard I: Learning Community, and Standard III: Collaboration, followed by Standard IV: Structures, Resources, and Roles. We believe we are moving closer to our vision of transforming both pre-service and in-service teacher preparation and K–12 schools by collaboratively creating a new model for effective career-long professional development within PDS.

More recently, the use of planning teams and the Peer Consultation model have created a culture of collaboration across the campus at Kansas State University. Thirty faculty from the College of Education, 30 faculty from the College of Arts and Sciences, and 70 teachers from our partner schools have designed new performance-based standards for future teachers. Content courses, methods courses, and field experiences have been critically examined and modified as necessary. As a result of this process, courses have now been aligned with K–12 content standards and our KSU performance-based teacher-education standards. University faculty and school partners now have a better understanding of each other's work environment, organization expectations, the reform movement in K–12 education and teacher education, effective teaching strategies, the needs of diverse learners, and of performance-based assessment. The Colleges of Agriculture, Arts and Sciences, Education, and Engineering frequently engage in joint ventures with one another and with our school partners. University and school faculty have attended conferences, made joint presentations, and implemented research projects together. PDS Partnership faculty participants collaboratively established the Faculty Exchange for Teaching Excellence. This group provides ongoing workshops and faculty SWAP Sessions. More than 60 college faculty have engaged in regular professional development opportunities during the year, including Summer Institutes, and have created a dynamic community of learners.

The College of Education and the partnership districts have jointly designed and implemented a mentoring program for new teachers. Three of our partner districts have formally adopted our partnership mentoring program. All new teachers in these districts participate in this program during their first three years of teaching. We are also creating a distance-mentoring process to provide support to graduates from our programs that are teaching in districts outside of our partnership. To provide professional development for our highly experienced teachers, we supported study groups and coached the K–12 teachers from our partnership districts who are preparing for NBPTS certification. Over 50 teachers from our PDS have participated in the National Board certification process and 21 teachers have achieved National Board certification.

PDS Impact on K–12 Student Achievement

To track student achievement gains across time at each PDS, we analyzed 1995–2002 state assessment data in mathematics. Kansas state assessments changed in 2000 for all content areas; therefore, data before 2000 cannot accurately be compared to data after 2000. Student achievement data will be reported in three groupings: from the 1995–1999 assessments, from the 2000–2002 assessments, and from two cases of change using the 2000–2003 assessments. The data reported represent school-wide average scores.

1995–1999 Results

We began our analysis of PDS impact from 1995 to 1999 by sorting our PDSs into three groups based on the length of time they have been a PDS (from 1, the most established, to 3, the newest PDS). We then examined student achievement gains in each school across time compared to the length of time each school has been a PDS. We looked for common patterns in achievement gains across sites, as well as uncommon trends unique to individual sites. Uncommon findings were subjected to further analysis using the wealth of longitudinal data that have been collected at each site.

The first pattern we noted across sites was that our oldest PDS (Group 1) showed greater gains in mathematics (19 percent), compared to our newest PDS, Group 3 (0.7 percent). However, an interesting trend was revealed with our Group 2 schools (26 percent gain) out-performing both our oldest (Group 1) and newest (Group 3) sites (see Figure 2.1).

To better understand this finding, we examined program documents, surveys, and interview data looking for differences among the three groups of PDSs. One trend we

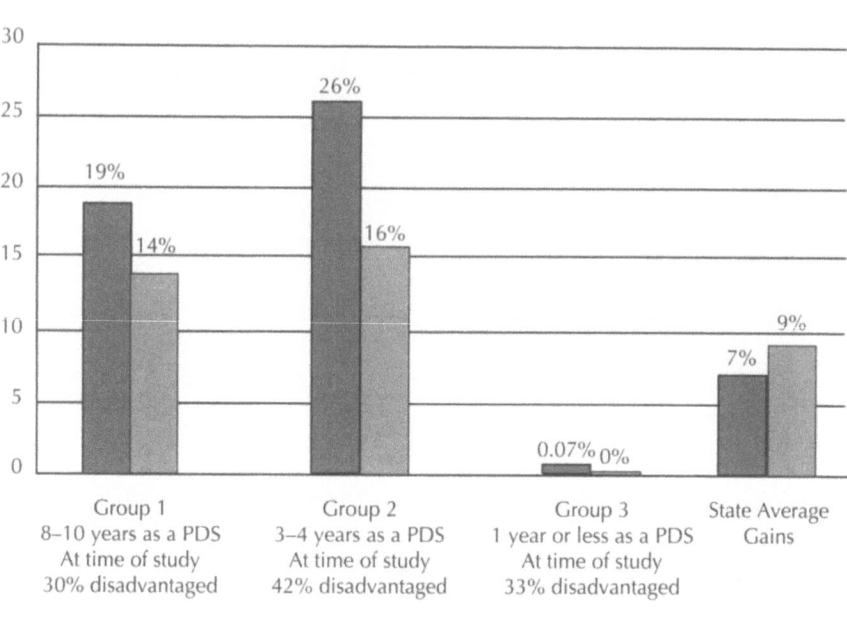

FIGURE 2.1. Student Achievment Gains in Mathematics Compared to Length of Time as a PDS (Comparison of average school scores on state assessments from 1995–1999).

noted was that teachers from Group 2 schools were more involved in professional development activities and grant projects offered through the partnership. To further explore this trend, we divided our PDSs into two groups (active and non-active) based on the level of teacher participation in each PDS. A school was classified as non-active if fewer than five teachers in a given school participated in less than half of the offered activities (see Figure 2.2).

As shown in Figure 2.2, student achievement gains are greater in PDSs in which teachers are more actively involved in professional development activities (23 percent gain) than those not involved (3 percent gain). To explore this idea even further, we decided to see if there was a relationship between student achievement gains and teacher participation in particular professional development activities. We examined our original Group 2 schools and found that many schools in this group were involved in Project Pride, an action research project conducted from 1995 to 1997.

Project Pride was a 2-year project that involved 8 PDSs in an effort to improve mathematical and scientific problem solving through the use of classroom-based and school-wide action research. Over the 2-year period teachers attended monthly professional development days and 2 month long summer institutes designed to enhance

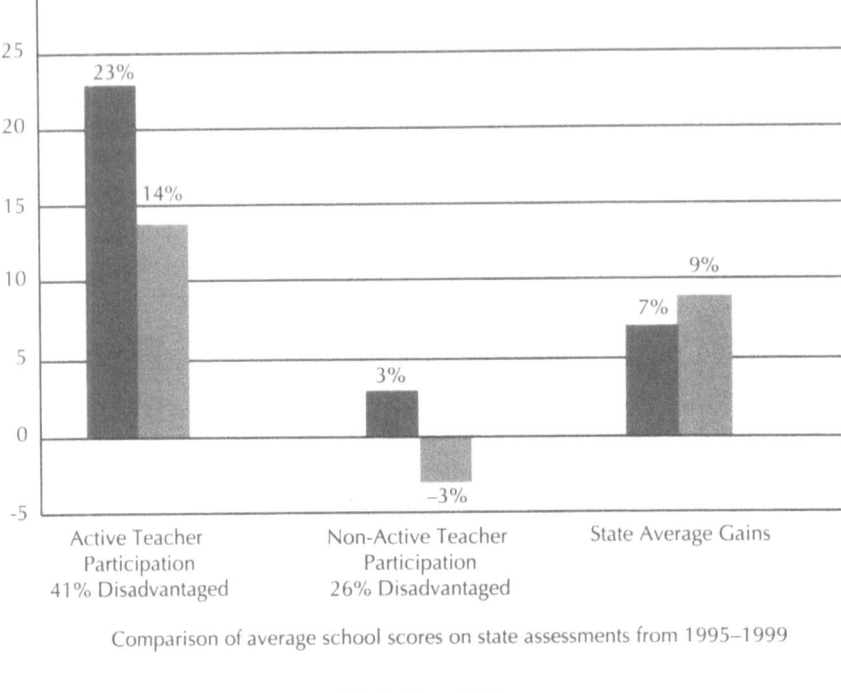

FIGURE 2.2. Student Achievement Gains in Mathematics Compared to Level of Participation in PDS Activities (Comparison of average school scores on state assessments from 1995–1999).

mathematics and science instruction. Teams of teachers from each of the 8 schools completed action research projects to assess the effectiveness of changes in their classroom practices in terms of student achievement. Although the teachers for each school participated as a team, the majority of the action research projects focused on individual classroom practices in science or mathematics. Three of the participating schools planned school-wide improvements in mathematical problem solving. Mathematics scores from all 8 participating schools were analyzed to compare achievement gains in action research schools with average state achievement gains using Kansas Assessment data from 1995–1999. On average, the 8 schools involved in this project saw a 19 percent increase in mathematical problem solving and a 12 percent increase in their total mathematics score from 1995 to 1999 compared to a state increase of 7 percent in problem solving and 9 percent in total mathematics. The schools that initiated school-wide action research projects saw a 28 percent increase in mathematical problem solving and an 18 percent increase in their total mathematics score from 1995 to 1999. One of these schools saw a 47 percent increase in mathematical problem solving from 1995 to 1999 (see Figure 2.3).

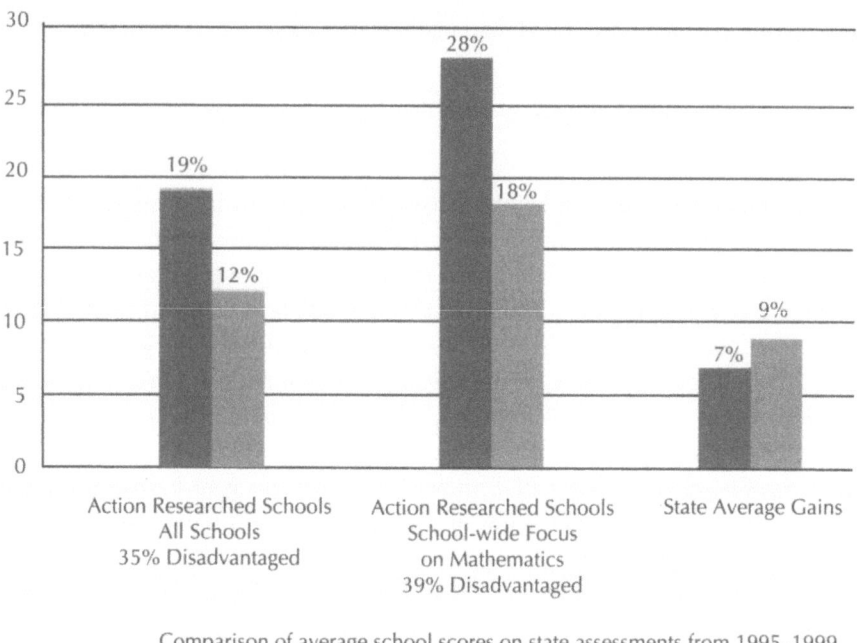

FIGURE 2.3. Student Achievment Gains in Mathematics Compared to Teacher Participation in Action Research Projects (Comparison of average school scoreson state assessments from 1995–1999).

Findings from this analysis indicate that schools that have been involved in continuous professional development and student-centered action research projects have seen significant increases in student achievement scores compared to average state increases. Schools with teachers involved in school-wide improvement projects have increased their scores even more than schools with teachers involved in individual classroom improvement projects.

As a follow-up to this analysis, scores for the action research project schools were examined using state mathematics assessment from 2000 to 2002. For five to seven years after the initial project, mathematics scores still showed a difference between participating and non-participating schools. Although they did not report the same increase in academic gains as compared to the other groups, the sites with a schoolwide action research focus consistently reported higher mean scores. In 2002, the PDSs that participated in school-wide action research projects reported a total mathematics score that was 10 percent higher than the state average. The other project schools participating in individual classroom-based action research projects reported a score 9 percent higher than the state average. KSU PDS sites that did not participate in the action research project had total mathematics scores 3 percent higher than the state average.

2000–2002 Results

We also examined state mathematics assessment data from 2000 to 2002 as a follow-up to our earlier comparison of student achievement gains in relation to length of time as a PDS. We maintained the same three groupings of schools. Since the state no longer provides a problem solving score, we compared the total math scores from 2000–2002. Whereas, the 1995–1999 data showed the greatest gains in Group 2, the 2000–2002 data indicate greater achievement gains in Groups 2 and 3 as compared to the scores of Group 1, which were more established sites. The Group 2 schools showed a gain of 6.3 percent while the Group 3 schools showed a gain of 11.8 percent. Group 1 PDS showed a 3.9 percent gain based on the same 2000–2002 data. State average gains in mathematics were 4.6 percent for the same time frame (see Figure 2.4).

These results continue to illustrate that there is not a simple relationship between student achievement and length of time as a PDS. Obviously, contextual factors within each PDS have an impact on student achievement. Further analysis of these contextual factors leads us to believe these gains are from partnership-supported mathematics improvement efforts. In 2000, we asked each PDS site to target an area for improvement using PDS partnership resources. The 2000–2002 data suggest that schools that targeted mathematics for improvement efforts (Groups 2 and 3) are making greater gains in this area. Specific examples of this collaborative improvement in mathematics in two partner districts are presented below.

2000–2003 Cases of Change

Kansas City, Kansas (USD 500) is a large, diverse, high-needs, urban district, that has historically performed poorly on state mathematics assessments. In the fall of 2001, as part of our collaborative renewal process, the elementary and middle school PDS decided to pilot NSF-sponsored standards-based curricula in mathematics, *Investigations in Number, Data, and Space* (TERC, 1998) and *Connected Mathematics* (Lappan, Fey, Fitzgerald, Friel, & Phillips, 2002). The district used this PDS as a test site prior to implementing the mathematics programs district-wide in the fall of 2002. The PDS Partnership Project worked together to support this pilot under the leadership of a mathematics educator, a mathematician, and a fifth- and sixth-grade teacher. The new curricula were introduced to teachers in a weeklong summer session, with implementation support sessions offered during the following two years. Teachers from Kansas City, Kansas visited teachers in Manhattan-Ogden (USD 383) who were already using the curricula, and teachers from Manhattan-Ogden traveled to Kansas

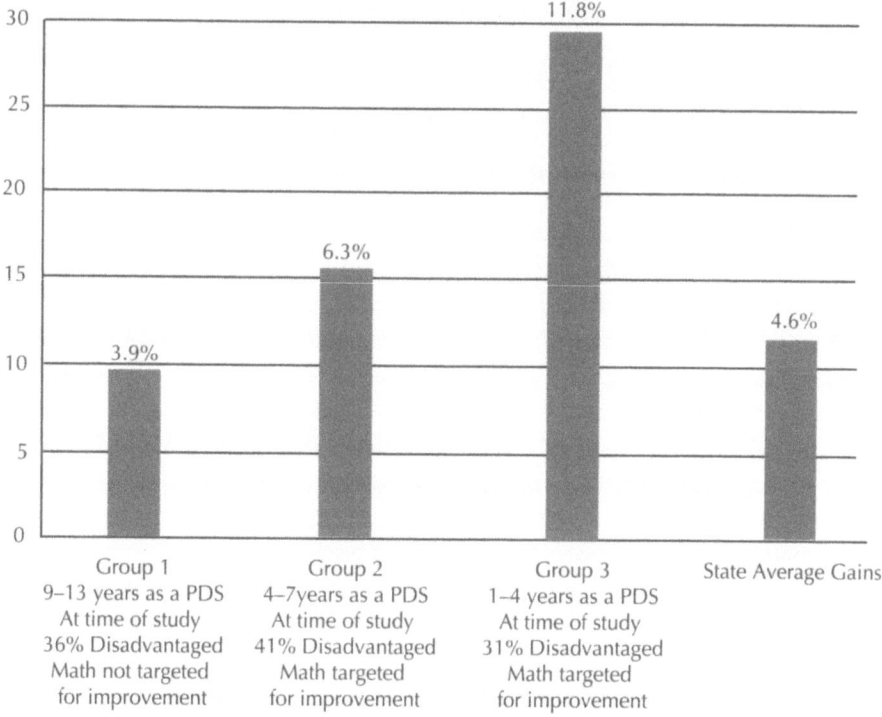

Comparison of average school scores on state assessments from 2000–2002

FIGURE 2.4. Student Achievment Gains in Mathematics Compared to Length of Time as a PDS and Involvement in Math Improvement Projects (Comparison of average school scores on state assessments from 2000–2002).

City, Kansas to demonstrate model lessons and participate on Peer Coaching teams. The pilot project has been a great success in terms of institutional change and student learning. We have tracked student achievement gains in mathematics using state mathematics assessment data. The elementary school has seen a 29.28 percent increase from 2000 to 2003, while the average gain in elementary schools across the state was 10.2 percent. The middle school has increased 14.15 percent while the average state middle schools increased 4.5 percent over the same years.

One high-needs school in the Manhattan-Ogden (USD 383) district also piloted and implemented a similar mathematics improvement project. The elementary school is located in Ogden, a small, low-income community adjacent to a military installation. The majority of the students in the school qualify for free and reduced meals (65 percent). Using the same model of workshops and implementation support used in Kansas City, including the utilization of KSU students (student teachers and math and science students from methods courses), the school has focused on improving student achievement in mathematics. Historically, the school has been

TABLE 2.1. Student Achievement in Targeted Schools: 2000–2003

School Site	2000 Score	2003 Score	% Increase	Average State Increase
USD 500 Elementary	32.1	41.5	29.28%	10.2%
USD 500 Middle School	31.8	36.3	14.15%	4.5%
USD 383 Elementary	52.8	69.3	31.25%	10.2%

one of the lowest performing in the district. However, in analyzing the year 2003 state assessment data, the school has shown an increase of 31.25 percent in mathematics scores between years 2000 and 2003. Additionally, the school achieved the State Standard of Excellence for the first time in mathematics. Table 2.1 summarizes these achievements.

Through the development of PDS, the Kansas State University's teacher preparation program has been enhanced, the teaching skills of participating teachers and faculty have been improved, and new collaborative relationships have been established between the College of Arts and Sciences, the College of Education, and the Professional Development School districts and their communities.

References

Bernstein, D.J. (1996). A departmental system for balancing the development and evaluation of college teaching. *Innovative Higher Education, 20,* pp. 241–248.

Bolick, M.E. (1996). *Socialization influences of the elementary environment on a beginning teacher prepared as a constructivist educator: An interpretive case study.* An unpublished doctoral dissertation, College of Education, Kansas State University.

Cooper, C.K. (1995). *Qualitative analysis of preservice elementary teachers' scientific ways of thinking, attitudes, and perceptions during collaborative earth science field-based experiences.* An unpublished doctoral dissertation, College of Education, Kansas State University.

Darling-Hammond, L. (1999). *Solving the dilemmas of teacher supply, demand, and standards: How we can ensure a competent, caring, and qualified teacher for every child.* New York: National Commission on Teaching and America's Future (NCTAF).

Daisey, P. & Shroyer, M.G. (1995). Parents speak up: Examining parent and teacher roles in elementary science instruction. *Science and Children,* Nov./Dec.

Fullan, M. (1991). *The new meaning of educational change.* New York: Teachers College Press.

Govindarajan, G. (1993). *Analysis of preservice elementary school teachers' collaborative problem solving in a constructivist-based interdisciplinary science course.* An unpublished doctoral dissertation, College of Education, Kansas State University.

Holmes Group (1995). *Tomorrow's schools of education.* East Lansing, MI: Author.

Interstate New Teacher Assessment and Support Consortium (1995). INTASC Core Standards. [online] *http://developo.ccsso.cybercentral.com/intasc.htm.*

Lappan, G., Fey, J.T., Fitzgerald, W.M., Friel, S.N., & Phillips, E.D. (2002). *Connected Mathematics.* Glenview, Illinois: Prentice Hall.

National Board for Professional Teaching Standards (1998). *What teachers should know and be able to do.* [online] http://www.nbpts.org/nbpts/standards/intro.html.

National Commission on Teaching and America's Future (NCTAF) (1996). *What matters most: Teaching for America's future.* New York: NCTAF.

National Commission on Teaching and America's Future (NCTAF) (1998). *Teaching for high standards: What policymakers need to know and be able to do.* New York: NCTAF.

National Council for Accreditation of Teacher Education (NCATE) (2001). *Standards for professional development schools.* Washington, DC: Author.

National Council for the Social Studies (NCSS) (1998). *NCSS Standards for Social Studies Teachers.*

National Council of Teachers of English and the International Reading Association (NCTE & IRA) (1996). *Standards for the English Language Arts.*

National Council of Teachers of Mathematics (NCTM) (2000). *Principles and standards for school mathematics.* Washington, DC: Author.

National Research Council (NRC) (2001). *Educating teachers of science, mathematics, and technology: New practices for the new millennium.* National Academy Press.

National Research Council (NRC) (1996). *National science standards.* National Academy Press.

Ramey-Gassert, L. (1996). A qualitative study of factors influencing science teaching self-efficacy of elementary-level teachers. *Science Education, 80*(3), 283-315.

Shroyer, M.G., Ramey-Gassert, L., Hancock, M., Moore, P., & Walker, M. (1995). Math, science, technology after-school clubs and summer magnet school: Collaborative professional development opportunities for science educators. *Journal of Science Teacher Education, 6* (2), 112-119.

Shroyer, M.G. & Wright, E.L. (1995). *Expertise in preservice elementary teaching in science, mathematics, and technology: Evaluation of an innovative model.* Paper presented at the National Association for Research in Science Teaching. San Francisco, CA.

Shroyer, M.G., Wright, E.L., & Ramey-Gassert, L. (1996). An innovative model for collaborative reform in elementary-school science teaching. *Journal of Science Teacher Education, 7* (3), 151-168.

Stalheim-Smith, A. & Scharmann, L.C. (1994). General biology: Creating a positive learning environment for elementary education majors. *The American Biology Teacher, 56* (4), 216-220.

Teitel, Lee (2001). *How professional development schools make a difference: A review of research.* Washington, DC: National Council for Accreditation of Teacher Education (NCATE).

TERC (1998). *Investigations in Number, Data, and Space.* Glenview, Illinois: Scott Foresman.

U.S. Department of Education. (USDOE) (2000). *Before it's too late: A report to the nation from the National Commission on Mathematics and Science Teaching for the 21st Century.* Education Publications Center.

U.S. Department of Education. National Center for Educational Statistics (1999). *Teacher quality: A report on the preparation and qualifications of public school teachers.* Washington, DC: U.S. Department of Education.

U.S. Department of Education (USDOE) (1998). *Promising practices: New ways to improve teacher quality.* Washington, DC: U.S. Government Printing Office.

Wilhite, K.T. (1995). *Changes in elementary science teachers during their participation in a science, mathematics, and technology teacher preparation project.* An unpublished doctoral dissertation, College of Education, Kansas State University.

Wilson, J. (1996). An evaluation of the field experiences of the innovative model for the preparation of elementary school teachers for science, mathematics, and technology. *Journal of Teacher Education, 47* (1), 53-59.

Wise, A.E. & Leibband, J.A. (2001). Standards in the new millennium: Where we are, where we're headed. *Journal of Teacher Education, 52* (3), pp. 244-255.

Zollman, D. (1994). Preparing future science teachers. *Physics Education, 29,* 271-275.

CHAPTER 3   *Jennifer E. Aldrich*

PDS First Steps
Baby Steps and Giant Steps

Introduction

A major education reform movement began in 1983 with the publication of the report, *A Nation at Risk: The Imperatives for Educational Reform* (National Commission on Excellence in Education, 1983), which prompted changes in the way teachers are prepared to teach and how they teach. Through these efforts, it has been proposed that future teachers attain knowledge and experience from practicing teachers along with their university teacher-educators. In a response to *A Nation at Risk,* two groups have promoted the idea of professional school partnerships as a method of restructuring the education of teachers: the Carnegie Forum on Education and the Economy (1986) and the Holmes Group (1990). The intent is to prepare teachers and support the professional development of practicing educators, in order to enhance their learning. Darling-Hammond (1998) writes, "Teachers learn best by studying, doing, and reflecting; by collaborating with other teachers; by looking closely at students and their work; and by sharing what they see" (p. 8).

Professional Development School partnerships have been one method for making a difference in the preparation of teachers and the continued professional growth of teachers in the field. The development of a PDS partnership is evolutionary and requires great effort. As an example, the Professional Development School partnership between a comprehensive regional university and several local public schools (the focus of this chapter) has been characterized by continual assessment and modification throughout its inception and development.

Theoretical Perspectives

Many commentators believe well-prepared teachers are the best hope for successful school reform (Association of Teacher Educators, 1986; Cobb, 2001; Goodlad, 1990; Ishler, 1995). The Holmes Group and the Carnegie Forum, for example, have emphasized that in order to prepare students for the future, schools, teachers, principals, and colleges of education must change to accommodate the diversity of America's citizens. Consequently, PDS partnerships have been posited as a means of enhancing teacher education (Goodlad, 1990). Minner, Varner, and Prater (1995) have reported that pre-service teachers "graduating from these programs are highly skilled, very confident, and well prepared to assume leadership roles in the schools where they will work" (p. 57). Likewise, Clark (1995) suggested the PDS is important in educating future teachers because the PDS model supports the [university] students' abilities to construct pedagogy skills, accumulate knowledge about the curriculum, and acquire the attitudes necessary to educate all learners.

The traditional program of teacher education is one in which students finish their coursework at a college or university and have one or more field placements in schools (including student teaching). The Professional Development School (PDS) program is a field-based approach in which education majors spend two or more semesters in a public school while completing coursework and practical experiences. PDSs follow different models with varying semesters, number of courses, and kinds of courses offered on-site. However, the overall PDS goals for future teachers are similar, even though the conceptualization of each partnership may differ. Commonalities include collaboration with teachers, administrators, and college faculties—all working together to change the preparation and induction of future teachers (Stallings & Kowalski, 1990). Planned outcomes are developed to "create a sustainable network of schools through which the schools prepare new teachers" and "supporting teaching practices that promote and assist all students in achieving high academic standards" (Cooper, 1998, p. 64). Currently, a greater emphasis is being placed on the need for teacher preparation efforts to center on the impact of that preparation on the students they will teach. Thus, university faculty, teacher candidates, and students have a stake in the collaborative efforts of PDS partnerships. Marshall (1999) reported "children benefit from having increased numbers of adults supporting their learning; in-service teachers learn new ideas from pre-service teachers; university professors need continued experiences working with children and in-service teachers in order to nourish their own instruction about teaching; and, teaching, like learning, is a dynamic experience for which one is never totally prepared and opportunities for tutelage come from a multitude of sources, including colleagues, mentors, students, and families" (p. 3).

One validation of the PDS is the recent development of standards for PDS by the National Council for Accreditation of Teacher Education (NCATE). Five standards address the characteristics of Professional Development Schools, and ten key concepts are embedded in the standards to describe the purposes and principles of the PDS (NCATE, 2001). The five standards are divided by the topics: learning community; accountability and quality assurance; collaboration; equity and diversity; and, structures, resources, and roles (NCATE, 2001, p. 6). The standards are meant to guide the development and continuation of partnerships, toward the overall goal of meeting the diverse learning needs of all learners. To supplement the standards, NCATE created developmental guidelines for four stages in the development of Professional Development Schools: beginning level, developing level, at standard, and leading level (NCATE, 2001).

Development of a Public School–University Collaboration

The history of one university's PDS partnership with two school districts began with a grant proposal submitted to the state Department of Education. This four-year grant helped in the beginning development and implementation of the PDS. Funds were used to hire a director, pay stipends to teachers, provide release time for university faculty, pay for two hours of graduate credit for participating teachers, pay for PDS teams to attend conferences, hold a Summer PDS Institute, provide money and supplies for action research projects, and provide professional development activities and supplies for teachers. The PDS continued the grant because there was a collaborative effort between the school districts and the university to maintain the program. Now, the PDS continues with support for the director's position, pay for graduate credit, holding an abbreviated version of the Summer PDS Institute, reduced release time for the university faculty, and the provision of professional development opportunities for teachers whenever possible. In addition, during the fifth year another early-childhood PDS site was added.

The goals and benefits of the PDS model speak to advancements in pre-service teachers' professional development and the schooling of public-school students. PDS goals include:

- promoting the development of effective pre-service teachers
- increasing student achievement in the public schools
- developing strong and collaborative professional relationships
- increasing the use of technology to enhance teaching and learning
- developing teachers in undertaking leadership roles
- assisting districts and pre-service teachers in determining a strong employment fit

In addition, the benefits derived from the partnership include better working-relationships between school districts and the university, university faculty having greater credibility through role reversals and a more complete understanding of the way schools function, a positive impact on K–12 students through interaction with university education majors, and better preparation of education majors. Specific benefits for the preparation of education majors include:

- a chance to learn about the culture of schools in a "low-stakes" environment (in contrast to student teaching when a teacher candidate has more responsibilities)
- interactions with clinical faculty in the classroom setting and when clinical faculty present on topics
- more and varied experiences for teacher candidates to engage with K–12 students
- additional opportunities to observe in P–16 classrooms
- more time in classrooms—two semesters instead of the previous practice of one semester (student teaching)
- conversations about teaching occurring on a variety of levels—between university and public-school faculty, between public-school faculty and university students, and between university students and their university faculty. This leads to sharing information about best practices, current research, latest materials, and so forth (Carter, 2002)

Consequently, the PDS partnership has had a positive impact on students and teachers, and the school district now has a policy to hire PDS graduates at step two on the pay scale, instead of step one for beginning teachers.

Description of the Steps in an Early-Childhood Professional Development School Partnership

At our university, education students may major in early-childhood education only, early-childhood/elementary-education double major, or elementary education only. All elementary majors and double majors are required to participate in a PDS experience as part of their senior block classes. However, the early-childhood education majors did not have a PDS experience available. During the fall semester, a new early-childhood PDS collaboration began. Details regarding the early-childhood PDS journey are displayed in Table 3.1.

The PDS director began collaborating with the principal of the school during the spring 2002 semester. Because the principal was interested in creating a partnership with the university, the university faculty member and PDS director were invited to attend a school faculty meeting. They talked with teachers in order to gauge their interest in a partnership with the university. The school faculty's response to the PDS was favorable, and the university faculty member rearranged the scheduled time for the Early Childhood Curriculum Course. The new schedule corresponded with the school schedule in order to provide the maximum interaction of interns (pre-service

TABLE 3.1. **PDS First Steps**

Step 1: Spring 2002	PDS director contacted desired PDS site principal.
Step 2: Spring 2002	PDS director and university faculty member met with interested teachers and principal at desired PDS site.
Step 3: Fall 2003	PDS director and university faculty member met with new principal and selected site coordinator (previous principal transferred).
Step 4: Fall 2003	PDS director, university faculty member, elementary faculty, principal met in focus group—beginning of collaboration, definition of PDS, expectations.
Step 5: Fall 2003	PDS director, university faculty member, elementary faculty, principal, university interns met—introductions, tour, expectations.
Step 6: Fall 2003	University interns met twice per week for class and to participate in mentor classrooms, and university faculty member visited classrooms twice per week.
Step 7: Fall 2003	University faculty member and elementary faculty met monthly to discuss progress of interns and students, and to report on and discuss a book.

teachers), teachers, students, and university faculty. The Early Childhood PDS partnership was launched.

It has been reported that collaboration between the university and elementary school is essential to the growth and success of Professional Development Schools. Collaboration determines the ability of schools and universities to accept the values, conflicts, failures, lapses in commitment, and most importantly, the erratic nature of progress toward the ultimate restructuring goal (Stirzaker & Splittgerber, 1991). The quality of collaboration between and among the stakeholders often becomes key to the success of PDS programs. One of the PDS NCATE Standards is based upon collaboration:

> PDS partners and partner institutions systematically move from independent to interdependent practice by committing themselves and committing to each other to engage in joint work focused on implementing the PDS mission. They collaboratively design roles and structures to support the PDS work and individual and institutional parity. PDS partners use their shared work to improve outcomes for P-12 students, candidates, faculty, and other professionals. The PDS partnership systematically recognizes and celebrates their joint work and the contributions of each partner. (NCATE, 2001, p. 23)

The PDS university-faculty member continued the process of collaboration begun by the PDS director and scheduled a meeting with the new elementary-school principal and the school faculty to discuss perceptions about PDS (none of the teachers had been involved in a PDS prior to this time), expectations, and assignments for the interns. The faculty participated in a focus group/collaborative brainstorming session with the PDS coordinator and university faculty member before school began. It is believed that this first collaborative meeting set the tone for the partnership and resulted in reciprocal respect and trust.

At the first meeting, the elementary-school faculty and principal listed some of their expectations and roles for the interns. Appropriate and professional dress and language, dependability, punctuality, and confidentiality were important considerations that the teachers stressed with the interns. They also stressed their desire for the students to interact with children and to participate in classroom activities. In addition, they listed specific jobs such as helping with journal writing, reading to individual children, and helping individual children in other learning activities.

Documentation of the Early-Childhood PDS Beginnings

A researcher selected a qualitative, case-study approach to describe the first stages of the Early Childhood PDS. Participants selected included elementary school teachers (n = 8) who had volunteered to mentor interns, the principal, and the PDS director. The observations, monthly meetings, and focus group sessions took place at the elementary school.

During the first meeting, a focus-group technique was used to determine the elementary-school faculty's familiarity with, and preconceived notions about, PDS partnerships. The focus-group method was used so the participating teachers' interactions would stimulate others to share the feelings, perceptions, and beliefs that they might not express if they were interviewed individually (Gall, Borg & Gall, 1996). The focus-group interview was conducted at the school in a non-threatening, relaxed, and comfortable environment so the participants could more readily share their ideas. The teachers who took major responsibility for stating their views and drawing out the views of others in the group asked the following discussion questions:

1. What is a PDS?
2. What makes a PDS work?
3. Who is involved in a PDS?
4. What roles do these people play?
5. Who benefits from a PDS?
6. How do they benefit?

The participating teachers' answers to the above questions guided later discussions. The questions, "What is a PDS?" and "What makes a PDS work?" generated the most responses and a variety of points of view. Many participants reflected on the benefits to the interns. One elementary teacher stated the PDS is an "opportunity for education students to get exposure/training in the trenches as pre-student teaching." Other participants focused on the interns as learners who need real classroom experience before teaching, time to observe teachers modeling age-appropriate practices, and as persons making a transition to prioritizing students' needs over their own.

Some of the teachers focused on their descriptions of a Professional Development School. Participants stated that a PDS is "a school who grows together and develops toward the best way to educate children" and "a way to grow as a teacher while working with a student just starting out." One teacher summed up what many others said when she said a PDS is "a format that allows professionals to work together to produce more effective new teachers, improved learning for students, and growth for faculty."

The elementary-school teachers discussed how teachers and interns are involved in a PDS. They responded that the role of the teacher is to be a "wise and loyal advisor," give "guidance," and serve as a "role model and mentor." In contrast, the role of the intern is "a young adult who is learning how to teach."

Benefits cited by the participating faculty included benefits to themselves and their students. They stated that they learned from the intern's ideas, are more able to be in touch with what young teachers think and are taught in college, and are able to participate in professional development activities. Benefits to the elementary students included increased one-on-one attention, documented observations, small-group work, additional help for children, individual interaction with their teacher, sets of helping hands, and more.

In order to facilitate the professional growth of faculty, it was decided that the elementary teachers and the university professor would meet monthly to discuss current literature of interest to the group. In addition, this provided everyone involved with time to discuss the program, the interns, the students, progress, and problems. Sandholtz and Finan (1998) stated, "the heart of the program (PDS) is the creation of a professional learning environment promoting teacher learning in various forms" (p. 3). After the first semester, two main themes were identified from the data regarding the implementation of the Early Childhood PDS: benefits to college interns as well as to kindergarten students who received more individualized attention.

This research has become an ongoing activity at one PDS site. Data will be collected during the next several years to determine if the PDS experience is advantageous to the elementary teachers and what changes need to be implemented to continue meeting the needs of teachers, students, and interns. A focus for further research will be the impact of collaboration, and change in teacher attitudes regarding the continuation of the PDS.

Conclusion

The PDS experience has presented a number of challenges, including the meshing of two different cultures (public school and university), time, space, travel, compensation, and equality of partnership. However, activities such as holding classes on-site at the elementary school, inviting the elementary teachers to teach the interns specific topics from the curriculum course, and job-embedded professional development for the classroom teachers led to success for all involved. Specifically, the input of teachers regarding expectations for interns assisted in building collaboration and communication, which is essential for healthy partnerships. While many of the findings are specific to one site, many of the general concepts, such as collaboration and communication, can be generalized to all PDS partnerships.

References

Association of Teacher Educators. (1986). *Visions of reform: Implications for the education profession.* The report of the ATE Blue Ribbon Task Force. J. Sikula (Chair). Reston, VA: Author.

Carnegie Forum on Education and the Economy. (1986). *A nation prepared: Teachers for the 21st century.* Report of the Carnegie Task Force on Teaching as a Profession. Washington, DC: Author.

Carter, S. (2002, October). *The public school–university connection: A win-win collaborative.* Paper presented at the Southern Regional Council on Educational Administration, Kansas City, MO.

Clark, R. (1995). *National network for education renewal: Partner schools.* Center for Educational Renewal. Washington University, Seattle, WA (ERIC Document Reproduction Service No. ED 380 418).

Cobb, J. (2001). The impact of a professional development school on pre-service teacher preparation, in-service teachers' professionalism, and children's achievement: Perceptions of in-service teachers. *Journal of Teacher Education,* 64–74.

Cooper, M.G. (1998). Building a collaborative that will last. *Teaching and Change, 6* (1), 64–74.

Darling-Hammond, L. (1998). Teachers for the 21st century. *Principal, 78* (1), 8.

Gall, M.D., Borg, W.R., & Gall, J.P. (1996). *Educational research: An introduction* (6th ed.). White Plains, NY: Longman.

Goodlad, J.I. (1990). *Teachers for our nation's schools.* San Francisco: Jossey Bass.

Holmes Group. (1990). *Tomorrow's schools: Principles for the design of professional development schools.* East Lansing, MI: Author.

Ishler, R. (1995). Tomorrow's teachers, schools, and schools of education. *National Forum, 75,* 4–5.

Marshall, C.S. (1999). Constructing knowledge about teaching and learning in early-childhood teacher education because of a partnership. *Education, 119.*

National Council for Accreditation of Teacher Education. (2001). *Standards for Professional Development Schools.* Washington, DC: Author.

Minner, S., Varner, M., & Prater, G. (1995). Lessons learned from school-based teacher preparation programs. *The Teacher Educator, 31* (1), 56–67.

National Commission on Excellence in Education. (1983). *A nation at risk: The imperatives for educational reform.* Washington, D.C.: U.S. Government Printing Office (ERIC ed 279603), p. 1.

Sandholtz, J. H. & Finan, E. C. (1998). Blurring the boundaries to promote school-university partnerships. *Journal of Teacher Education, 49,* 13–15.

Stallings, J.A. & Kowalski, T. (1990). Research on professional development schools. W.R. Houston (Ed.), *Handbook of research on teacher education.* (pp. 120–132). New York: Macmillan.

Stirzaker, N.A. & Splittgerber, F. (1991). *Professional development schools.* Unpublished manuscript. University of South Carolina, Columbia.

PART II

Maintaining, Sustaining, and Supporting the Professional Development School

CHAPTER 4

Martha M. Mobley
& Nancy Norris-Bauer

Cross-Currents of Change
PDS Maintenance

Background

When taking stock of the progress of Professional Development Schools within the state of New Jersey, one might arrive at two conclusions. The first is the high level of commitment of teacher candidates, cooperating teachers, administrators, and clinical instructors. The second is the need for the same PDS participants to celebrate the PDSs as sites for educational change, bringing together the best in theory, practice, and research.

Two metropolitan universities (collaborating as partners in a grant) focused on establishing PDS partnerships. The universities selected local school districts with which to work on redesigning teacher education and enhancing the professional aspects of teaching. The field-experience directors of these universities realized that growth in Professional Development Schools was related to new work for schools and universities. On a daily basis, any PDS that moves beyond "courtship" into establishing a community of learners confronts new rules, new and changed responsibilities, different constraints, time allocation, and other concerns and issues. In *Modern Approaches to Understanding and Managing Organizations,* Bolman and Deal (1992) offer an organizational approach that provides a holistic framework for understanding the origins and growth of PDSs, their governance, personnel, rituals, and politics.

Bolman and Deal outline four major lenses—structural, human resources, political, and symbolic—through which basic issues of organizations can be viewed.[1] These lenses are useful in considering the struggles to develop and maintain fledgling and fragile PDSs into Year 2 and beyond.

The structural frame delineates the traditional edges of organizations and the basic issues of their design. It represents formal agreements, guidelines, role definitions, and PDS governance structure. Human-resource frames center on the people who work within the organizations. Subsumed within this frame are professional development and professional values, the belief in the power of education to make long-term change while feeling good about the work that is accomplished. The political frame presents the contrast and conflict within, and, in the case of PDSs, the agendas for the allocation of resources. Money, time, contracts, and collaboration continue to be among the different scarce resources around which conflict and power issues arise. These three—structural, human resources, and political—frame the varying degrees of certainty, rationality, and long-term stability of organizations.

Symbolism, the final frame, conveys organizational mysteries, myths, the magic of awards, banquets, T-shirts, and banners. These rites and ceremonies form the cohesiveness of an organization through word-of-mouth histories and grapevine stories.

Organizational events can be explained through these frames, each suggesting a special and unique approach to examining an organization and, by extension, its management. The four frames, in combination, form the inclusive lens that can be used to view the realities, power thrusts, and counterthrusts of an organization. For those who have breathed life into a PDS, the organizational frames appear to categorize major components of the new work resulting from the hybridization of a school-university partnership.

The intent in this chapter is to report the progress of 18 PDS partnerships of the two institutions, using Bolman and Deal's organizational frames, and then identify specific elements of the remaining 15 PDSs through their second and third years of existence (major elements for maintenance of our PDS are displayed in Appendix 4.A). The focus on work that is blended or combined from each of the institutions' schools and universities into "new" work is reflective of a new organization. The four included in this chapter are governance (structural frame), clinical instructors (human resources), union concerns (political), and celebrations (symbolic). From this approach to Professional Development Schools, it is apparent that the four PDS elements are used to concentrate attention on necessary "new" work, as outlined below, in order to maintain the lifeline of our PDSs.

Governance: Structural Frame

In our PDS network, governance is defined as a structure with membership that is representative of the university, school, and district, which is responsible for PDS oversight and management.

Expected Outcomes

- collaboration between university and school/district on issues of teaching and learning

- increased communication between partner institutions
- increased involvement of school/district personnel in the renewal of teacher education
- increased support for teacher candidates and induction-year teachers through
- collaboration undertaken by university faculty members and school personnel
- increased involvement of university faculty in school renewal
- heightened levels of mutuality in exchanges and achievement

Reality

- collaboration sometimes limited to issues related to finances and other resources
- decreased participation of school district personnel in the governance structure
- diminished leadership participation by the principal, albeit attendance in planning meetings remained constant
- shift of thinking from a "we" perspective to a singular focus on teacher candidates
- limited collaboration efforts that engaged the community of participants
- immediate retirement of a teacher leader and grave illness of the spouse of a second
- lack of an overall governance structure, one to bring together PDS personnel on a regularly scheduled basis; thus, governance remained school-based
- isolated successful PDS partnerships
- site-based school management teams serving as PDS governance
- standardized test scores of P–12 students not reflecting short-term increases in PDS partnerships

Description of PDS Governance

The objective of bringing together dissimilar institutions into a structure, while fostering commonality of purpose, goals, and outcomes, is seen as new work. The outcome of the university (a thirteenth-century glacier with an unchanged mission) interacting as a peer institution with public schools (with a daily refocusing of need) has been a merry-go-round of missteps, misstatements, and mishaps. However, common mission statements have been developed and put into place, with goals, objectives, and planned activities as part of the painful and necessary new work.

Clinical Instructors: Human Resources Frame

The clinical instructor is a university faculty member who is resident in school two full days each week—an experienced school administrator (principal or supervisor) hired for this position.

Expected Outcomes

- cohorts of selected teacher candidates placed in schools
- prospective teachers better prepared and capable of teaching a diverse student population
- higher retention rate of teacher candidates prepared in the PDS than in traditional placements
- increased support for induction-year teachers through the joint efforts of a clinical instructor and school personnel
- willing participation of teachers in preparation for their role as cooperating teachers

Reality

- high retention of university interns in the PDS through completion of requirements for teacher certification; interns self-selected to be placed in a PDS
- greater amount of time spent in PDS by clinical instructors than two days per week, yet pay remains static
- cooperating teachers disinclined to believe they need preparation for the mentor role
- induction-year teachers initially were not folded into the site/scenario
- the clinical supervisor's role may be considered as the most successful element of PDS efforts

Description of the "New" Work of a PDS Clinical Instructor

The role of clinical instructor is critical to the success of the model PDS described here. No two PDS partnerships are identical; thus, the roles and responsibilities of the clinical instructor vary by school. However, there are several themes of new work that cut across all PDS sites, including communication among in-service and pre-service teachers, and action research and professional development for teacher candidates, induction-year candidates, and certified professional educators.

Union Concerns: Political Frame

Expected Outcomes

- increased involvement of local teachers' associations and the New Jersey Education Association (NJEA)
- representation of teachers' unions in PDS governance structure
- assessment and accountability concerns

Reality

- university faculty and school faculty are unionized but in different unions
- union contract delineates the number of professional days that a teacher can participate in out-of-district professional development opportunities
- union contracts dictate remuneration to be paid to a teacher for each hour of participation outside of a school day or year
- teachers do not believe they should be assessed in their role as mentors

Description of Union Concerns and Their Impact on PDS "New" Work

- reward systems for university faculty do not include traditional work in public schools or districts
- change is a process requiring time for common planning, collaborating, and embedded professional development opportunities

Celebrations: Symbolic Frame

Expected Outcomes

- opportunities to celebrate openings of each school year, student achievement, and pre-service candidates in each PDS
- certificates awarded for exemplary achievements, action research, and accomplishments
- publications and presentations that disseminate ongoing work and success stories of a PDS partnership

Reality

- welcome orientations for incoming teacher candidates
- annual celebratory gathering of all PDS personnel
- plaques for partner schools to display
- limited individual school recognitions—retreats, bags, pencils, notebooks, T-shirts, etc.
- presentations at conferences by university and school participants
- newspaper articles in local and national publications

Lessons Learned

A number of lessons have been learned, with a primary one being that having high hopes, good intentions, and a belief in the educative process are insufficient to move a PDS to a stable position of invulnerability. Also, it is imperative that there be data about the growth and performance of teacher candidates with data needed regarding the excellence of PDS graduates. However, the fundamental philosophy of the PDS is sound, therefore, PDS is worthy work.

Concepts about the forward motion and the professional development of in-service and pre-service teachers have not been realized in these PDS partnerships. The improved performance capacity of interns can be documented, but there has been less success in making changes with the faculties of either institution. Further, action research is a unifying topic and a "new" work idea that may be turned into an effective activity by each university and implemented at the school sites. Also, action research has revitalized one PDS, thereby awakening teachers to its useful and rich possibilities for change.

Action research was begun originally as an assignment for teacher candidates, and their enthusiasm convinced the cooperating teachers of its value. It continues to be used more and more in the school. For instance, 24 out of 28 teachers are seeking answers to classroom-based research questions. Each semester, there are eight or nine interns in this PDS, and the school culture encourages and supports action research to the extent that the district staff developer delivers informational sessions about it throughout the district.

The first year of a PDS is like a first waffle from the grill—slightly malformed, and undercooked. The hope is that for subsequent years there will be a stability and consistency to the PDS that, to this point in time, has not been easy to accomplish. For example, two PDS partnerships were closed for the predominant reason that the schools were not ready for the development of a PDS relationship. Finally, it has been found that school and university leadership needs to be committed to the PDS if there is to be success.

Future steps include obtaining resources to continue funding the PDS. Perhaps, too, the NJEA will find reasons to join ranks with the universities and public schools, and help to invest in PDS partnerships as beacons for school reform and teacher improvement. Bolman and Deal (1992) did not design the organizational frames to address schools, universities, or their PDS stepchildren. Yet, the belief is that the four frames offer cogent and focused lenses through which to plan, implement, and examine PDS partnerships and their growth.

Note

1. The authors wish to thank John Wiley & Sons, Inc. for permission to use the framework created by Bolman & Deal (1992).

References

Bolman, L.G. & Deal, T.E. (1992). *Modern approaches to understanding and managing organizations.* San Francisco: Jossey-Bass.

APPENDIX 4.A. Crosscurrents of Change: PDS Maintenance

Structural (Coordination for Common Direction)	Human Resources (Individual Need)	Political (Networks of Special Interest)	Symbolic
Advisory Committee	Clinical Instructor	Action Research	Advertising
Contracts	Cooperating Teachers	Assessment	Awards/Certificates
Goals	Faculty	Change	Brochure(s)
Governance Structure	School Leaders	Collaboration Inter/Intra	Celebrations
Mission Statements	Leadership/Power	Conflict	Electronic Portfolios
Organizational Chart	Mentoring/Entry-Level Teachers	Curriculum Requirements	Exhibits/Photo Essays
PDS Guidelines	Parents	INTASC	Leadership
Power	Professional Development	Membership/Partnership	News Spots
Roles and Responsibilities	Mini-conferences	NCATE	Planning
	COE Faculty Meetings	NCLB	Posters
	School Faculty Meetings	NJCCCS	Presentations
	On-site Courses	NJEA	Signs & Banners
	Teacher Visitations	Power	T-shirts
	Student Visitations	Resources	Values & Appearances
	Retirements	UFT	Vision
	Roles	Union Issues	
	Students P–12		
	Teacher's Life Cycle		

Certainty, Rationality, Linearity ⟶   ⟵ Imagery ⟶

CHAPTER 5   *Clare Kruft*

PDS Collaboration
Providing Opportunities for Systemic Change

Life is, by nature, highly interdependent. To try to achieve maximum effectiveness through independence is like trying to play tennis with a golf club—the tool is not suited to the reality.
—STEPHEN COVEY,
The Seven Habits of Highly Effective People, p. 51

Professional Development Schools exist to collaborate. First piloted in the early 1980s, by innovators who sought to blur university and P–12 teaching boundaries for better education for all, the Professional Development School movement has gained increasing momentum as a practice in the initial and ongoing development of teachers. Although the National Council for Accreditation of Teacher Education (NCATE) reports that only about one-third of its accredited schools currently function with PDS sites as a cornerstone of their teacher preparation programs, it is clear that PDS involvement is a benchmark for quality teacher-training initiatives.

Introducing a New Vision for Collaboration

The question arises on how to institute quality PDS networks within the college preparation of pre-service teachers. As more colleges and universities test the waters of PDS collaboration, some basic research has begun to emerge on ways to conceptualize a PDS partnership network that will meet the needs for continual improvement among all constituents: pre-service interns, teaching staff at P–12 schools, university faculty, and perhaps most important, P–12 students themselves.

Testimonials from various PDS programs and anecdotal generalizations abound in the literature. This first phase of process evaluations of PDS schools is vital to the growing body of knowledge about the PDS. Sites using the PDS model for more than a few years attest to its inherent validity, and professional sources within teacher education are beginning to disseminate successful philosophies and practices embedded within PDS partnerships. A recent thematic issue of the Association of Supervision and Curriculum Development's (ASCD) widely read journal, *Educational Leadership,* relates (McBee & Moss, 2002):

> At its best, the professional development school is a place where paths of college faculty crisscross so regularly with the daily routines and expectations of school teachers, students, and administrators that interchange and mutual support are standard; college professors become trusted colleagues rather than idealistic, "clueless" interlopers. The professors become an integral part of the professional development school, bringing with them new ideas, techniques, research findings, and pre-service teachers. School life intimately engages the professors, imbuing them with a sensitivity to teachers' professional contexts. (p. 4)

In addition to the daily "crisscrossing" that blurs distinctions and forges new boundaries in the PDS, more deliberate partnerships within one college's sites (and possibly among a consortium of various colleges' sites) can benefit professionals in a more structured venue. In this way, many perspectives from various PDS sites can be shared. As Marsha Levine, a NCATE senior consultant for PDS, writes: "Professional development school partnerships pool the knowledge, skills, and resources of higher education institutions and pre-K–12 schools and bring them to bear collectively on teacher preparation and development and student learning" (2002, p. 67).

Creating Systemic Change through Collaboration

Peter Senge, a pioneer in systems-thinking and organizational development, explains how interrelated parts of a system need to reconceptualize themselves away from the fragmentation felt when experiencing challenges from disparate perspectives. He notes:

> From a very early age, we are taught to break apart problems, to fragment the world. This apparently makes complex tasks and subjects more manageable, but we pay a hidden, enormous price. We can no longer see the consequences of our actions; we lose our intrinsic sense of connection to a larger whole. . . . [It is] similar to trying to reassemble the fragments of a broken mirror to see a true reflection." (1990, p. 3)

Linked specifically to the educational system, Senge's remarks underscore the power of PDS to reunite disparate parts of teacher preparation programs, and to create learning. The university is primarily concerned with creating excellent beginning teachers, but without a strong link with P–12 schools, it perpetrates fragmentation in the undergraduate education that it provides. Conversely, elementary and secondary schools are primarily concerned with helping to facilitate the achievement of their P–12 students, but without viable connections to research-based and theoretically sound practices in higher education, they may operate in a practical but more limited cycle of "best practices." By employing a systems perspective, PDS schools bring together the best both cultures have to offer in a give-and-take of theory and practice to help increase student achievement and learning for all.

The concept of everyone learning within a learning community, as created with effective PDS partnerships, is central to the best practices outlined by many researchers and change agents (Hargreaves, & Manning, 2001; Bellanca, 1995; Deal & Peterson, 1999; DuFour & Eaker, 1998, and others). As DuFour, a former superintendent and highly sought educational speaker, and Eaker, a dean of education, write collaboratively:

> The basic structure of the professional learning community is a group of collaborative teams that share a common purpose. Some organizations base their improvement strategies on efforts to enhance the knowledge and skills of individuals. Although individual growth is essential for organizational growth to occur, it does not guarantee organizational growth. Thus, building a school's capacity to learn is a collaborative rather than an individual task. (1998, pp. 26–27)

PDS schools create structures and systems to sustain professional growth. The effectiveness of a PDS partnership can be measured in greater learning through the learning of all.

How Do We Network?

One way collective expertise can be harnessed is through the institutionalization of PDS network-wide meetings that can be called for a variety of purposes. These meetings can be a catalyst for collaboration, the kind of professional dialogue that is the hallmark of the PDS.

There are many purposes for which mentor-networking forums or PDS network articulation meetings can be conducted. One way to frame the thinking of PDS collaborative efforts is to use guiding principles established by the Holmes Group, a group of research institutions in the field. Their guidelines for the PDS (Holmes Group, 1990), list the following categories, all of which could be the focus for networking meetings:

- teaching and learning for understanding
- creating a learning community

- teaching and learning for everybody's children
- continuing learning by teachers, teacher educators, and administrators
- thoughtful, long-term inquiry into teaching and learning by school and university faculty working as partners
- inventing a new institution

Another helpful way to conceptualize the types of meetings and opportunities that could be provided for PDS partnerships is advanced by the Learning Coalition, a group of Auburn University PDS partnerships (Kochan & Kunkel, 1998). Their partnership includes goals to measure progress and to frame the process for articulation and growth:

- improving pre-service education
- providing an exemplary education for P–12 students
- developing collaborative learning communities
- providing continuing education for all professionals, and
- conducting joint research and inquiry

Auburn University's PDS Coalition used these categories so that participants could rate their progress in these areas of articulation, collaboration, and growth. In clarifying their ratings of these purposes, the process of collaboration itself seemed to supercede the individual outcomes. Kochan and Kunkel (1998) report:

> Although improving pre-service education was rated as the primary purpose of the PDS effort, when reporting on benefits as a whole, respondents ranked the creation of partnerships and their collaborative activities as of the most benefit to them. This may illustrate their understanding of the value of such connections. (p. 333)

Knowing that informal and formal collaborative opportunities are important for the vitality of the PDS, the next step is to devise opportunities for collaboration. Some reflections on effective large-scale networking opportunities from the Auburn University collaborative provide a map for others interested in pursuing structured networking sessions:

> The Coalition has committed to becoming a learning community as well. Semiannual meetings help create this community. Each meeting features large and small group affective activities to enable individuals and groups to form closer working relationships between and among teams. Time is spent in sharing progress, problems, and dreams, thus permitting the groups to support and inform one another. Guest speakers from throughout the nation attend each meeting and present their programs as ideas related to school-university partnerships. We are establishing a technological linkage through a listserve and hope to initiate a newsletter in which we can share information across sites between meetings. (Kochan & Kunkel, 1998, p. 329)

A Model for Networking Meetings: Loyola College in Maryland

The driving force behind the networking opportunities designed by Loyola College in its PDS network of P–12 schools is the creation of effective collaboration for clearly defined results; that is, to change the educational system for the better.

Loyola College is a Jesuit institution with approximately 3,500 undergraduate students; 300 of them are education majors or minors. As of the spring 2001 semester, all elementary and secondary education students began their pre-service teaching in a multi-semester, PDS placement for their student-teaching internship. Ongoing relationships with Loyola's 15 PDS sites are nurtured as mentor-teachers within each site work with the same intern for a full year or more. Trust between mentors, college coordinators for each PDS site, and interns develops as these groups work together within PDS classrooms.

Loyola College also has developed a tradition of going beyond informal learning opportunities provided through professional discussions, faculty meetings, and intern seminars provided at each PDS site. For the past five years, Loyola has conducted semi-annual networking meetings devoted to mentor-teacher development. Developments in coaching and evaluating the intern-portfolio process provide the capstone of the PDS experience. During the last two years, Loyola has begun to diversify its networking focus, affording opportunities for mentor-teachers and college faculty to explore concepts and concerns in the field of education. The following section is an overview of the 2001–2003 networking opportunities Loyola College has conducted with mentor-teachers. Sample agendas and key handouts are included, where appropriate, to illustrate concepts vital to each type of experience. Meetings are categorized according to purposes for PDS partnerships as outlined in the Maryland Professional Development Schools Standards (Maryland Partnership for Teaching and Learning K-16, Superintendents and Deans Committee, 2001).

Standards I and II: Developing Collaborative-Learning Communities

Community Action Team

A strong commitment to the PDS model is part of the infrastructure of Loyola's Education Department. Strategic planning within the Teacher Education Program (TEP) faculty yielded three major goals to be addressed: curriculum development, assessment, and community. Action teams, comprised of groups of tenure-track/clinical and new/experienced faculty began to work on setting measurable goals and activities to enhance an exemplary sequence for teacher candidates. This Community Action Team focused its efforts on two goals:

- Creating a climate among constituents of the Learning Community rated as "good" or better by at least 80 percent of the members
- Involving over 50 percent of students and faculty in outreach efforts to P–12 students and teachers in PDS schools and schools with substantial needs within the Baltimore area

To accomplish these goals, the group surveyed PDS and college faculties to match needs and strengths, working with a student-driven "Education Society" for collaboration and articulation among students and faculty, as well as planning social activities for all members of the learning communities.

Needs Assessment for College and PDS Faculty

Seeking to expand the collaboration among Loyola College Education Department faculty and the faculties at the 15 PDS sites, the Community Action Team developed a survey to assess areas of expertise and need that could be used to strengthen learning on campus and at each PDS school. This activity is based in other national PDS efforts. For example, one collaborative effort of universities in Utah wrote, "We continue to look for ways for university faculty to ground their theoretical perspectives in the often messy reality of classrooms full of children, while at the same time providing teachers with multiple opportunities to see and experience the value of theory and research in their own work" (Hobbs, et al., 1998, p. 50).

Loyola College's efforts began with a survey sent to tenured and clinical faculty members within the Education Department. A companion survey was drafted and delivered to each PDS site by the clinical faculty member assigned to that site. This initiative was designed to find ways to institutionalize the types of collaboration that have developed naturally or sporadically over the last two years. Examples of piecemeal collaboration include a graduate assistant professor of counseling speaking to parents at an inner-city PDS site about conducting successful parent conferences with their children's teachers; an assistant professor of reading speaking at the request of a suburban-PDS elementary site—helping teachers focus on vocabulary development approaches in light of new statewide testing requirements for No Child Left Behind; and a racially diverse, working-class PDS site inviting all the professors who were teaching education courses to the interns currently working within their school to observe/participate in lessons at their school.

Standard III: Accountability

Portfolio Assessment Process

Training in the PDS portfolio-assessment process, and in methods for interviewing interns, is a long tradition at Loyola College. Developed as a holistic approach to evaluating interns at the conclusion of their student-teaching experience, a team analyzes and discusses each candidate's portfolio to determine if the candidate is ready to become a primary-teacher-of-record upon graduation. This process involves key people related to the candidate's development. It is hoped the analysis will demonstrate a foundation of evidence of teaching that is exemplary, according to the Interstate New Teacher Assessment and Support Consortium (INTASC) and Maryland's Essential Dimensions of Teaching (EDOT) Standards. This includes reflective self-analysis performed by the intern in preparing rationales and responding to intensive questions from the portfolio interview team (see Appendix 5.A for the Maryland EDOT standards, based on the more familiar national INTASC standards).

The portfolio-review team is comprised of two mentor-teachers with whom the intern has been placed, the intern's PDS coordinator (who has supervised the intern in student teaching over a two- to three-semester period), a case manager/facilitator, and one or two outside evaluators who have not seen the intern in the field. The team members take a half-day to analyze the intern's portfolio and write evaluative comments about the progress the candidate has shown in terms of the ten INTASC or EDOT standards. The case manager compiles these comments and brings them to the portfolio-assessment interview (about 1.5 hours per intern). During the assessment meeting, the team discusses the ratings, comments, and questions for each standard, and then invites the intern to answer specific questions and to share reflections of his/her success, areas of growth, and insights gained about the profession while completing the portfolio and the internship. The final segment of the conference is devoted to commendations and suggestions for further growth. The team shares decisions on whether they are recommending the intern as being ready to be hired as a teacher.

Action Research Coalition or Network

Cited in the literature on PDS implementation as the most challenging issue, action research is the stepchild of the movement (Holmes, 1990; Kochan & Kunkel, 1998). P–12 and university cultures must change to embrace more opportunities for theory-driven, field-based research within a context of continual diagnosis and assessment. This "good idea" of placing teachers as researchers is likely to take a stronger role in driving educational innovation that will improve learning for all stakeholders. However, the current milieu in PDS practice is much different. As Kochan and Kunkel (1998) write about their Alabama collaborative:

> The major benefits of the Coalition partnerships focus on four of the five PDS purposes: developing collaborative learning communities, improving pre-service education, providing an exemplary P–12 education, and providing continuing education for professionals. No responses dealt with benefits related to involvement with research and inquiry. (p. 332)

At Loyola College, action research is the goal of the present and future. In spring 2003, a study and planning group from the ranks of college faculty, mentor-teachers, and intern teachers met for three extended sessions to study the literature on action research and to propose possibilities to enhance undergraduate and graduate-level experiences. An interactive symposium followed during summer 2003 to bring together interested mentor-teachers and college faculty with eight teacher researchers from another institution, who had successfully conducted action research. This launched a yearlong focus on intensive coaching from a college action-research facilitator with interested mentor-teachers conducting action-research projects in their classrooms and receiving mini-grant funding to do so. This plan emerged as one of many facets that the Teacher Education Program faculty at Loyola have discussed in order to weave together all undergraduate and graduate teacher preparation sequences. Inquiry into effective practices should be a natural part of teachers' repertoires, and a focus on action research is a natural vehicle to accomplish this important goal within our PDS network.

Standard IV: Organization, Roles, and Resources

Mentor Forum: Focus on Fall Senior Courses

The first in a series of Mentor Forums was held during fall 2003 for PDS network schools. These forums were designed to provide a means for discussion and feedback among mentor-teachers, administrators, PDS coordinators, and regular college faculty so that they could collaborate on topics of interest to the network. The first forum had a focus on an intense semester for elementary education majors during the fall semester of their senior year. This is the semester designed to be at the beginning of the interns' student teaching for at least 100 days, and spread over two consecutive semesters (a mandate from the Maryland State Department of Education). At Loyola College, this process places elementary interns with their mentor-teachers in their PDS settings during the spring of their junior year for one-half day each week. As the interns enter their senior year, they return to the school two weeks early to rejoin their mentor-teachers for the first week of professional development, and the first day of school for students. When classes begin on campus, the interns settle into a schedule of serving in a student teaching capacity at their PDS sites for one or more days a week and taking classes on campus.

Other work during the Mentor Forums included Loyola's faculty as they coordinated field-based assignments with their other courses, in order to develop a matrix of due dates and spread their requirements as evenly as possible throughout the semester. Evaluative comments for this Mentor Forum opportunity were quite positive. The mentor-teachers felt their opinions mattered in constructing the tasks interns were being asked to perform as they applied theory to practice. Typical comments included:

- "We really got a nice, overall picture of each class and what is expected of each student."
- "We were glad to hear about the books to add to our professional library and the schedule calendar of assignments."

Future Mentor Forums will focus on other pertinent topics, but will always be centered on program improvement. A helpful framework for this effort is described in an article by Elton and Ranae Stetson (1997):

We have learned to establish regular feedback processes whereby all partners in the program address four critical questions: (1) what is my current primary role in the program; (2) what are my greatest benefits; (3) how could my role change to make it better and more effective, and (4) what could I suggest to make the overall program more effective and profitable for all customers? (p. 492)

Professional Development Sharing

During the last three years, Loyola's PDS coordinators have sought to enhance collaboration in professional growth activities. Personnel at PDS sites have begun to move beyond the traditional seminar in education conducted by the college coordinator. They now host site-based training on specific topics of interest, which is organized and presented by mentor-teachers. In many sites, these sessions have turned into a collaborative effort through inviting interns from other PDS sites, inviting new faculty (fewer than five years of experience) at the PDS site, and having all faculty at a site attend valuable convocations with audiences of interns and experienced teachers. Additionally, opportunities for sharing insights throughout the network have grown as PDS coordinators and mentor-teachers visit one another's sites for seminars and chances to observe and discuss the PDS model being implemented in another school. Finally, Loyola has committed grant funding and College funds to send representatives from the Education Department and the 15 PDS sites to national PDS conferences. An additional component to this year's national conference attendance is a follow-up collaboration opportunity in which participants will be invited to an evening session to describe one or more "best practices" or ideas gained at the conference.

Conclusion

The PDS is not a panacea to solve all of the challenges of educating pre-service and experienced teachers, but it is a promising model for integrating the best of their respective worlds. Systemic change in undergraduate and experienced-teachers' professional development can be enhanced through a partnership in which the university and schools communicate, teach, and learn together. As Fulghum (1989) wrote,

> Show-and-Tell was the very best part of school for me, both as a student and as a teacher. . . . As a kid, I put more into getting ready for my turn to present than I put into the rest of my homework. Show-and-Tell was real in a way that much of what I learned in school was not. It was education that came out of my life experience. . . . As a teacher, I was always surprised by what I learned from these amateur hours. A kid I was sure I knew well would reach down into the paper bag he carried and fish out some odd-shaped treasure and attach meaning to it beyond my most extravagant expectation. It was me, the teacher, who was being taught at such moments. (pp. ix–x)

References

Bellanca, J. (1995). *Designing professional development for change.* Arlington Heights, IL: IRI Skylight Training and Publishing.

Bullough, Jr. R.V., Hobbs, S.F., Kauchak, D.P., Crow, N.A., & Stokes, D. (1997). Long-term PDS development in research universities and the clinicalization of teacher education. *Journal of Teacher Education, 48*(2), 85–95.

Covey, S. (1989). *The seven habits of highly effective people.* NY: Simon and Schuster.

Deal, T.E. & Peterson, K.D. (1999). *Shaping school culture: The heart of leadership.* San Francisco: Jossey-Bass.

Duffy, G.G. (1994). Professional development schools and the disempowerment of teachers and professors. *Phi Delta Kappan, 75*(8), 596–590.

DuFour, R. & Eaker, R. (1998). *Professional learning communities at work: Best practices for enhancing student achievement.* Alexandria, VA: Association for Supervision and Curriculum Development.

Fulghum, R. (1989). *It was on fire when I lay down on it.* New York: Villard Books.

Hargreaves, A., Earl, L., Moore, S., & Manning, S. (2001). *Learning to change: Teaching beyond subjects and standards.* San Francisco: Jossey-Bass.

Hobbs, S.F., Bullough, Jr., R.V., Kauchak, D.P., Crow, N.A., & Stokes, D. (1998). Professional development schools: Catalysts for collaboration and change. *The Clearing House, 72*(1), 47–50.

Holmes Group. (1990). *Tomorrow's schools: Principles for the design of professional development schools.* East Lansing, MI: Author.

Hudson-Ross, S. (1998). A discipline-based professional development faculty: A case for multiple-site collaborative reform in the disciplines. *Journal of Teacher Education, 49*(4), 266–275.

Ishler, R.E. (1996). The future of schools of education: Is there one? *National Forum, 76*(4), 3–4.

Kochan, F.K. & Kunkel, R.C. (1998). The learning coalition: Professional development schools in partnership. *Journal of Teacher Education, 49*(5), 32–38.

Levine, M. (2002). Why invest in professional development schools? *Educational Leadership, 59*(6), 65-68.

Maryland Partnership for Teaching and Learning K-16, Superintendents and Deans Committee. (2001). *Professional Development schools: An implementation manual.* Baltimore: Author.

McBee, R.H. & Moss, J. (2002). PDS partnerships come of age. *Educational Leadership, 59*(6), 13-66.

Neubert, G.A. & Binko, J. B. (1998). Professional development schools: The proof is in performance. *Educational Leadership, 55*(5), 44-46.

Odland, J. (2002). Professional development schools: Partnerships that work. *Childhood Education, 78*(3), 160-161.

Rice, E.H. (2002). The collaboration process in professional development schools: Results of a meta-ethnography, 1990-1998. *Journal of Teacher Education, 53*(1), 55-67.

Sandholtz, J.H. & Finan, E.C. (1998). Blurring the boundaries to promote school-university partnerships. *Journal of Teacher Education, 49*(1), 13-25.

Senge, P.M. (1990). *The fifth discipline: The art and practice of the learning organization.* New York: Doubleday.

Stetson, E. & Stetson, R. (1997). Overhauling teacher education: It takes a collaborative. *Education, 117*(4), 487-495.

Appendix 5.A.

Maryland's Essential Dimensions of Teaching

The highly effective classroom is one in which every student is fully engaged at all times with curriculum that is inviting, motivating, and personally relevant. To achieve this,

TEACHER CANDIDATES AND TEACHERS WILL:

1. Demonstrate mastery of appropriate academic disciplines and a repertoire of teaching techniques.
2. Demonstrate an understanding that knowledge of the learner's physical, cognitive, emotional, and socio-cultural development is the basis of effective teaching.
3. Incorporate a multicultural perspective that integrates culturally diverse resources, including those from the learner's family and community.
4. Demonstrate knowledge of strategies for integrating students with special needs into the regular classroom.
5. Use valid assessment approaches, both formal and informal, which are age appropriate and address a variety of developmental needs, conceptual abilities, curriculum outcomes and school goals.
6. Organize and manage a classroom using approaches supported by research, best practice, expert opinion, and student learning needs.
7. Use computer and computer-related technology to meet student and professional needs.
8. Demonstrate an understanding that classrooms and schools are sites of ethical, social, and civic activity.
9. Collaborate with the broad educational community including parents, businesses, and social service agencies.
10. Engage in careful analysis, problem solving, and reflection in all aspects of teaching.

CHAPTER 6   *Carol Frierson-Campbell*

Sound Ways of Learning
Anchoring Music Education to the PDS P–16 Reform Movement

At some point in your boating career you will probably want to anchor.
—INTERNATIONAL MARINE EDUCATORS *(2002a)*

Anchoring has several meanings, but it is rooted in the seafaring world. It is a useful metaphor for contemplating the role of music in schooling, and particularly for thinking about the implications of including music in the Professional Development School movement. If one thinks about it, the importance of anchoring is particularly obvious when a ship pulls away from the dock in a foolhardy way, without planning a voyage, recruiting a crew, plotting a route, and choosing appropriate anchors.

Of interest, the literature on boating safety stresses that no single anchor will work in every circumstance. Differences in the size of the vessel, the depth and current of the body of water, the subsurface topography, and the weather determine the type of anchor and the method of anchoring. Thus, even for a single voyage, it may be necessary to have several anchors aboard.

These maritime metaphors aptly describe the emerging PDS relationship between a state university and the music educators from three high-needs school districts in northern New Jersey. In 1999, the College of Education at William Paterson University (WPU) joined two other New Jersey universities to form the New Jersey State Teacher Quality Enhancement Consortium. The consortium was created to implement a five-year, federal Teacher Quality Enhancement grant that was awarded to a number of university coalitions across the country. The grant was intended to support efforts to develop PDS partnerships between Colleges of Education and high-needs, culturally diverse urban schools in the region served by those universities.

The William Paterson University College of Education initially selected five schools from three city school districts in New Jersey as preliminary PDS sites. A College of Education faculty member was recruited to serve as a liaison between each PDS site, as well as to plan and coordinate partnership activities at the site. Arts and Science faculty at the university and public school level were required to be involved in the partnership. Once the PDS site coordinators were in place, the recruiting of other faculty began. I was invited as a music-education faculty member to join this voyage in the second half of Year 2 of the grant.

While the stated mission of the partnership was clear about the importance of including the arts in the PDS model, details were sketchy as to what that might mean. This is consistent with much of the school-reform literature—the importance of the arts in education is often stressed but seldom given form or substance. This is not necessarily a bad thing, but it does necessitate the involvement of arts (in this case, music) faculty from the university and the partnership schools if a meaningful collaboration is to be realized.

Sending an untrained crew on an untried ship into uncharted waters can be a recipe for aimlessness, if not disaster. In contrast, a working fleet has to allow enough leeway for each member ship to find anchorages that are profitable for its crew and beneficial to the fleet. This is the dilemma faced by school reformers. With limited time and budget, slacking the lines so arts educators can seek similar (but not identical) anchorages is a risk many are afraid to take.

The grant administrator, the university's faculty liaisons, and the school administrators allowed the music faculty and the partnership's music teachers to decide whether or not to become part of the master PDS plan (a single ship) or create a plan specifically for music teachers in the schools (a ship in a fleet with a common mission). Early in the PDS conversation, it was noted that the Holmes Group suggested that improving teaching depends upon giving teachers the opportunity "to contribute to the development of knowledge in their profession, to form collegial relationships beyond their immediate working environment, and to grow intellectually as they mature professionally" (1986, p. 56). Realizing that the isolation of music teachers—teaching mostly one to a site—created limited opportunities for collegial relationships, a collaborative group of music teachers was created called the Coalition Music Teachers (CMT). This group was formed to provide curricular support for music education in all of the partnership schools. The initial explorations led to suggesting that it is possible to adjust the traditional PDS model (based primarily on classroom teaching) to meet the co-collegial needs of music teachers, other specialist teachers, and the arts-related interdisciplinary needs of classroom teachers. The remainder of this chapter will include a description of the "maiden voyage," and a sharing of the plans and excursions envisioned for the future.

Mapping the Voyage

In order to find the way safely from place to place on the water one must depend on road signs just as is done on land. Navigational aids are the road signs on the water.
—INTERNATIONAL MARINE EDUCATORS *(2002b).*

School/arts partnerships often are characterized as "a sort of 'drive-through' approach to education" where content learned in any given place is separate from the next experience. Little effort is made to connect these related experiences into a meaningful whole (Robinson, 1998, ¶8). In other words, reliable maps to guide co-collegial partnerships between music educators, PDS colleagues, and university music faculty are rare. Indeed, the voyage and its potential anchorages are largely uncharted. Still, there are suggestions as to how the PDS model might meet the needs of teachers who teach specialized content and serve in limited number at a given school site. Zimpher (2001), for instance, suggests that while most instances of PDS partnerships involve single school sites, "the professional development school notion might accommodate networks of types of classrooms; for instance, a number of sites for music educators, reading resource teachers, or the special education classroom across a district" (p. 44).

From reviewing the PDS literature, three partnerships were found involving music or art teachers at the Ohio State University, the Eastman School of Music, and the University of North Texas. Parsons (2000) and several colleagues at the Ohio State University (OSU) created a partnership with the art teachers from four school districts in their region. The purpose of this partnership was to address the need for discipline-specific training and collegiality for art teachers. Parsons and the others decided upon some specific criteria. Participants needed to be successful teachers in schools where student teachers were frequently placed and share the methodological philosophy of the OSU Art Department. The participants' institutions needed to have administrators who supported art education, including specialized in-service activities, prior to establishing the partnership. There were three purposes for the collaboration: pre-service education, in-service learning, and research. Parsons offers a telling description of the co-collegial nature of art teaching as he describes "the tension between viewing the teacher as an independent subject-matter specialist and as a school faculty member" (p. 224). This is an important characteristic of all arts teachers, and a similar tension was found pulling at the music teachers in this partnership. Writing in Year 4 of the OSU partnership, Parsons noted that the contexts of institutional priorities and individual personnel leave much to chance, especially with a fledgling partnership and even with those that are established.

The music-education PDS relationships described by Conkling at the Eastman School of Music and Henry at the University of North Texas (Conkling & Henry, 1999) are similar to the traditional PDS model: professors partner with an excellent pedagogue in their region to co-teach methods classes. While efforts like this one have done much to vitalize pre-service music teacher education in their respective institutions, the collegial relationships addressed by their partnerships are limited to the teacher(s) they work with directly.

One reason for the dearth of musical involvement in the PDS movement may be that most music school faculty see their role in clinical training, for a music teacher's certification, as limited to the pre-service or novice teacher. The idea that the university and public school share responsibility for pre-service training, in-service teacher quality, and student achievement is foreign to many responsible for music teacher education (¶6). In addition, as is the case at William Paterson University and in each of the partnerships described, music departments or schools are often housed separately from colleges of education. For this reason alone, collaboration at the university level is a rarity, simply because of the geographic limitations of the institution. This limitation carries through to most public-school sites where music rooms, if they exist, are removed from other classrooms. Also, music teachers do not share preparation time with other teachers (indeed, they usually provide it).

Realizing that existing navigational systems had little experience plotting a journey like this one, at the outset, there were only a few pre-set map points. The New Jersey State Teacher Quality Enhancement Consortium, of which this partnership was a member, was guided by the following goals:

1. Create regional and statewide K–12-IHE (Institution of Higher Education)-Public Partner committees to integrate curriculum reform, teacher preparation, and educational policy reform activities.
2. Recruit and prepare a diverse group of new teachers to reform pre-service teacher education.
3. Create professional development and assessment regional and statewide K–12-IHE-Public Partner committees to integrate curriculum reform, teacher preparation, and educational policy reform activities.
4. Address issues critical to New Jersey's "high-need" schools, especially increasing student achievement.

New Jersey's Core Curriculum Content Standards for the Visual and Performing Arts also provided guidance in plotting the course. These standards include:

1.1 All students will acquire knowledge and skills that increase aesthetic awareness in dance, music, theater, and visual arts.
1.2 All students will refine perceptual, intellectual, physical, and technical skills through creating dance, music, theater, and/or visual arts.
1.3 All students will utilize arts elements and arts media to produce artistic products and performances.
1.4 All students will demonstrate knowledge of the process of critique.

1.5 All students will identify the various historical, social, and cultural influences and traditions which have generated artistic accomplishments throughout the ages and which continue to shape contemporary arts.

1.6 All students will develop design skills for planning the form and function of space, structures, objects, sound, and events. (New Jersey Department of Education, 1996)

In addition, the following additional perspectives served as personal navigational points:

1. Belief in importance of music as a discipline for students of all ages and cultures.
2. Desire to become involved in urban music education as researcher and colleague.
3. Belief in interdisciplinary education that is true to all disciplines, both in a discrete and a multi-disciplinary sense.

Thus, these anchorages were the only ones deemed unacceptable:

1. The idea that music education is purely for "relaxation" or "enjoyment" without a disciplinary or skills base in the curriculum.
2. The idea that the purpose of music education is to enrich other academic subjects without recognition of the academic nature of musical skill and knowledge.

Preparing for Storms

> *At certain times of the year weather can change rapidly and one needs to continually keep a "weather eye" out, especially to the west, in order to foresee changes that might be impending. Storms on the water can kick up suddenly and without warning.*
> —INTERNATIONAL MARINE EDUCATORS *(2002c)*

In the PDS relationship, a storm can mean a change in the priorities of an institution or an administrator, a change in the structure of government or institutional funding, or a change in personnel. To prepare for such an occurrence, the CMT partnership was structured so that teachers are poised to become an independent curricular-support group for urban music educators at the end of the grant period. It is likely the New Jersey Music Education Association (NJMEA) will sponsor curricular-support aspects of the CMT vision. In addition, NJMEA used the Needs Assessment model developed through the project to plan in-service days for urban music teachers in other regions of the state during the 2003–2004 school year. The music teachers' partnership, then, is less likely to be swamped if a sudden storm threatens the future of the partnership.

Pulling Away from the Dock

> *Prior to getting underway, one should implement an undocking plan with the help of passengers. This is done by considering the traffic in the area, the direction of wind and the current, and the depth of the water.*
> —INTERNATIONAL MARINE EDUCATORS (2002d)

The partnership literature speaks of the fits and false starts that characterize the beginnings of any partnership relationship, and this one was no different. The first year of the CMT partnership was characterized by site visits and unstructured interviews with the music teacher and administrator in each partnership school. The typical PDS model involves a single university faculty member working as a partner with one or more public school faculty members, co-teaching classes and sharing responsibility for student teachers. This model worked well for the two most successful sites in Year 1 of the partnership. Thus, initially, it was envisioned that working as a co-teacher with individual music teachers in several schools, and then bringing those teachers together on occasion to talk about their work, would be an effective process. It turned out that while the music teachers were happy to talk about what they were doing a few times (one principal said they thought the CMT director was "harmless"), they did not share their classrooms on a regular basis.

In retrospect, this stage of the relationship was referred to as the "who are you and what do you want?" stage. This is not a comfortable stage to be in, since after committing to a partnership vision and being provided with resources, there is an expectation that the project will suddenly take off. It seems, however, this is a necessary stage that is frequently mentioned in the literature. Examples are the concept of "a time before the beginning" in the NCATE PDS standards (2001, p. 3), and Robinson's (2000) review of literature related to arts-in-education partnerships.

The Ship's Log: Year 1

March 27, 2001

As I ponder my role in the partnership, there is not much information about exactly what is happening and what is needed at each site in terms of music.

April 5, 2001

It would not benefit anyone for me to just show up with some "grand idea" to impose upon the school. It was said, "they'd kick you right out of here"—meaning the teachers at H5. Also, I know little about urban education (other than what I know about education in general) and do not know much about education in New Jersey. The best way to proceed is to establish a relationship for a prescribed amount of time and see what happens.

May 31, 2001

What would I have thought in my classroom if a professor had shown up to help solve music problems in my schools? What would it have taken to allow one of those folks to have access to me and to my classroom? This teacher is being incredibly gracious to let me walk in and take up his time practically sight-unseen.

June 7, 2001

I am starting to have a better sense of what is needed. Both teachers have confirmed the thoughts that the arts get left out of school reform. It may be by design or default.

June 14, 2001

What do we have to offer a partnership? The most obvious benefit (and quickest to establish) is collegiality. Meetings can be set up between the music teachers in the three schools to help them determine what they need, and perhaps, some of those things can be funded through the partnership.

Coalition Music Teachers, Year 2

By the time Year 2 of the CMT partnership arrived, it was obvious that developing music-teacher collegiality and understanding the role of music in schools would be a big part of working together. Guided by the research suggesting that activities rather than goals propelled collaboration through initial stages (Lieberman, 1986, as cited in Robinson, 2000), the music teachers in the Partnership schools were invited to the university campus for a series of meetings that served as small-scale needs assessments. These meetings began the process of building the CMTs into a coherent group.

The first meeting consisted of getting acquainted and brainstorming about music-teacher needs. In the second meeting, the focus was on four primary goals:

- Developing a program to bring chamber music into partnership schools by providing training for pre-service music education students. This would be a benefit for PDS students and WPU students

- Creating a mission statement related to the importance of music in urban schools and disseminating it to policymakers and institutions of higher learning
- Investigating ways to bring greater professionalism to urban music teachers
- Planning a symposium on urban music education for some time in the future

At the third meeting, it was decided that a main focus would be the creation of a mission statement, in order to foster the impetus of becoming a public voice in support of urban music education. The CMTs suggested they would like to gain further input from their peers in their respective school districts before writing the mission statement. They felt that a needs assessment similar to that which occurred during the first meeting (brainstorming, followed by discussion, followed by decision making) would be of greater benefit to them, and to their colleagues, than would simply following their own opinions. This propelled us into Year 3 of our journey.

The Ship's Log, Year 2

February 9, 2002

There is a strong sense among the CMTs that they need a collective voice with the power to speak about the needs of urban music teachers in a more public forum. It must be noted that many of these needs are related to the overwhelming nature of their task. They are charged with teaching music in a meaningful way when they see students only once a week, meeting the musical needs of students who are from "around the world," carrying teaching materials around "on a cart." They often have no office or classroom wherein they could work, write on the board, and post materials. They often work with students whose reading and math levels are so low that having them read the words to songs is difficult. They were asked if they would like to meet again. The response was: "Yes, if it goes somewhere." To this end, they suggested a series of meetings during the remainder of the school year. They decided to create a mission statement in the final meeting.

Perhaps the reason music is left out of school reform is because it is invisible to administrators who plan the "hands-on" acts of reform. Few knowledgeable reformers leave music out of the picture (e.g., Gardner, 1999), but when it gets down to the district and school level, music does get left out. Also, the grant administrator made a good point: One of the reasons no one ever sees the music teacher is because there are always children in their rooms—they are always working. But, this means the administrators and other powerbrokers do not know what music teachers are doing.

Coalition Music Teachers, Year 3

In Year 3 of the CMT partnership, the focus on drafting a mission statement has changed the direction of the CMTs (at least for the time being) from activities revolving around the PDS sites to analyzing and responding to the needs of the greater-urban music-education community in the North Jersey region. Thus, in September 2002, a full-day needs-assessment and professional development day was planned for all music teachers in the districts served by the partnership. The needs assessment followed the three-phase model suggested by Altschuld and Witkin (2000). Briefly, during the pre-assessment stage, a committee is formed to decide whether there are needs to be met; CMT teachers served as the committee. The assessment stage also involves the formal assessment of a constituent group for the purpose of understanding and prioritizing perceived need. The professional development day provided quantitative data for the needs assessment. Qualitative data, including observations and unstructured interviews, were collected and analyzed after that time. The post-assessment stage involves identifying and selecting solution strategies. This stage was designed to last for a year after the other data were analyzed.

Prior to the formal needs assessment, the CMT teachers were trained as facilitators for the in-service workshop. The day was designed to enable the music teachers to network and discuss common problems, their solutions, and to prioritize needs. The needs assessment, then, was based on the question: What is needed to take urban music education from where it is now to where it could be?

At the start of the workshop, the music teachers were divided into focus-type groups of approximately nine people. First, the participants had an opportunity to talk with one another in order to get to know each other and share a few useful teaching techniques. Next, they were asked to discuss answers to the "question of the day" by creating a "mind-map" of their ideas. Afterwards, each individual shared them with a partner and then with members of their groups. Each group created a priority list based upon similarities in each individual's mind maps. Finally, each group presented a list of their eight or ten priorities to the teachers in attendance.

To further clarify the data, participants were asked to complete a questionnaire related to their professional needs. The questionnaire was based on one developed by Fiese and DeCarbo (1995). Results of the needs assessment showed that music teachers in the partnership districts consistently placed the following needs at the top of their priorities:

- facilities and supplies
- administrative support and collegial (non-music) support
- validation of music as a legitimate subject

Results from the combination of music teacher prioritizing and questionnaire will help to plan future voyages.

Choosing Anchors

The first step in anchoring is to select the proper anchor. In spite of claims to the contrary, there is no single anchor design that is best to be used in all conditions (International Marine Educators, 2002a). Scholars and researchers endorse the idea of anchoring music to school reform efforts. There is widespread belief that music is itself a worthwhile discipline for study (Eisner 2001; Gardner, 1999), and there is conjecture that music aids other types of academic achievement in schools (MENC, 2002; New Jersey Department of Education, 1996). The question to be answered, then, is: What are the best ways of anchoring music education to the PDS P–12-reform movement?

The data gathered in the formal needs assessment, and through unstructured interviews and observations, suggested that four anchors have potential for connecting the combined educational visions of music educators and PDS planners: building level collegiality, discipline-specific collegiality, interdisciplinary training, and connection to pre-service education. The music teachers in the study stated a great need for administrative and collegial support. In addition, each of the interviews with administrators provided at least some mention of the power of music to connect to other disciplines, and the need for the music teachers in their schools to develop skills in that area. On this basis, it was suggested that the PDS model include interdisciplinary teams of classroom teachers, music teachers, and other special area teachers in each building who would meet on a regular basis to work on interdisciplinary content. Such a team would foster the building-level collegiality needed by music teachers, and would enable classroom teachers and others to access music teachers' specialized knowledge. This kind of team is in line with state standards. The New Jersey Core Content Curriculum Standards for Language Arts Literacy note that "brain-based research clearly shows implications for student learning when there are links to the arts, like classical music, and the real world" (New Jersey Department of Education, 2002a, ¶9). The state standards for social studies make an even stronger case for arts-integrated curricula, citing an influential New Jersey law related to educational equity:

> Thorough and efficient [education] means being able to fulfill one's role as a citizen, a role that encompasses far more than merely registering to vote. It means the ability to participate fully in society, in the life of one's community, the ability to appreciate music, art, and literature, and the ability to share all that with friends (Abbott v. Burke 119 NJ 287, 1990, pp. 363–364 in New Jersey Department of Education, 2002).

The creation of a network of music teachers, preferably with a university- or district-based coordinator, to provide discipline-specific collegiality and curricular support is equally crucial for anchoring music education to the PDS model. The twin roles of faculty-member music teacher and subject-matter specialist are in constant tension (Parsons, 2000), and the teachers in the partnership noted a specific need for mentoring and collegiality with their music-teaching peers. Although initiatives between buildings or between districts are not common as a practice in the PDS model, the results of the needs assessment suggest music teachers believe this kind of collegial contact to be crucial for professional success. Since music teachers and school administrators noted a need for interdisciplinary training, this should be a topic for interdisciplinary and discipline-specific teams. Finally, it was suggested that a connection to pre-service education could foster co-collegial connections between pre-service music educators and classroom educators. In this way, pre-service educators can overcome the disciplinary and collegial boundaries that impede the utilization of the many resources music teachers have to offer in schools.

Given the tenuous nature of partnership relationships, it was further suggested that planners of PDS networks for music teachers make a connection with the Music Education Association in their state. Many MEAs are investigating ways to support urban music educators and would welcome the opportunity to collaborate in a university-school partnership. Further, making a connection with the state organization is seen as providing music educators in the partnership with a means of curricular reinforcement not dependent upon the university or school administration for support.

An Invitation to a Journey

The William Paterson CMT partnership has been supported by a grant from the New Jersey State Teacher Enhancement Consortium. This year is the final year in which the partnership will be funded in this way. The travels, thus far, have resulted in strong foundation and provided the experience to navigate in deeper waters. The next stage of the voyage will result in visiting the five anchorages: building level collegiality, discipline-specific collegiality, interdisciplinary training, and connection to pre-service education.

Music and the other arts are a crucial part of the educational fleet with which to educate our children. Join the journey in the continuing quest for anchoring music education to the P–16 Professional Development School model.

References

Abbott v. Burke 119 NJ 287. (1990). Abbott v. Burke II, pp. 363-364 in New Jersey Department of Education, 2002). Retrieved August 26, 2003, from http://www.nj.gov/njded/cccs/11socintro.html.

Altschuld, J.W. & Witkin, B.R. (2000). *From needs assessment to action: Transforming needs into solution strategies.* Thousand Oaks, CA: Sage Publications.

Conkling, S.W. & Henry, W. (1999). Professional development partnerships: A new model for music teacher preparation [Electronic version]. *Arts Education Policy Review, 100*(4), 19–23.

Eisner, E. (2001). Music education six months after the turn of the century. *Arts Education Policy Review, 102*(3), 20–24.

Fiese, R.K, & DeCarbo, N.J. (1995). Urban music education: The teachers' perspective. *Music Educators Journal, 81*(6), 27–31.

Gardner, H. (1999). Keynote address. *Bulletin of the Council for Music Education, 142,* 9–21.

Holmes Group. (1986). *Tomorrow's teachers: A report of the Holmes Group.* East Lansing, MI: Author.

International Marine Educators. (2002a). Anchoring. *Nautical Know How—Basic Boating Safety Certification Course.* Retrieved on February 3, 2003, from www.boatsafe.com/ nauticalknowhow/ boating/74.htm.

International Marine Educators. (2002b). Aids to navigation. *Nautical Know How—Basic Boating Safety Certification Course.* Retrieved on February 3, 2003, from www.boatsafe.com/nautical knowhow/ boating/5_3.htm.

International Marine Educators. (2002c). Awareness of environmental conditions. *Nautical Know How—Basic Boating Safety Certification Course.* Retrieved on February 3, 2003, from www.boat safe.com/nauticalknowhow/ boating/ 5_3.htm.

International Marine Educators. (2002d). Docking and undocking plans. *Nautical Know How—Basic Boating Safety Certification Course.* Retrieved on February 3, 2003, from www.boatsafe.com/ nauticalknowhow/ boating/ 7_2.htm.

MENC: The National Association for Music Education. (2002). *Academic achievement and music.* MENC Website. Retrieved on December 9, 2002, from http://www.menc.org/ publication/ articles/academic/academic.htm.

National Council for Accreditation of Teacher Education. (2001). *Standards for Professional Development Schools.* Washington, DC: Author. Retrieved on December 9, 2002, from http://www.ncate.org/2000/pdsstands_10-00.pdf.

New Jersey Department of Education. (1996). *The New Jersey Core Curriculum Content Standards for the Visual and Performing Arts.* Retrieved on August 26, 2003, from http://www.nj.gov/njded/cccs/02/.

New Jersey Department of Education. (2002). *New Jersey Core Curriculum Content Standards for Language Arts Literacy, July 2002.* Retrieved on August 25, 2003, from http://www.nj.gov/njded/cccs/ 02/s3_lal.htm.

Parsons, M. (2000). A PDS network of teachers: The case of art. M. Johnston, P. Brosnan, D. Cramer, & T. Dove. (Eds.) *Collaborative reform and other improbable dreams* (pp. 223-231). Albany: State University of New York Press.

Robinson, M. (2000). *A theory of collaborative music education between higher education and urban public schools.* Rochester, NY: Unpublished doctoral dissertation, Eastman School of Music of the University of Rochester.

Robinson, M. (1998). A collaboration model for school and community music education [Electronic version]. *Arts Education Policy Review, 100*(2), 32–39.

Zimpher, N.L. (2001). Creating Professional Development School sites. *Theory into Practice, 29*(1), 42–49.

CHAPTER 7   *Teena R. Gorrow & John R. Bing*

Using Literature Circles to Research Instructional Strategies

In Professional Development Schools, future teachers, practicing teachers, and university faculty collaborate to support the initial preparation of pre-service teachers, continuing professional development of current teachers, and the performance of P-12 students. In this community of learners, stakeholders collaborate to identify, examine, implement, and refine instructional strategies to promote student achievement (Gorrow, 2002).

One of the strategies in support of activities in a "community of learners" is the use of literature circles. According to Allen (2001), the use of literature circles is one strategy that engages students in their learning by promoting discussion among group members. Students assume a variety of roles that may include discussion director, passage master, connector, and illustrator. The use of literature circles can be modified to suit the needs of a particular classroom.

There is research supporting the use of a variety of instructional strategies. Specifically, Marzano, Pickering, and Pollock (2001) examined and recommended a number of research-based instructional strategies including:

- identifying similarities and differences
- summarizing and note taking
- reinforcing effort and providing recognition
- homework and practice
- non-linguistic representations
- cooperative learning
- setting objectives and providing feedback
- generating and testing hypotheses
- cues, questions, and advance organizers

In their review of the literature, Marzano, Pickering, and Pollack found that effective teachers, more than any other factor, make a difference in student learning, and that student achievement can be improved by improving teacher effectiveness.

While examining the ways in which teachers effectively instruct diverse student populations, Tomlinson (2001) stresses that learners have individual needs. In an effort to describe the ways in which individual student needs can be met in current diverse classrooms, she states that, "a differentiated classroom provides different avenues to acquiring content, to processing or making sense of ideas, and to developing products so that each student can learn effectively" (p. 1).

In this chapter, we describe professional development opportunities at PDS sites for prospective teacher candidates. These credential candidates participate in a community of learners who use literature circles to engage in researching and learning about instructional strategies. The goals of this research were to:

1. increase prospective teacher candidates' knowledge and use of literature circles
2. increase prospective teacher candidates' knowledge of research-based instructional strategies for diverse student populations
3. apply prospective teacher candidates' knowledge of instructional strategies for diverse student populations to the development of lesson plans

Method and Procedures

Fifty-seven prospective teacher candidates were enrolled in one of two sections of Learning and Assessment, an undergraduate education foundations course for elementary-education majors at a four-year public university located on Maryland's eastern shore. The prospective teacher candidates were required to complete the course prior to admission to the professional teacher education program. The course was designed to examine concepts, principles, theories, and research related to teaching, learning, and assessment. Learning experiences included a variety of individual assignments, collaborative projects in which technology was used, and a minimum of 20 hours of field experience in a PDS setting. One of the collaborative projects, *Going in Circles* (Bing & Gorrow, 2001a), was developed in order to foster PDS partnerships, increase knowledge of literature circles, increase knowledge of research-based instructional strategies, develop skills in writing lesson plans, and increase the use of technology. Norton (2001) suggested the use of "webquests" as a particularly effective instructional strategy for engaging students in real-life problem solving.

In the *Going in Circles* project, prospective teacher candidates previewed *Classroom Instruction That Works* (Marzano, Pickering & Pollock, 2001) to identify the instructional strategies they would most like to investigate; they then formed literature circles for each strategy based upon preferences identified by the candidates. They were required to complete a webquest designed to enable them to: (a) develop knowledge about literature circles (b) work in literature circles, and (c) provide a variety of resources to facilitate the research of each instructional strategy (Bing & Gorrow, 2001a). The preservice teachers posed questions to guide their inquiry, conducted online research to answer their questions, and met in person and online to communicate their findings. Members in each literature circle then developed a PowerPoint presentation to teach classmates about their assigned instructional strategy in a mini-conference, thus providing a professional development opportunity by sharing the results of their inquiry.

At the conclusion of the project, the prospective teacher candidates reflected upon their learning experiences and identified ways to implement the strategies into classroom instruction. The course instructors encouraged them to collaborate with on-site mentor-teachers, observe the instructional strategies being practiced, and develop lesson plans to incorporate the strategies. Then, the prospective teacher candidates formed new literature circles to study differentiated instruction and collaborated to create unit plans (Bing & Gorrow, 2001b). They were encouraged to teach the lessons collaboratively at their PDS sites. Due to time constraints, they were unable to teach students in schools. At the conclusion of the course, they presented their collection of lessons during a second mini-conference to their classmates and/or to practicing mentor-teachers in a Professional Development School.

Conclusion

The project provided benefits to prospective teachers as they developed knowledge about, and worked in, literature circles. They increased their knowledge of instructional strategies that promote student achievement in diverse populations, and developed lesson plans that could be implemented in a PDS setting. Conversations between prospective teacher candidates and their classroom mentor-teachers during the development of lesson plans, observation of strategies being implemented in the classroom, and the presentation of the lesson plans during the mini-conferences provided further evidence of the kind of positive collaboration that is characteristic of a "community of learners" in a PDS setting.

References

Allen, R. (2001, summer). *English teachers fight back: Connecting literature in an image-driven world.* ASCD Curriculum Update. Alexandria, VA: Author, from http://www.ascd.org/framecup date.html.

Bing, J. & Gorrow, T. (2001a). Going in circles: A research-based instructional strategy webquest for pre-service teachers using literature circles. Retrieved on September 6, 2004, from http://faculty.salisbury.edu/~trgorrow/going_in_circles_webquest.htm.

Bing, J. & Gorrow, T. (2001b). Going in circles, again: A differentiated instruction webquest for pre-service teachers using literature circles. Retrieved on September 6, 2004, from http://faculty.salisbury.edu/~jrbing/going_in_circles_again.htm.

Gorrow, T.R. (Ed.) (2002). What is a professional development school? *PDS Passages*. Salisbury, MD: Salisbury University.

Marzano, R.J., Pickering, D.J. & Pollock, J.E. (2001). *Classroom instruction that works: Research-based strategies for increasing student achievement.* Alexandria, VA: Association for Supervision and Curriculum Development.

Norton, P. (2001, July) *Oh, sh. .! And now I'm supposed to do technology too!: Some thoughts on using technology from Priscilla Norton.* Paper presented at the PT3 Salisbury University/Frostburg State University Summer 2001 Technology Institute. Salisbury University, Salisbury, MD. from http://Mason.gmu.edu/~pnorton/PT3_files/frame.htm.

Tomlinson, C.A. (2001) *How to differentiate instruction in mixed-ability classrooms* (2nd ed.) Alexandria, VA: Association for Supervision and Curriculum Development.

CHAPTER 8

*Frank Sweeney, Roberta Strosnider,
& Jo Ellen Smallwood*

Empowering Interns as Partners in Mentoring

Introduction

Hood College, a small liberal-arts school in western Maryland, offers initial teacher-certification programs in early childhood education, special education, and secondary education. An integral part of the teacher-education programs is the Professional Development School (PDS) partnerships with two local public-school systems, which enable students from the college to participate in extensive internships in all three program areas. Internships begin during the first education course and continue throughout the program, culminating with an extensive internship during the last two semesters. In addition to having a mentor-teacher in the schools, interns receive support from a college supervisor during the final semester of the internship. Also, they participate in an internship seminar with faculty from the college's Education Department.

It is widely accepted that students learn best when highly skilled teachers teach them. This leads to the issue of how to best prepare teachers for today's schools. More and more colleges and universities across the country have moved away from the traditional teacher-preparation model that has been organized into two primary components: college courses and student teaching. During the first phase of the traditional model, students are expected to learn the content, pedagogy, and methodology necessary to become effective teachers. Opportunities for in-school experiences in classrooms, where teachers are actively engaged in teaching and learners are engaged in learning, are limited to short-term field experiences as part of methods courses. At the most, interns may teach one or two lessons developed in a college class and presented to students with whom they have had previous experience. Most of these field experiences involve observing experienced teachers and reflecting on what the interns have observed.

The second phase of the traditional model is the student-teaching component in which pre-service teachers are required to work in schools with experienced teachers for a specified period of time, typically from 8 to 16 weeks. For many aspiring teachers, this is their only extensive in-school experience. To further dilute this experience, usually the intern and cooperating teacher have had no previous experience working together. Darling-Hammond (1999) believes this brief clinical experience offers few connections with previous learning. She contends that, unless university and school-based faculty plan or teach together, interns will face different practices from those they studied in their college courses. Morrison and Marshall (2003) support this contention and note it is critical that the practices interns see modeled in their field experiences are consistent with the practices they are taught in their university programs. They report a need for university programs to be informed by the practices of classroom teachers, as well as classroom practices being informed by research.

Many teacher-education programs help interns make the connection between theory and practice by increasing opportunities for extensive in-school experiences. Extensive internships in schools have created a new role for teachers as they move from being *cooperating* or *supervising teachers* for student teachers to that of being *mentor-teachers* for teacher-interns. The extensive internship provides pre-service teachers with more firsthand learning opportunities and increases the amount of support provided by mentor-teachers. The success of teacher-interns during this extensive internship is dependent upon the support received from their mentor-teachers.

There are several formats and structures for PDS partnerships with a strong convergence around four goals: the improvement of student learning, new teacher education, the professional development of educators, and research and inquiry into improving practice (Teitel, 1998). This kind of collaborative effort enables teachers and interns to view themselves as members of a professional community, as opposed to working in isolation, allowing numerous opportunities for beginning teachers to gain experience.

The PDS model increases the amount of time college students spend in schools working directly with P–12 students and under the supervision of experienced teachers. Teacher candidates from Hood College complete an internship with a mentor-teacher for a minimum of 120 days over two consecutive semesters. The semesters are comprised of a part-time teaching internship experience for one semester and a full-time teaching internship experience for the other semester. This experience is enhanced with interns having had opportunities to participate in less intensive internships of one-half day or one day per week prior to the extensive internship. Additional in-school experiences are provided as part of methods courses that are offered at the PDS, with interns experiencing firsthand theory evolving into practice (Strosnider, Sweeney & Gill, 2004).

A primary objective of the Hood College PDS partnerships is to support teachers in their development for becoming effective mentors for beginning teachers and teacher-interns. This is of utmost importance since approximately 30 percent of teachers leave the profession within three years (Halford, 1998). Odell (1992) contends this rapid exodus from teaching can be offset by providing adequate support through mentoring for beginning teachers. She found the attrition rate for teachers receiving one year of mentoring was only 16 percent, about half the national attrition rate. It has been reported that novice teachers who are provided adequate support tend to stay in the profession and are more likely to involve students in more complex learning. They make better decisions about curriculum, classroom discipline, and practice more reflection about their teaching (Saphier, Freedman & Aschhiem, 2001).

Training Program for Mentors

As reported by Strosnider, Sweeney, and Gill (2004), Hood College has offered mentor training programs for the past four years in order to prepare teachers in PDS schools. These programs were designed and facilitated by faculty and the PDS was funded by a grant from the Maryland State Department of Education. The training programs were offered during the summer, and from 15 to 22 teachers attended. Teachers were paid a stipend at the in-service rate they would receive if they were enrolled in a summer professional-development activity conducted by the school system in which they were employed.

As teachers considered the possibility of becoming mentors to interns during the first year of the partnership, they shared questions and concerns relating to their past experiences of working with "student teachers." A common theme was confusion over the effectiveness of their past actions on behalf of the "student teacher." These discussions provided baseline data for the initiation of the training program. Although mentor training for teachers who work with college interns is an integral part of the PDS partnership, a central focus for one of the partnerships is to support each school's efforts in mentoring new teachers.

The initial training workshop for mentor-teachers was a three-day program offered on campus and conducted by two Education Department faculty members. Of the 20 teachers enrolled, 15 teachers participated all three days while five teachers attended one or two days. The program goal was to promote an understanding of mentoring for mentors; therefore, the workshop focused on understanding the role of a mentor-teacher and developing effective mentoring skills in the following:

- identifying personal strengths
- working with adult learners
- developing effective conference skills
- understanding college expectations
- developing an action plan

Teachers who participated in the training program reported that it "prepared me to be an effective mentor after identifying the roles of mentors and interns, and the characteristics of an effective relationship. After a negative experience with a student teacher last fall, the training has encouraged me to be a mentor again." Another teacher reported, "It helped me learn how to conduct effective conferences and reflection." Others reported that an understanding of the kinds of issues they may encounter helped them feel less stressed and more comfortable working with interns and beginning teachers. Evaluation feedback indicated that the workshop participants were more prepared and more confident to be mentors (Strosnider, Sweeney & Gill, 2004).

The mentor training programs during the following two summers adhered to the same foci. The third session had 18 teacher participants, while in the fourth, 22 teachers participated. Feedback from both groups was positive and was similar to that from the first two sessions.

Training Programs for Interns

As part of the first summer training program, a separate three-day orientation to mentoring was conducted for five special-education interns to help them understand what it means to have a mentor. The interns received a small stipend for participating. A staff member from Hood College who had participated in the training program for mentor-teachers facilitated the workshop. In addition to addressing similar topics covered in the mentoring workshop, this program included such topics as how to approach office personnel, where to find the copy machine, how to find out about general school procedures, and what could be expected of an intern for assuming management duties, such as lunchroom supervision and bus duty. There were also discussions about maintaining confidentiality, avoiding "teacher-lounge complaining," and working within the expectations and requirements of the college.

As they were observed during their extensive internships, the interns were found to be somewhat ahead of their peers in terms of understanding school procedures. In the early stages of the internship they required less guidance from the PDS coordinator for understanding general school information, and they asked more questions of their mentors about classroom-related issues such as schedules and routines, behavior management practices, and lesson plan format (Strosnider, Sweeney & Gill, 2004). The behaviors of these interns seemed to mirror, to a lesser degree, the developmental stages of in-service teachers. Yet, beginning teachers need to deal with lower-level concerns about self and management before they address higher-level concerns related to students and achievement (Odell & Huling, 2000).

Building on the premise that it is beneficial for mentors to develop a common understanding of what mentoring is, it was posited that interns who understand how to benefit from the mentoring process are more successful in the internship experience.

During the final semester of the extensive internship, the interns who had participated in the first orientation program were observed, and these observations were used for planning a summer training program for interns. This was a more formal program and was conducted at the same time as mentor training. Eleven interns representing early-childhood, secondary, and special-education chose to participate in this program. They received a stipend. Although the second program was more structured than the first and included discussions of the role of mentor-teachers and program expectations, the focus was primarily on procedural concerns and managerial issues.

Over time, there was a change from the first program in that the programs for mentors and interns were offered simultaneously. This allowed mentors and interns to meet together for a half-day session. Together they viewed a video clip of teachers in a large urban high school and were asked to analyze what they thought they saw. Both groups were surprised at the different perspectives each had on what they saw. This provided the format for a discussion of the fact that beginning teachers do not always perceive events the way experienced teachers perceive these events. According to Boreen et al. (2000), dissonance can encourage the consideration of another perspective. A limitation to this activity was that most of the teachers would not serve as mentors to the interns who participated with them in the session, but would serve as mentors to other interns.

As the interns moved into their final student-teaching internships, they demonstrated behaviors similar to those interns who participated in the previous summer training program. They appeared to be at a higher level of readiness for assuming class responsibilities as they began the internship than the interns who did not participate in the summer training. They required less guidance in assuming general duties and responsibilities and they asked fewer questions about expectations and reasons for basic procedural and managerial functions.

A more formal two-day program was developed for a third summer training, with a focus on practicing effective communication skills inherent in developing and nurturing a trusting relationship between mentors and interns. Interns practiced strategies for asking questions, accepting feedback, actively participating in conferences, and reflecting on feedback from mentors. Similar activities were offered to participants in a mentoring workshop for teachers, but there was no opportunity for interns and mentors to practice together since the programs were offered at different times.

In this program, the 16 interns who participated were comprised of traditional and non-traditional students. The four focus areas for the workshop were: (1) managing anxiety; (2) becoming a member of the school learning community; (3) developing effective observation skills; and (4) using effective communication skills. As a result of their focus on these four areas, the interns reached specific conclusions, an explanation of which follows.

Managing Anxiety

Anxiety rested in the context of expectations, personal and professional. Five areas of anxiety were identified: student achievement, balancing personal/family responsibilities with school responsibilities, personal expectations, PDS expectations, and college expectations and requirements. The interns explored strategies for dealing with these anxieties and identified resources to support them during their internship.

Becoming a Member of the School Learning Community

In previous short-term field experiences, interns felt they were more like visitors than participants. With the extensive internship experience, they became immersed in the culture of the school. Questions arose as to how to know when it is appropriate to take initiative or when to hold back. They began to articulate the importance of participating in collaborative professional development activities with their mentors and other school personnel.

Developing Effective Observation Skills

A critical part of the extensive internship is observing competent teachers instructing students. It was evident that interns could identify effective practices, but they often could not connect what they observed to why it worked. Guiding the interns in how to observe and what to observe in classrooms provided the framework for making the observation experience more meaningful.

Using Effective Communication Skills

If mentors and interns are to develop a trusting relationship, they must be able to communicate effectively. Interns practiced communication strategies for future success. In response to expressed concerns about initiating communication with their mentors, interns developed strategies for establishing a communication system with their mentor-teachers: times for meeting, types of formal and informal feedback, using written communication, etc. One intern asked: "What if my mentor keeps telling me I am doing fine? How will I know what I need to do to continue to grow as a teacher?" This was a good lead-in to sharing strategies for opening communication with mentors. The importance of body language, phrasing questions, and reacting to feedback and criticism were all explored.

The facilitators observed that as the interns progressed through the program, they moved from a focus on self to a focus on students and students' learning. Their questions and concerns during days preceding their active involvement began with topics such as, "What is the first day like?" and "Do I have to maintain the same hours as my mentor?" Once interns were actively involved in the classroom, these topics were quickly replaced with issues addressing instruction, such as, "I'm afraid I will miss that *teachable moment*" and "How do I capture their motivation?" Interns who completed this program reported they felt better prepared to begin their teaching internships, and felt especially comfortable in being able to communicate with their mentors. One student stated that she "felt empowered" to be an active participant in the mentor/intern conferences rather than just a receiver of feedback from her mentor.

"Getting Started"

Building on the success of previous training sessions for interns, the program evolved to an even higher level of support for the interns and was entitled, "Getting Started: Building a Team of Support for the Intern." This new program was designed as a two-day effort with college supervisors joining the interns and their mentor-teachers in the first day of training. The intent was to give the interns, mentor-teachers, and college supervisors an opportunity to get to know each other better and have them begin to develop a team approach prior to the student-teaching internship. Daloz (1999) contends that a successful mentoring program depends upon developing a trusting relationship between mentors and their interns. He states that "to engender trust" is central to the relationship and that mature trust is sustained by the commitment of each partner.

The program initiated in spring semester 2003 was for those students who would be going into their student-teaching internship the following fall semester. It was offered again in December 2003, to support those students who would be doing their teaching internship during spring semester 2004. A total of 28 interns (13 secondary education, 11 early-childhood education, and four special education) participated in the training. In addition, 38 mentor-teachers (early childhood education and special education interns have two teaching placements), and eight college supervisors attended the two days of training. In total, 86 percent of the teaching intern teams (a triad of intern, mentor-teacher, and college supervisor) were intact that day. Hood College's Professional Development Schools staff facilitated the program, and the coordinators for each of the initial teacher-certification programs assisted them.

As in the past, the first day began by recognizing that interns feel anxious about the teaching internship. This allowed the interns the opportunity to share their anxieties with their mentors and college supervisors, and to receive assistance in addressing these issues. Participants identified those items that would make the teaching internship a good experience and those issues that might lead to a negative experience. Responses were recorded and shared, providing a framework for common understandings of how team members can support each other by being proactive in preventing potentially negative issues from occurring.

A valuable part of the training was devoted to having all participants get to know each other better. To do so, everyone participated in a personality inventory activity. This was a first step in building a trusting relationship and exploring ways to work together effectively. Many discoveries were interesting. For example, an intern, her mentor-teacher, and college supervisor discovered that they feel most comfortable when things are harmonious and peaceful—they are nurturers who see the best in others. The intern commented that because of this, the mentor-teacher and college supervisor might be hesitant to criticize her teaching. She openly gave them permission to deliver hard messages to her so that she could grow. Another intern discovered that he appreciates spontaneity, freedom, and risk-taking; however, his mentor-teacher values order, routines, and security. This led to an interesting discussion about what they must remember about each other as they work together. Similar discussions among everyone present eased anxiety and initiated meaningful conversations about how people with different personalities can effectively work together.

Working with each other provided participants with a framework for looking at effective communication strategies. Thus, the next part of the program focused on giving and receiving effective feedback. After a discussion on the art of giving feedback and the importance of trust and open communication, participants practiced giving and receiving feedback. Activities were designed so the participants recognized the importance of "non-verbals" and probing for specificity. Again, the underlying intent was for the group to begin building a relationship and experiencing what it felt like to give and receive positive and critical messages. Feedback from the interns at the end of the program indicated that this was valued by them: "I feel more empowered because I have some tools for promoting positive, constructive criticism/feedback," and from another, "I feel more prepared to ask for feedback and glad that my mentor-teacher and I discussed the importance of this aspect of my teaching experience." These are representative of the comments made by others and in the responses of the program evaluation feedback provided by participants.

In addition, expectations for the teaching internship were reviewed. It was important that everyone heard the same message at the same time and had the opportunity to ask for clarification about any aspect of the program. Roles and responsibilities were defined, and mentors and supervisors had time to talk with interns about how they would function in their roles. This time also allowed mentors and supervisors to begin to develop a collaborative working relationship with each other.

Further, time was provided for the interns and their mentor-teachers to continue to develop a professional relationship through planning for instruction, scheduling times to continue meeting prior to the beginning of the semester, and discussing expectations. Results of a survey administered at the end of this session indicate this was the part of the program that the interns seemed to value most. A great deal of anxiety was eased for the interns from learning what unit they would be teaching, with which students they would be working, and what materials would be available. This provided a context in which the interns could practice some of the communication strategies they had learned early in the training.

In response to a survey administered to mentor-teachers at the end of the training, they, too, appreciated the opportunity to have this experience. The following comments were representative of all of them: "Nice to know what Hood's expectations are. Loved the personality inventory—gives you an idea of your [intern's] personality and how you can expect to work best together. Helped to ease some of the anxiety that goes along with the [teaching internship]." "It was nice to have the opportunity to meet with my student teacher [intern], spend time getting more acquainted, and plan before the 'stress' begins." "Reviewing expectations *together* helps set appropriate standards."

The college supervisors also recognized the value of the day spent with their interns and their mentor-teachers. Their comments mirrored this statement made by one of the supervisors: "Meeting interns and mentor-teachers 'broke the ice' and gave me the opportunity for forming a professional and trusting relationship. My learning about personality types will surely help me to be open and sensitive as I work with my interns and mentor-teachers. Thanks for helping us all to 'begin on the same page.'"

The second day of the training program was designed for interns and facilitated by PDS staff. The focus was on planning strategies to deal with their anxieties, initiating honest communication, and clarifying expectations. Interns indicated at the end of the day that they felt relieved to have been able to share anxieties with each other (and realized that they were not the only one feeling this way), and that they had considered ways to deal with their anxieties. In addition, several commented that the discussion of communication strategies provided means to use to continue building a positive mentor/intern relationship.

Interns also reviewed the work that addressed "good" and "bad" experiences of beginning teachers. The interns worked in teams to identify ways to convert the bad experiences into good experiences. They explored ways in which they could be proactive in preventing issues from occurring or escalating into a problem for themselves or others. The intent of this activity was for them to gain control over the many things that can happen during the internship and to begin the experience with confidence.

A session was devoted to viewing a video of a teacher who was an extremely effective motivator for students in an inner-city middle school. It was during discussions about this teacher's effectiveness that the facilitators were able to help the interns identify what was occurring that was effective, while the facilitators began to make the link as to why it was effective. This provided the basis for the interns to develop an understanding of observation techniques, which enabled them to understand why certain strategies are used and why certain outcomes are attained.

The interns met in groups according to their program disciplines—early-childhood education, secondary, or special education—for a concluding activity. This allowed them to discuss issues pertinent to their area of specialization. They concentrated on ways in which they could continue to be supportive of one another throughout the internship and expressed enthusiasm that the mentors and college supervisors were working as a team to help them be successful.

As a result of this program, interns expressed that they felt more confident about beginning their teaching internship. For example, "I feel more inspired to teach. There are lots of people there to support me—this is a nice feeling!" Another intern stated,"It's time to stop talking about teaching. I'm ready to go." Overwhelmingly, all groups who participated in the training program—interns, mentor-teachers, and college supervisors—felt more ready to begin the teaching internship as a result of their participation in the program.

Support for "Getting Started"

Although the financial support for "Getting Started" came from a grant from the Maryland Higher Education Commission, it was the collaborative efforts of the PDS partners that enabled the program to occur. Principals were supportive of previous programs for mentor training, but those sessions were offered during the summer and did not impact the operation of the school or disrupt teachers' schedules. In order to have time with their interns at the end of the college semester prior to the teaching internship, principals agreed to release the mentors from school and get substitute teachers to cover their classes. The college offered support by allowing interns to remain in their dorms after the date when they are normally closed. The college also arranged for space so the program could be held on campus.

Active involvement by interns in this process can be viewed as an initial step in collaborative professional development that should be encouraged and reinforced throughout their teaching careers. In addition to participating together in school-based and system-sponsored professional development activities, funds from the grant were used for mentors and interns to attend local, state, and national conferences where they shared their insights about this collaborative mentor/intern training.

Conclusions and Recommendations

Based upon the four-year history of the program, it is evident that preparing interns to understand the role of mentors is imperative to involving them as partners in the mentoring process. The interns felt more prepared to begin their internships after participating in training that included their mentor-teachers and college supervisors. The three interns who attended the "Getting Started" program without their mentor-teachers reported they found the experience to be helpful, but stated that it would have been greatly enhanced if their mentors had also attended the training.

A resulting challenge is to document how interns use the skills and knowledge they gained from this program as they assume more and more responsibilities during their final teaching internship. It is also important that mentor-teachers and supervisors understand each other's roles and responsibilities if they are to work together as a team. PDS staff will continue to collect data to measure the effectiveness of the training during the internship semester. In addition, information relevant to interns' performance that applies to the purposes of the training program will be reviewed during regularly scheduled seminars as part of the teaching internship.

As a result of qualitative feedback, mostly anecdotal, revisions were made each time the program was held. It started out as a time to focus on teachers mentoring interns as they focused on integrating the arts. It was so well received that a course for mentors was developed. The course provided the knowledge and skills for a larger group of participants. However, it was necessary to continue mentor and intern training specific to the undergraduate program. The feedback provided by participants during and following each of the summer trainings supplied the faculty with information that guided their decision making as they planned the next program. Thus, the program has evolved to the point described.

This process for preparing mentors and interns will be enhanced by having school administrators participate as members of the teams. Administrators' participation will demonstrate support for mentor-teachers and enable them to have a more in-depth understanding of the role of a mentor, which can lead to such things as arranging schedules so mentors have time within their workday to plan and confer with interns and college supervisors. Principals also must continue to provide release time for teachers to be involved in the process, and teachers and interns must commit time for further planning over the summer and winter break. Due to extremely demanding schedules, especially while school is in session, it will continue to be a challenge for principals to commit to participation in the training.

The college and the local school system must find funds to continue the mentor and intern training program. Having this as a targeted item in college and school-system budgets will offer more of an assurance for continuing the program rather than depending upon funding from grants.

A final recommendation is to expand the training program to three days. A third day will enable interns and mentors to develop their skills in giving and receiving feedback and will enable early-childhood and special-education interns, who have two placements, to have equitable time for planning with both mentor-teachers. It will also allow more time for teambuilding activities for mentors, interns, and college supervisors. Interns cited the time allotted for planning in partnership with their mentors as one of the most meaningful aspects of training; more time for this activity would certainly enhance their training.

References

Boreen, J., Johnson, M.K., Niday, D., & Potts, J. (2000). *Mentoring beginning teachers: Guiding, reflecting, coaching.* York, ME: Stenhouse Publishers.

Daloz, L. (1999). Mentor: Guiding the journey of adult learners (2nd ed.). San Francisco: Jossey-Bass.

Darling-Hammond, L. (1999). Educating teachers: The academy's greatest failure or its most important future. *Academe, 85,* 1.

Halford, J.L. (1998). Easing the way for new teachers. *Educational Leadership, 55,* 5.

Morrison, K.L. & Marshall, C.S. (2003). University and public schools: Are we disconnected? *Phi Delta Kappan, 85,* 4.

Odell, Sandra J. (1992). Teacher mentoring and teacher retention. *Journal of Teacher Education, 43,* 3.

Odell, S. & Huling, L. (2000). *Quality mentoring for novice teachers.* Indianapolis, IN: Kappa Delta Pi.

Saphier, J., Freedman, S., & Aschheim, B. (2001). *Beyond mentoring: Comprehensive induction programs.* Newton, MA: Teachers 21.

Strosnider, R., Sweeney, F., & Gill, H. (2004). Perceptions of mentor-teachers: Reflections before, during, and after mentor training. In Gartland, D. (Ed.). *Mentoring.* Towson, MD: Small Special Education Programs Caucus.

Teitel, L. (1998). Professional development schools: A literature review. In M. Levine (Ed.), *Designing standards that work for professional schools.* Washington, DC: National Council for Accreditation of Teacher Education.

PART III

Shaping the Professional Development School through Standards

CHAPTER 9   *Marsha Levine & Roberta Trachtman*

Co-Constructing an Accountability System for Professional Development Schools

Professional Development Schools are innovative institutions formed through partnerships between professional education programs and P-12 schools. Their mission, analogous to that of a teaching hospital in medicine, includes professional preparation of candidates, faculty development, clinical research, and enhanced P-12 student learning. This is accomplished through a program of professional education and clinical research performed in the context of practice. PDSs are real schools that have been specially staffed and structured to support these multiple functions.

The potential impact of a PDS is one of its unique features—they are strategically positioned at the intersection of teacher education and school reform. These two sectors of education traditionally have found it difficult to bridge their differences, although each has a large stake in the success of the other, and each has much to contribute to that success. They call upon partners to share responsibility for professional and children's learning, and to commit and reallocate resources to this new setting and new kind of work. Partners are also called upon to be accountable, professionally and publicly, for the outcomes of all PDS participants.

Context for the Project

From 1995 to 2001, the National Council for Accreditation of Teacher Education conducted a project to develop and field test standards and assessments for Professional Development Schools. Over the course of six years, NCATE and their PDS partners in the field refined their understanding of Professional Development Schools and how they function, and used this new knowledge to construct standards and assessment processes to advance and support this innovation. Two contextual factors influenced the approaches that were taken in the project. First, the relative newness of Professional Development Schools heightens concerns about developing standards prematurely. The second and counterbalancing factor was the growing commitment in the broader education community to establishing standards and assessments as the primary strategy for accountability. These two factors led to a search for a way to develop standards that could support and assess vulnerable, new institutions.

Professional Development Schools had come to be recognized as a potentially powerful innovation for teacher education and school reform. Many institutions claimed to have PDS partnerships. Although there was general consensus about the PDS mission in 1995, there was a broad range of practices that characterized partnerships. Some PDSs were innovative institutions, while others were traditional student-teaching programs with new names. On the one hand, PDSs needed to be defined more clearly and be shown to make a difference, or they would disappear or remain forever on the margins of teacher education and school reform. On the other hand, many advocates of Professional Development Schools were concerned that, as an innovation, PDSs needed more time to develop. Standards were viewed as a premature imposition on a fragile institution, and a threat to further creative development. In 1996 the PDS Standards Project began, with full awareness of these concerns.

As to the second contextual factor, the growing move toward standardization, the Standards Project work took place in an era of educational accountability. Therefore, it was not surprising that the task of developing standards was viewed as an innovation that could make a difference. Education reform in the last decade has been driven by a powerful call for accountability and quality assurance. Policymakers demanded greater skills and knowledge from students and teachers. Standards and assessments (usually meaning tests) have been the pre-eminent approach, but challenges abound in any standards-based approach to education reform. Knowing one's purpose is critical. Some standards are meant to serve a gate-keeping function; others are designed to define. Authority imposes some standards; others are grassroots generated. Whatever the purpose, certain universals must be met if standards and assessments are to be useful and credible. In other words, standards must reflect what is important and assessments must appropriately measure proximity to that standard. If standards and assessments are to be useful for developmental purposes (e.g., building capacity), they must provide useful information to guide future activity. Given the state of the art in PDSs at the time, the project took on the challenge of creating a set of standards that would support development in PDS partnerships and be used to make judgments about them.

It was within this context that the NCATE initiated a project to develop standards for Professional Development Schools. The project received funding from the AT&T Foundation to do the first phase of the work.

Expectations

The standards were intended to have several uses. First, they would bring rigor to the concept of Professional Development Schools so their potential would not be lost. Second, they would provide a framework for PDS partnerships to use in guiding their development. An appropriately designed assessment process would provide feedback to PDS partners about their work. Policymakers at the national, state, and local level might use the standards to shape incentives, statutes, and programs for encouraging PDS development, and the standards would help them link PDS to the teacher quality agenda. Finally, the PDS standards could provide a much-needed framework for conducting and evaluating research that addresses the question of learning outcomes in PDS partnerships. In each of these ways, standards and assessments could be tools to support PDS development and to leverage their impact on P–12 and teacher education reform.

Between 1996 and 1998, NCATE staff, working with leaders from across the constituencies of PDSs, developed a set of draft standards for Professional Development Schools. The next step was to take the draft standards into the field to authenticate them. A three-year field-test project was funded by the Wallace Reader's Digest Fund to accomplish the second phase of the work.

The first part of this chapter recounts the methodological approach taken in this activity. Research questions are identified, and participants and processes are described. The partnering strategy is explained, and the process of data collection and analysis is described. Part II presents a discussion of important outcomes of the effort, including what was learned about PDSs and about the design and development of standards and assessments. Part III presents a discussion of the broader implications of this project for designing systems of accountability.

Phase 1: Designing Standards That Work

In 1995, NCATE initiated the Professional Development School Standards Project with three goals: to establish a consensus about quality and good practice in PDSs; to design standards that reflect the fact that the PDS is still evolving as a new institution; and to use standards as part of the development of an infrastructure to support and sustain PDSs. Activities were designed to achieve these goals. In June 1995, a National Advisory Group was established, composed of representatives of the constituencies of PDSs—teacher educators, teachers, administrators, national, state and local policymakers, teacher unions, and education researchers with special knowledge about teacher education and teacher learning. Out of this large group, several smaller working groups were formed to guide the project. These groups were organized around research, policy, finance issues related to PDSs, and the drafting of the standards. Several consultants were engaged throughout the project implementation and a number of professionals donated their time on advisory and working groups.

While support for PDSs had grown over the years, by 1995 it had become clear the PDS "movement" was in some danger. Viewed as an important innovation, PDSs had proliferated rapidly with little attention paid to their definition and quality. Under such circumstances, there was concern PDSs could become an empty promise and a lost opportunity. As interest from national, state, and local policymakers increased, it became clear that definition and a way to identify quality were imperative.

The creation of institutional standards represented an appropriate response to supporting and sustaining the PDS. However, there was concurrent concern about how to set standards, given the fragile and complex nature of the institution. Three characteristics presented the greatest challenge. First, PDSs were collaborative institutions. The partners belonged to different sectors of the education community, each with its own history, culture, and governance structure. Second, each partnership is somewhat unique to its locality. Could standards be designed to further help PDS development, yet not attempt to standardize PDSs? And finally, PDSs are at varying stages of development. Could there be standards that would help the partnerships move from one stage to the next?

Developing the Draft PDS Standards

A set of studies and analyses were commissioned to provide information for the deliberations of the working groups and the development of the draft standards. In his paper "Worthy of the Name: Standards for the Professional Development School," Sykes (1996) developed arguments in favor of and against the development of standards for PDSs. He asserted that if standards were to serve as instruments for reform, they would have to identify what was important in PDSs, define the conditions necessary for growth, and connect to an assessment mechanism that allows partners to identify quality and support individual and institutional development.

Through his extensive literature review, Teitel (1998) confirmed the generally held view that there was little agreement on the definition of a PDS. Policymakers, practitioners, and researchers were applying the term "PDS" to a broad range of activity, which extended from traditional student teaching (but in cohort placements), to wholly restructured teacher education programs that were developed in full collaboration with schools and other partners. Much of the existing literature was descriptive, including a growing number of case studies. Out of this descriptive material, however, a general agreement emerged regarding the four functions of a Professional Development School: teacher education, professional development, enhanced student learning, and inquiry directed at the improvement of practice. Importantly, the research review also revealed little evaluation or research on outcomes related to PDSs. Teitel's work helped reinforce concerns regarding the vulnerability of this new institution and contributed to the identification of consensus regarding its purpose.

After reviewing the literature, practices in the field were examined. Trachtman (1998) completed a survey among 28 well-developed PDSs nominated by their peers. The survey analyses produced a set of findings about what was happening within these partnerships and the challenges confronted by individuals and institutions. The data suggested that participants held a shared vision of learning that was constructivist, contextual, and oriented toward higher levels of thinking. While survey responses provided more than a hint about the ways in which participants were integrating three of the PDS functions, very few sites were doing anything they could describe as inquiry. The data indicated that PDSs served all kinds of students and existed in different contexts. Most partnerships indicated they lacked a critical mass of participants, strongly suggesting the need for more institutional commitment. The data also suggested a lack of parity between the university and school. For example, survey participants noted that university faculty members were described as being teachers and facilitators rather than "learners" in the PDS. The findings also clarified the nature of development within a PDS and began to show three stages of PDS evolution: pre-threshold, threshold, and quality attainment.

Overall, the picture that emerged from the survey was of an extremely vulnerable, young institution. Values, beliefs, and goals were articulated, but often partners were not able to describe the ways in which they were being enacted. Further, participants voiced a need for safety and buffers to shield themselves and their work.

Findings from these studies suggested directions for the content and structure of the standards. They pointed toward the creation of a structure to emphasize the integration of the functions of a PDS rather than the development of standards around each separate function. Also highlighted was the need to identify the practices associated with partners' commitments and beliefs.

In February 1996, two representatives from each survey site, other PDS participants from across the nation, and Project advisors and consultants examined the survey findings in a highly interactive conference in Chicago. Mining the subtleties of these conversations, Freeman (1998) identified four deep structures in the PDS terrain, namely: (1) roles and relationships; (2) time, results, and rewards; (3) evolution, acknowledgment, and gate keeping; and (4) core values and processes. His analysis furthered the commitment to finding ways in which the standards would respond to the specific needs of the developing institution, reinforce the integration of functions, and support stages of development. Also, the conversational format of the conference revealed that PDS participants often held different meanings or uses for the same terms. These differences suggested that standards-development designers would need to navigate carefully between various local "languages" used by PDS participants and the language employed in the national standards.

During the conference, participants directed the discussion toward imagining ways in which the PDS standards could be used. Echoing Sykes's (1997) earlier conceptualization, PDS partners argued that the standards and a process for using them were two sides of the same coin. In response, Wilson (1998) was invited to develop a conceptual argument for co-joining the development of standards with the creation of a PDS institutional assessment process.

Snyder (1998) completed the final research study, which served as a foundation for the creation of the draft standards. His work provided critical findings related to the kinds of financial and policy supports necessary for implementing and sustaining PDSs. Most important among these findings was the observation that in mature, effective PDSs, pre-service teachers represented a value-adding resource rather than a "drain" on teachers' energy and time. In well-developed PDSs, the regular participation of pre-service and university-based teachers in the life of the school provided a unique form of support for students and for the development of excellent educational programs.

Phase 2: The First Review of the Draft Professional Development School Standards

In June 1996, NCATE released its Professional Development School Draft Standards. By building on written descriptions of PDS participants' lived experiences (Trachtman, 1998), their reflections and responses at a national conference (Freeman, 1998), the deliberations and advice of a national advisory committee, and mounds of extant anecdotal and empirical evidence (Teitel, 1998), the PDS standards designers decided to construct two levels within the draft standards. The first level, referred to as "Threshold Conditions," sought to capture how well partnering institutions were committed to and understood what it would take to form a new hybrid institution. The second level, called the "Quality Standards," represented the characteristics or attributes of participants and partner organizations as they worked toward achieving their PDS mission.

As a first step in revising the draft standards, NCATE Project staff invited school- and university-based PDS teachers and administrators to review the draft. They wanted to learn how PDS practitioners might use the threshold conditions and the quality standards to examine and improve their work, and whether these conditions and standards captured what was most essential about their Professional Development Schools. Based upon the experiences of other standards-setting groups and newer conceptions of standards as capacity-building mechanisms (Sykes, 1997), it was decided to refine and expand the draft standards by taking them into the field for in-depth review.

The seven PDS sites that examined the draft standards included all regions of the country, all school levels (elementary, middle, and high schools), and small, medium, and large public and private colleges and universities. In each setting, university- and school-based teachers and administrators reviewed the draft standards in advance and participated in focus-group discussions or individual interviews. Participants also provided written reflections at the end of each discussion.

Refining and Expanding the First Set of Draft Standards

For the most part, during this initial examination in the field, participants offered support for the two levels of the draft PDS standards. Importantly, however, they made several recommendations that found their way into the next draft:

- A pre-threshold stage was added to the draft after participants explained the critical importance of the time before the PDS actually began. As described by PDS insiders, during this initial period school- and university-based educators begin to learn about each other by engaging in collaborative activities.
- As participants reported they needed more concrete examples in order to understand the document's two levels and to use the framework to examine their own practices, the next draft included multiple examples and indicators of PDS work.
- Given the conviction that PDSs were grounded and dependent upon relationships, participants effectively argued for adding a Collaboration Standard to the draft.
- Concerned by the linearity implied in the threshold conditions and quality standards, the revised introduction to the draft standards articulated a strong statement about the varied ways in which PDS partnerships grow over time.

Potential Conflicts between the PDS Standards and Current Practices and Policies

Participants identified a set of conflicts between current policies and practices and the draft standards. While these conflicts were not resolved in the revised draft, they served as valuable touchstones for the development of the next phase of field-testing. State- or county-mandated accountability measures sometimes seemed to contradict the PDS focus on developing teachers with an inquiry orientation who built an interdisciplinary curriculum. In most cases, pre-service, university, and school-based teachers volunteered to participate in the PDS. The draft standards implied recruitment, selection, and evaluation processes for participants that might run counter to current and past personnel practices. Further, large-scale teacher education programs would continue to need a broad array of clinical placement opportunities for their pre-service teacher candidates. They believed they could not meet the clinical needs of all pre-service students in Professional Development Schools. And teacher-union seniority rules posed potential conflicts with the Professional Development School's need to retain their specially prepared school-based teacher-mentors.

Using the Standards

Participants theorized multiple uses for the threshold conditions and standards. For some, the standards were seen as a tool for driving school improvement, for engendering support for their time and work, for increasing the construction and generation of new knowledge, for recruiting new members, and for inquiring about and assessing their practices. Others suggested the standards were like a shield that protected participants from external, conflicting demands, affirmed the uniqueness of this form of school-university collaboration, and supported the inherent fragility of cross-institutional partnerships.

Overwhelmingly, participants saw the set of PDS standards as a catalyst and guide for growth and change. They used words like "blueprint," "target," and "framework" to describe how the standards might be used to steer their work. The standards would help them build capacity in order to improve (see Sykes, 1997 for a conceptually congruent discussion).

The Beginnings of an Assessment Process Emerge

Participants recommended multiple ways in which sites might demonstrate how they were meeting the PDS threshold conditions and standards. Throughout these discussions, however, they were careful not to define an evidence "hierarchy" or a fixed set of indicators. Although focus-group members and interview informants seemed to put forth some recommendations more strongly than others, the participants remained committed to tying PDS processes and progress to local conditions. The sites were unwilling to establish generic parameters for distinguishing between more and less compelling evidence or between negotiable and non-negotiable indicators. Yet, because they recognized the need for the PDS to demonstrate its impact, they supported the development of an assessment process to assure insiders and outsiders that PDS work made a difference. Importantly, these participants, and hundreds like them throughout the years of the field test, would argue that the PDS assessment process needed to align with the standards and with the culture and the norms of the PDS as a unique, educational institution. As the next phase of the field test began to take shape, Project staff would repeatedly return to the data provided during these initial examinations of the draft PDS standards.

Phase 3: The Partnering Strategy

The success of the field test depended upon the interest and commitment of PDS sites to use the draft standards and develop a process for assessing institutional quality. Project staff required willingness on the part of the PDS institutions for self-reflection and inquiry.

The Application and Selection Process for the Field Test

The draft PDS standards formed the centerpiece of the field-test application. In essays no longer than ten pages, applicants had to describe their goals and activities in terms of the standards, including the ways in which they were accountable to stakeholders. They had to select and explain the PDS attributes about which they had strongest resolve. Also, they had to predict the benefits and problems they expected from engaging in the field test.

The Project staff invited ten reviewers to help select the PDS sites for the field test. In addition to depending upon the considerable PDS experience brought by each member of this Selection Committee, four criteria were developed to guide the review process:

1. sites represented the range of PDS developmental levels: pre-threshold, threshold, and quality attainment;
2. sites represented the array of PDS configurations, including one-university–one-school site model; one university–multi-school site model; and a multi-university–one-school site/multi-school site model;
3. each site demonstrated a willingness and capacity to design an assessment strategy and refine and validate the draft standards; and
4. sites were likely to benefit from participating in the field test.

Selection Process
Thirty-nine partnerships involving 90 schools from across the nation responded to the Invitation to Apply. Applicants included school-university partnerships committed to the four goals of a Professional Development School, including the preparation of new teachers, the support of children's learning, the continuing professional development of experienced teachers, and practice-based inquiry within a school setting. The university partners were NCATE accredited, or candidates/pre-candidates for NCATE accreditation.

Two selection committee members read and scored each application. The members reviewed the applications that received the highest scores at each developmental level. They raised questions about the applicants and solicited information from other members who knew these sites well. Committee members selected 20 partner sites based upon scores and the previously established criteria.

Project partners committed to engaging in a three-year process of gathering standards-related data, designing and field-testing a new assessment process, visiting each other's sites, and examining the impact of the standards and the assessment process on their own PDSs. Modest stipends (a total of $12,500) were provided to offset some of the costs related to the Project's work. While all 20 invited partnerships accepted their invitations to become part of the field test, seventeen engaged in all phases of the Project.

Field-Test Activities

As specified in the Invitation to Apply, the field-test partners undertook four major activities:

1. standards refinement and validation: partner sites worked with each other and Project staff to refine and validate the PDS standards;
2. assessment design: partner sites and Project staff constructed, piloted, and refined a PDS assessment process;
3. national Project and site-driven inquiries: partner sites identified PDS learning outcomes for children and participating adults; and
4. impact analysis: partner sites examined and reported on the impact of using PDS standards and engaging in the PDS assessment process.

Field-Test Roles

By design, the field test required the PDS partners to create new roles and engage in new work. Each partnership had to identify a site contact, two site visitors, and a research liaison. The site contact was responsible for acting as the "point person" to school and university-based PDS colleagues and Project staff. After participating in a multi-day training program, each PDS site visitor had to leave his or her own school for about five days to visit with and assess another PDS partnership in the Project. The research liaison in each partnership took primary responsibility for implementing the partnership inquiry activities. In some sites, a few individuals played more than one of these roles.

The Design Team. Individuals from within the Project's partner sites and from the broader PDS community were invited to commit to developing the new process for assessing PDSs. Called the "Design Team," the members met two or three times during each Project year to develop and revise the PDS assessment process.

The Standards Revision Group. Like their Design Team colleagues, the "Standards Revision Group" included participants in the partnerships and others who had worked in PDSs or were education policy analysts. Informed by data provided during the field test, the members revised the initial set of PDS draft standards.

Phase 4: Using the Initial Standards Review to Initiate the Self-Study Process

The partner sites began to play a critical role in refining the draft standards through their "Initial Standards Review Activity." The research liaisons engaged their colleagues in an examination of the draft standards as their first Project-related work. Through this process, two goals were to be accomplished: increasing sites' awareness and understanding of the standards; and providing an initial set of reflections and recommendations for refining the standards. The process also required each site to recruit and select members for a "Field Test Steering Committee," a group that would take responsibility for all Project work during the following three years.

Task and the Outcomes

The Task
The PDS Draft Standards contained an introduction, five Threshold Conditions (with indicators and evidences), and five Critical Attributes (with indicators and evidences). The sites closely examined each section and then responded to a series of questions relating the standards to their own lived experiences.

The Outcomes
The sites' responses were organized into three domains: (1) using the standards; (2) connecting the parts to the whole; and (3) naming what or who was missing from the standards document.

(1) Using the Standards. Overwhelmingly, participants indicated the standards could serve as a catalyst and a guide for growth and change. It was suggested that the standards would help to build capacity in order to improve the PDS. Some "younger" sites suggested that this close examination of the standards raised their awareness and anxiety about the field-test project, and the more general expectations embedded in the work of participants in Professional Development Schools. Finally, many sites called for simplifying the standards and for making the language less clinical.

(2) Connecting the Parts to the Whole. Participants recognized that the draft standards were complex because they identified the developmental nature of Professional Development Schools, the institutional commitments that were required to support PDSs, and the attributes or characteristics of highly developed PDSs. During their initial discussions, many partner sites seemed to struggle with the document's density, and the relationship between each part of the document to the whole. These struggles informed the members of the Standards Revision Committee during their deliberations on the following dimensions:

- *The Checklist Dilemma.* While some sites indicated that, although they valued the naming of specific beliefs and practices through the inclusion of indicators and examples, they resisted the ways in which the indicators and examples seemed to represent a checklist for participants and/or visitors. Some added that the use of several of the same indicators for more than one standard would confound future attempts to provide evidence from the work done on each standard.

- *The Stages.* Although the sites supported the ways in which the standards reflected the developmental nature of PDSs, they rejected the linearity implied by the three stages. For example, some partners explained that the stages in the document did not reflect their experiences because they had already made considerable progress on some of the critical attributes listed as Stage 3 characteristics, but they had not yet met one or more of the Threshold Conditions included in Stage 2.
- *The Functions and the Whole.* Although the sites accepted the four PDS functions described in the standards, they raised questions about the ability of a PDS to be able to focus on all four functions at each stage of development. Some suggested the decision to embed the functions throughout the document diminished their presence. According to some sites, embedding the functions prevented the standards document from emphasizing the importance of integrating the functions in a PDS. Finally, many sites indicated that student learning and inquiry functions were underdeveloped or underemphasized in the document.
- *The Standards and the Assessment Process.* As partners in the Field-Test Project, the sites were committed to developing a PDS assessment process. They recommended that the standards be clearly linked conceptually and "practically" to the newly created assessment process.

(3) *Naming What or Who Was Missing from the Standards Document.* The sites identified some elements as missing from the standards. These included:

- *The Power of the Local Context.* According to partner sites, the PDS was uniquely affected by variations in the local context. For example, the PDS as a developing, collaborative entity depended upon the successful integration of participants from different cultures; or, the PDS sometimes took resources away from valued programs or initiatives; or, the PDS might expose institutional or individual weaknesses. Consequently, the standards needed to acknowledge and make room for the opportunities and constraints created by local conditions.
- *Others in the Partnership.* The sites concluded that school and university partners were represented throughout the draft standards. However, several partners concluded that the standards needed to name additional PDS partners, especially parents, the community, non-education school faculty, school-district members, and non-teaching school-based personnel.
- *Institutions and Individuals.* The PDS is grounded in institutional and individual commitment. For some participants, the standards did not go far enough in delineating the work of individuals and the responsibilities of the institution.
- *The Equity Attribute.* Many sites described the underdevelopment of this attribute as a critical weakness in the standards. They recommended that issues of equity be given prominence throughout the document as well as within this single standard.

Using the Results

The initial standards-review activity appeared to open new kinds of PDS discussions among longtime participants and among those at each site who were newer to PDS work. From the beginning, Project participants used these early findings about the standards to guide their development of the PDS assessment process. Specifically, the field-test Design Team members integrated the findings from the standards-review activity into the initial self-study template and the training workshops created to prepare visit teams and visit chairs.

Phase 5: Initiating, Implementing, and Assessing the Assessment Process

Research Questions and a Research Process Emerge

The project began with five overarching questions. These included:

1. What is a Professional Development School?
2. What revisions are needed so the standards can identify what is most important in a Professional Development School?
3. How can alignment between standards and the assessment process be assured?
4. Can the same set of standards and assessment process be used to support PDS development (internal accountability) and assess a PDS partnership (external accountability)?
5. What are the connections between the PDS standards and assessment process and local, state, and national policies? What are the disconnections?

Two critical research decisions were made related to the Project research and development agenda. Although participants' suggestions continued to be collected after the initial review activity, the draft standards were not revised until the Project's final phase. In contrast, the emerging PDS assessment process was revised *during* the Project in response to partners' and visitors' lived experiences.

Data Collection I: Focusing on the Self-Study in Relation to the Draft Standards

Field-Test Design Team members drafted a first outline of the PDS assessment process by building upon Wilson's (1996) framework for school inspections. The PDS designers created a three-part process that included a self-study, a visit by a team of PDS participants, and a follow-up internal review six months after the visit had been completed. During its first meeting, the 12 members of the team evaluated each proposed assessment strategy in relation to how well the strategy reflected their shared understandings of the PDS process. This commitment influenced the team members' work, from the creation of the first self-study template into the final PDS Handbook. Thus, early on, the team firmly established the stance for all participants and activities in the PDS assessment process.

The Self-Study Process
By spring 1999, all partner sites completed their self-study reports. Serving as pilot-pilot sites, three partnerships also hosted visits that spring. After each visit, these sites engaged in focus-group conversations with Project staff to reflect on their self-study experiences and on the visit by the PDS external team. At three additional sites, Project staff engaged the research liaisons in discussions about their sites' experiences with the self-study process. At the remaining sites, self-study data were collected through written questionnaires.

Seventy-two participants in the Project responded to a 33-item questionnaire about their experiences with the newly developed Self-Study process. These respondents came from 11 partnerships participating in the Project. While the response rate of 74 percent was acceptable for exploratory research, there was caution about generalizing these results to all of the partnerships within the field test and to the larger world of PDSs.

As a group, the respondents were positive about their experiences related to completing the self-study. They indicated that the steering committee was an effective structure for completing the tasks. They gave high scores to the ways in which engaging in the self-study benefited them, and they valued the process that required them to use their professional judgment to evaluate their own practice. The self-study had asked them about having to use the Draft Standards, and the participants also reported this to be a positive experience.

The questionnaire analyses yielded one main effect due to size. The partnerships that involved only one site reported statistically higher means than did the multi-site partnerships on their experiences in using the draft standards during the self-study process. This finding highlighted the Project's initial beliefs about one-site partnerships. During remaining visits, more would be learned about how the standards and the assessment process needed to reflect the multi-site nature of most PDS partnerships. Rather than designing a process for visiting one college or university and one school, the process would need to incorporate strategies for assessing the relationships and outcomes of PDS work among a group of connected PDS schools and their higher-education partner.

Data were used from the visits to the pilot-pilot sites, the focus groups, and the self-study questionnaires in order to revise the initial-visit process design and to create the program for visitor training. In August 1999, approximately 70 individuals, representing most of the PDS partner sites and several Project advisory board members, participated in an intensive site-visitor training session. With participation from two of the visited sites, a visit was simulated using video, documents, and interviews. Five months later, the final visit chairs were engaged in a training session based upon what had been learned earlier. Again and again, the attempt was to make the most of early findings to refine the evolving PDS assessment process.

Data Collection II: Focusing on the Visit in Relation to the Draft Standards

The PDS Design Team members worked hard to construct the visit as a collaborative, equitable, inquiry-driven process. While each visit team gathered evidence to help the Project validate and refine the structure and content of the draft PDS standards, the visitors also sought to provide useful feedback to the partnership sites. There were two agendas. First, site visitors were asked to learn how participants integrated the four functions of a PDS. As part of the field test, Project staff needed to know whether or not using the standards helped the partners become more accountable to each other and to their publics. Since the draft standards and initial assessment process had been designed mainly for single-site partnerships, the visitors also needed to collect data related to how the standards and the assessment process could be used in multi-site configurations. Further, given the distinct phases identified in the draft, the visitors also needed to determine how the PDS changed over time. Did the PDS move deliberately through the phases identified in the draft standards?

Second, for visitors and for those who were visited, preparing for and engaging in the visit required the development of new skills related to collecting and using data. As report presenters, the visitors developed insights into the politics of sharing information in unfamiliar public settings. Thus, for all participants, an unintended consequence of the visit process was the development of new ways of knowing, speaking, and making sense of the world of the PDS.

Data Collection III: Focusing on Outcomes in Relation to the Draft Standards

As part of its research and development agenda, Project staff and the research liaisons designed an inquiry process for capturing PDS outcomes for teacher candidates and children in PDSs. The following questions were developed and mirrored the interests of policymakers who wanted PDS outcome data:

Children's Learning

1. What impact does the PDS have on children's learning? How do you know?
2. How does inquiry—the processes engaged in and the results identified—affect children's learning in the PDS?
3. Which conditions and circumstances in the PDS correlate with children's learning?

Teacher Candidates' Learning

1. What opportunities for learning do teacher candidates have in a PDS? How do these opportunities differ from those in non-PDS sites?
2. How does the engagement by teacher candidates in action research affect their learning?
3. How do key PDS structures—such as school-based responsibility for candidate learning and integration of university faculty into the learning environment for teacher candidates—affect the ways in which children learn?

Although few of the partnerships completed their outcomes research during the remaining months of the Project, staff incorporated this outcomes orientation into the revised PDS standards. As the final section in the standards, the "Developmental Guidelines" orient readers to using outcome data to move a PDS partnership from one level to the next. Additionally, the Design Team members integrated the collection of outcome data into all components of the PDS assessment process.

Phase 6: Mining the Self-Studies and Visit Reports to Refine the Standards and Assessment Process

As described previously in this chapter, the partnerships completed self-studies, the visit teams constructed formal reports, and Project staff set out to examine data from these (and other) sources to refine the draft standards and the PDS assessment process.

Step 1
The self-study process required the partners to provide evidence about their PDSs by examining their work through the lens of the draft standards. Similarly, visiting team members who visited each partnership site identified evidence of how the PDS partnership used the draft standards.

Organizing Questions for Document Analysis. The self-study data analysis was guided by four sets of questions:

1. Did the evidence affirm the draft standards? Did the evidence cluster around the draft standards and the elements in each draft standard?
2. Did the evidence gathered from the pilot partnership sites suggest other important characteristics of a PDS not represented in the draft standards? What new characteristics were suggested?
3. What was the relationship between the developmental level of a PDS partnership and the critical attributes represented in the draft standards?

4. How were the four functions (teacher preparation, staff development, practice-based inquiry, and student achievement) represented in the work of the PDS partnership?

Step 2
An array of demographic characteristics was used to code each bit of data extracted from the partnership documents (e.g., level of maturity, number of school sites). Early reviews of these data revealed some general patterns. First, there was considerable overlap among the stages of development identified in the draft standards, and the standards themselves appeared to overlap. While substantial clusters of evidence were associated with each of the draft standards, new clusters emerged as well. The basic PDS functions appeared throughout the data, but this was represented unevenly. While children's learning, for example, was one of the basic functions of the PDS, in their self-studies partners did not regularly write about how the PDS focused on children. Most evidence related to the preparation of preservice teachers and the professional development of staff. These clusters were not surprising since they were consistent with PDS activities described in the literature (Teitel, 1998).

Step 3
During this step of document analysis, Project staff began to focus on the relationship between the level of development or maturity of the PDS and the evidence provided for each of the draft standards. In this analysis, the evidence, coded by source, was arrayed for each standard. The frequency and kinds of evidence differed from site to site with the age of the PDS appearing as an important factor, although not the only factor that might account for the differences.

Step 4
Next, Project staff sought to understand what the evidence revealed about best practices. In this step, the focus was on the self-studies and visit reports from nine selected sites. These partnerships were selected for this analysis for two reasons. First, during the initial review it was indicated that these sites were engaging in "mature" PDS practice. Second, at that time, staff had access to the self-study and visit reports.

Using the draft framework, the evidence was examined from these nine sites for each standard and each threshold condition. From this fine-grained analysis, "unexplained" clusters of data emerged and they were incorporated into the draft framework.

Step 5
Because PDSs embrace professional and student learning, staff wanted to see what the self-studies and visit reports could say about how learning takes place. Therefore, the next step was to examine which learner(s) were associated with what clusters of evidence from the mature sites.

Anecdotal reports and descriptions in the literature had suggested that, although many partners were attempting to address each PDS function separately—teacher preparation, staff development, children's learning, and inquiry—few, if any, had sufficient resources to follow through on all of these. The analysis of the documents from the mature sites revealed these partners were no longer engaging in "parallel pursuits." Instead, in the mature PDS sites, the partners were doing work that integrated all four functions. Their PDS work examples led to an understanding of how these partners pursued their goals: they engaged in systematic inquiry and professional learning in order to meet the needs of children.

Step 6
In this step, staff combined the findings from the self-studies and the visit reports with focus-group, interview, and questionnaire data to develop new understandings about the PDS sites.

Step 7
In order to refine the PDS assessment process, staff re-examined the data. These analyses indicated the process helped PDS partners define their goals, describe their work, inquire about what they do, and examine what they accomplished. Additionally, the assessment process raised stakeholder awareness, built stakeholder commitment, promoted sturdier connections among institutional and individual partners, and supported the development of inquiry dispositions and processes.

Step 8
From the beginning of the field test, participants wrestled with whether or not a PDS partnership with multiple-school partners would be able to use the draft standards. The self-study data suggested the draft standards were biased toward single-school PDS partnerships. In order to test this concern in relationship to the assessment process, visitors to three PDS partnerships that included multiple-school partners undertook an examination of this question. Together, the visitors learned how to organize their work so the standards and the assessment process could be made applicable to PDS partnerships with multiple-school sites.

By combining the findings from these visits with recommendations from the Design Team members and advisors, Project staff incorporated a definition of multi-site partnerships into the standards, and expanded the assessment process to support participants in multi-site settings who were interested in using the standards to support and judge their work.

Discussion

In order to frame the discussion of the findings and implications of the work of the PDS Standards Project, it is important to return to the five questions that shaped the data collection and analyses activities.

What Was Learned about Professional Development Schools?

Affirmation of Critical Attributes
One of the central goals of the Project was to bring better definition to the concept of Professional Development Schools. Working in partnership with PDS sites around the nation, we were able to enhance the understanding of what a PDS is and how it functions. The field-test process affirmed and refined several key concepts generally recognized by the PDS community and embedded in the draft PDS standards (Freeman, 1998). These included:

Partnership. The understanding of partnership was considerably refined. While school and university faculty were affirmed as the principal PDS partners, staff observed how the university, the school, and the school district needed to support the work of participating individuals. The breadth of the partnership was found to be critical; that is, PDS partnerships extend beyond the principal partners and partnering institutions to include parents, community members, and professional associations and unions. Also, university and school leaders are important to the effectiveness of the partnership.

PDS Mission. Prior to the field test, there was general consensus that teacher preparation, staff development, inquiry, and enhanced student achievement were the key functions of a PDS partnership that defined its mission. As field-test data affirmed this mission, project participants learned a great deal about the interaction among these functions in an effective PDS.

Importance of Relationships and Establishing Trust. The importance of the "time before the beginning" of the partnership was affirmed as the period when relationships and trust are established.

Boundary Spanning. The draft standards spoke to the new roles and relationships of university and school faculty and administrators that extended across traditional institutional boundaries. This concept was affirmed and detailed.

Blending of Resources. The importance of blending financial, human, and intellectual resources across institutional boundaries was embedded in the draft standards. The field test provided an opportunity to observe how this takes place. Most notable was that more mature PDSs viewed teacher preparation candidates as an important resource, including them in the implementation of research and instruction.

Leveraging Change. The idea of PDSs as instruments of change in P–12 and professional education was present in the draft standards. The field test permitted staff to observe how PDS work influences policies and the practices of the partnering institutions. Project participants also learned that PDSs regularly compete with other institutional priorities that may not be aligned with PDS practices.

Standards-Bearing Institutions. The important role of PDS partnerships, as institutions, to model good practices and be accountable for outcomes for their learners was articulated in the pilot sites. The diverse ways this occurs was observed in the PDS partnerships that carried out this responsibility.

Project learning, however, went beyond these refinements and affirmations. Because the assessment process focused on the concrete work of the partnership, a more subtle understanding was gained about how teaching and learning for all participants took place in these innovative and collaborative institutions.

New Knowledge about PDSs

The research design and field-test approach allowed us to identify several new, and core, understandings about PDSs and how they function. These understandings were used to revise the standards and to refine the assessment process. They are discussed in some detail below.

PDS Work. When this project began, there was general agreement that the mission of Professional Development Schools included new-teacher preparation, staff development, practice-based inquiry, and support for student achievement. Anecdotal reports and case studies, however, revealed that few PDS partnerships were being successful at carrying out all parts of that mission. Most often, the inquiry agenda was left unattended and new-teacher preparation was the area most developed. This was not a surprise, considering the way in which most PDS partnerships were addressing this complex mission. They tended to think about each function as a separate strand of activity. As a result, they rarely had sufficient time, energy, resources, or people to engage in each strand. However, when PDS partners integrated these functions, rather than attempting to pursue them in a parallel way, it became possible to address each of them. The integration of the strands resulted in a unique kind of teaching and learning, which came to be to referred to as "PDS work."

PDS Work Focuses on Student Learning. This understanding represents an important refinement in the developing notion about PDS work. PDS work attempts to integrate the four strands of the PDS mission and is undertaken collaboratively by the

PDS partners. Integration is possible when the focus of such work is on students' needs. PDS partners and candidates focus on identifying and meeting students' diverse learning needs by drawing on their unique knowledge bases in academe and practice. In a teaching hospital, the patients provide the curriculum and focus for medical students, residents, staff physicians, and medical-school faculty. In the same way, P–12 students provide the focus for candidate learning and faculty development in a PDS. This is how professional and student learning are both supported.

Inquiry Is a Tool in PDS Work. The understanding of what is unique about teaching and learning in a PDS evolved even further by understanding how professional and student learning are integrated through the process of inquiry—the function often receiving the least attention in many PDS partnerships. In PDS work, candidates and faculty use a process of inquiry to identify and address the diverse learning needs of P–12 students. PDS partners engage in inquiry in order to identify and meet students' learning needs, to effect candidate learning, and to determine their professional development agenda.

PDSs Go through Important Stages of Development. Early versions of the standards acknowledged the importance of building PDS partnerships on a foundation of shared interest, mutual commitment, and trust. This foundation is often laid by individuals from schools and universities working together over some period of time. Partners either need to have this pre-existing relationship or need to spend time in their initial stages building it before they can enter into the very difficult work of the partnership. In the field test, this early work was observed and recognized as what Sarason (1972) described as "the time before the beginning." Through data collected during the field test involving PDS partnerships at varying stages of development, staff came to understand that the Standards apply to all stages of development and that what varies is the degree of commitment, level of expertise, the degree of institutionalization and support, and the impact the PDS partnership has outside its partnering institutions. Further, it is only in the more developed stages that one could expect enhanced outcomes for both student and professional learners.

Defining the Unit
At the outset, the term "PDS" meant different things to different partnerships. Some used it to refer to the partner school; to others, it meant the partnership. Some reserved the term for a single-school/university partnership; others included multiple-school partnerships in their definition. The drafting of standards and the design and field-testing of an assessment process ran into these ambiguities. The field test included visits to several multiple-school partnerships that attempted to use the draft standards and an assessment process that addressed the multiple-school configuration in a variety of ways. On the basis of data derived from field test activities, Project par-

ticipants reached the following understandings:

- A Professional Development School is a P–12 school in partnership with a university or college of education.
- Some PDS partnerships include more than one PDS.
- While it is critical to assess PDS work at the level at which it occurs within the PDS and the university, it is also useful to look across the entire partnership, including multiple schools.
- Each of the standards can be applied across the entire multiple-school site partnership in meaningful ways, but this assessment must be based on, and therefore be preceded by, application of the standards within each PDS in the partnership.

The revised PDS standards and the self-study and visit processes, address single PDS and multiple PDS partnership configurations.

Effects of Context. Pilot-site participants continuously pointed out the importance of context in the review of the standards and application of the assessment process. Field-test sites were chosen to reflect diversity of context: large and small university programs; public and private institutions of higher education, elementary, middle, and high schools; urban, suburban, and rural environments; programs fully committed to PDSs for all their candidates' field experiences; and programs that offered PDS placements to a small percentage of their candidates. It was not surprising to find that institutional commitment varied, often in relation to context, as did the PDS partnership's ability to address diversity and equity. In the revision of the standards and assessment process, attention was paid to the need for the PDS partnership to identify those factors in the context they deemed important in their ability to address the standards. Overall, however, the experience indicated that standards and the assessment process had relevance across the broad range of contexts in which PDS partnerships exist.

What Revisions Needed to Be Made to the Draft Standards?

Substantive Changes
As a result of these findings, significant changes were made to the substance and structure of the draft standards. Each of the standards and all of its parts now reflect this new understanding of PDS work. Professional and student learning are addressed throughout as integrated functions. Inquiry is woven throughout the standards to give emphasis to the important role it plays in effecting all other parts of the mission. Attention to student learning, as the core of PDS work, also can be found throughout the standards.

Revisions were made to the standard addressing equity. Project participants came to understand that the standard needed to directly address equity and diversity and not to confuse the two. The PDS was seen as having an explicit role in addressing gaps in student achievement, as well as ensuring that candidates were prepared to meet the needs of a diverse student population.

Other substantive changes were made to reflect new understandings about how PDSs function. The revised PDS standards now identify "principal" and "institutional" partners. Principal partners are the faculty and administrators who do the work of the PDS. Institutional partners are the organizations they represent and the people in them who can lend support to the work of the PDS through policy and practice.

The definition of "learning community" was expanded to include parents, community, and other educators. The standards emphasize the importance of features such as the boundary-spanning roles, joint governing councils, and collaborative research that can act as triggers for changes in institutional policies and practices.

Structural Changes Made to the Standards
In addition to the substantive changes, the field test yielded data pointing toward other changes. The most important change was the creation of "Developmental Guidelines" for each standard. Four levels of development were gleaned from the data and used to construct the guidelines. While each standard is relevant at all four levels, the assessment criteria for each level vary. Thus, the criteria progress from planning activities at the beginning stage to having systemic impact in mature PDS partnerships. These developmental levels and their criteria are as follows:

1. Beginning: Beliefs, verbal commitments, plans, organization, and initial work are consistent with the mission of PDS partnerships.
2. Developing: PDS partners pursue the mission of a PDS partnership with partial institutional support.
3. At Standard: The mission of the PDS partnership is integrated into the partnering institutions. PDS work is expected and supported, and reflects what is known about the best practices.
4. Leading: Advanced PDS work is sustaining and generative, leading to systemic changes in policy and practice in the partner institutions as well as impact on policy at the district, state, and national levels.

Threshold Conditions in the draft standards were embedded throughout the stages based upon the more refined understandings of PDS work and PDS development.

How Was Alignment between Standards and Assessment Addressed?

Co-construction Strategy

The approach used to revise the standards and develop the assessment process was collaborative, as well as data-driven. The initial draft standards were generated by a working group of PDS constituents, researchers, and policymakers. They were informed by the available PDS literature and commissioned papers. Further input was sought through a survey, from focus groups, and during a highly interactive conference attended by representative PDS partnerships. The draft standards were revised through a three-year field-test process engaging PDS participants in 18 sites as partners in the Project, together with NCATE staff, consultants, and advisors. These participants constructed, field-tested, and revised the self-study and the visit-team assessment processes. The PDS standards and assessment process represented the participation of many partners in an inquiry-oriented, data-driven approach.

Co-construction, however, has another meaning in this endeavor. It refers to the interaction between the draft standards and pilot assessment processes that resulted in refinement and/or revisions to both. Too often, standards are developed and an assessment process follows. The assessment process may not be well aligned with what is most highly valued in the standards; and assessments are rarely seen as a means for making revisions or refinements to the standards. In the case of the PDS Standards Project, the assessment process was developed by Project participants to reflect what was most important in Professional Development Schools and to help learn more about the work that goes on in them, in order to make revisions to the standards that would reflect the institution and its functioning.

This approach to standards and assessment development was fostered by concerns and objectives articulated by Project partners. They had identified two critical features for the assessment process. First, they asserted that the assessment process needed to mirror the PDS concept if it was to be acceptable to partners in the field. Second, the process needed to get at the heart of PDS partnerships (i.e., the teaching and learning of candidates, faculty, and students). The two-phase assessment process became the source of critical data used to refine and revise the draft standards. Reciprocally, revisions made to the standards at the end of the field test were used to inform the revisions made to the assessment process. This approach assisted Project staff in achieving an authenticity and alignment often lacking in other accountability systems.

Changes Made to the Assessment Process
The pilot assessment processes focused on identifying and evaluating PDS work. As a result, there was a much better understanding of how the functions of a PDS were integrated. The self-study and the visit were revised to ensure that participants focused on all learners, emphasizing outcomes and examining the role of inquiry in addressing each standard. Changes made to the structure of the standards had implications for the assessment processes as well. PDS participants engaged in self-studies or as visiting team members needed to know how to use the developmental guidelines that were created and how to interpret the elements and indicators that were introduced.

In addition to changes resulting from substantive and structural changes to the standards, the research that was done yielded important findings on how to improve the process itself. Design Team members, then, were able to further define the relationship between the self-study and the visit. A process was developed so team members could focus on gathering and evaluating outcome data, or identifying its absence. Twenty self-studies and 18 team visits resulted in clarification of participants' roles for visitors and those being visited. The role of the visit-team chair was refined and the visit was reduced from four and a half days to three and a half days.

A major challenge was to determine how an assessment team could function in a multiple-school PDS partnership visit. This process was designed on the basis of data from the several visits made to multiple PDS partnerships (NCATE 2001b).

What Are the Connections between the PDS Standards and Assessment Process and Local, State, and National Policies? What Are the Disconnects?

An examination of the alignment between local, state, and national policy and the PDS Standards on teacher quality and accountability is worth the effort, yet is beyond the scope of this chapter. Nevertheless, a few key observations can be made.

Project participants recognized the potential of Professional Development Schools to reform teacher education and P-12 schooling. In order to fulfill these promises, PDS partnerships need to be aligned with policies at the local, state, and national level in some areas. The two most important of these are teacher quality and accountability. The PDS standards are a mechanism to support such alignment.

PDSs as a Part of the Teacher-Quality Agenda
The PDS standards are aligned with the teacher-quality agenda in scope and content. The broad PDS mission addresses every phase of professional development from early preparation through internship, induction, ongoing professional development, and enhanced teacher roles and responsibilities, all of which are incorporated into the revised standards. The PDS standards acknowledge stages of teacher development and create appropriate roles for practitioners at various levels of expertise. Candidates, for example, are incorporated into the instructional program but not assigned as the teacher of record, fully responsible for a class of students. Candidates are continuously mentored by expert faculty members who have been specifically prepared for their mentoring roles.

In terms of content, the PDS standards address important concepts related to teacher quality. First, the importance of school-university partnership in the preparation and development of practitioners has been acknowledged for some time (see, for example, Goodlad, 1988; Kroll et al., 1997; Schlechty, 1988; Sirotnik & Goodlad, 1988; Stoddart, 1993). The standards articulate the ways in which partners can bring to bear their respective knowledge, skills, and resources on the preparation of candidates and more experienced faculty. The standards also address how the respective programs of partnering institutions can be strengthened through the partnership.

Second, clinical experience has been identified as a critical component of professional preparation, although it has often been poorly implemented (see for example, Zeichner, 1996, 1980; Guyton & McIntyre, 1990). The standards are instructive for creating a rich environment that supports learning in the context of practice.

Accountability

In the standards, the importance of educators being accountable to the public and to themselves is recognized in terms of what students and candidates learn in the PDS setting. The standards were designed to incorporate the professional, student, and curriculum standards prevailing in each local and state context. Candidates, as well, are held accountable for the skills, knowledge, and dispositions required by local and state jurisdictions. The PDS is called upon to publicly make known how candidates and students perform on a range of assessments, including local and state standardized tests. Candidates and PDS faculty members are expected to implement curriculum standards in classrooms and to be able to meet the needs of a diverse population of students.

In addition to public accountability through alignment with local, state and/or national standards and assessments, the standards call for PDS faculty members to use a process of practice-based inquiry to identify and address the needs of the students they teach. This process places students' needs at the core of PDS work and defines the curriculum for candidate learning and the professional development agenda for more experienced faculty. In this way, PDS participants are held professionally accountable for creating and maintaining a continuous cycle of inquiry, teaching, and assessment focused on student achievement. Further, it is important to note that recent studies on teacher retention, candidate performance, and gains in student achievement in the PDS are all suggestive that school districts and states would do well to consider alignment and long-term investment in Professional Development Schools (Wise & Levine, 2002; Teitel, 2001).

Can the Same Set of Standards Be Used to Support Internal and External Accountability?

Policymakers and practitioners in P–12 and higher education have struggled with the tension created by external requirements for accountability, and internal needs for standards and processes that support development. Staff and participants in the Project were aware of the tension of these competing demands and struggled to create a system that would support PDS development and provide a basis for evaluating PDS partnerships. One way in which this tension was addressed was to focus on alignment between standards and assessments.

Each of the new findings about the PDS suggested a corollary for the design of standards and assessments. Since PDS work is not just a set of parallel activities (that is, each function carried out in a separate strand of activity), the building of standards and assessments are not separate endeavors. Project participants came to understand the value of standards and assessment building as integrated activities, reflecting and informing each other. The co-construction of these mechanisms for accountability has allowed for better alignment between standards and assessments, and for the creation of a system for continuous refinement and revision. Thus, standards can be periodically revised based upon data collected through the assessment process; and the assessment process is revised to reflect what is most important in the revised standards.

As the nature and significance of PDS work became understood, there was a need to add that understanding to the focus of the standards and the assessment process. Since the standards and the assessment process are oriented toward identifying actual practices and associated outcomes within the partnership, the assessment process provided feedback to the partnership on practices that make a difference.

An understanding of how inquiry is instrumental in PDS work led to an emphasis placed on inquiry in the standards and the assessment process. The process requires partnerships to name their PDS work. Then, through a process of data gathering, drawing tentative conclusions, raising questions, more data gathering, and discussion, participants arrive at a point where they are able to formulate conclusions about how, and how well, the partnership meets standards. Sources from which evidence can be drawn include, but are not limited to, data on learning outcomes for all learners, reports of the history or progress of the partnership, policy statements and handbooks, interviews with members of the various constituencies of the partnership, analysis of candidate placement, candidate journals, and minutes of meetings. Direct observations of interactions within the partnership, too, are a critical source of evidence. Conclusions based on consideration of the data can lead to a statement of standing for each standard, and then to recommendations. In this way, the PDS participants and colleagues engage in an inquiry process that mirrors the role of inquiry within the PDS and can be used to improve the partnership.

The identification of stages of development in the life of a PDS partnership made it possible to construct developmental guidelines for the four levels, each with its own criteria. The assessment process recognizes that a PDS partnership may be at different stages of development on each of the standards.

The standards and assessment provide a mechanism for internal accountability. It is somewhat remarkable, however, that the standards are not self-determined or defined, as is often the case with internal accountability. The PDS relies on external standards developed through a public process. During the field test, partner sites grew to accept external standards as a way of assessing themselves. Now, many PDS partnerships have adopted the use of these standards to guide their development and assess their progress. For example, they have been adapted by Maryland for use in their mandated PDS partnerships. Other states have used them as a framework to guide statewide initiatives to support PDS partnerships for teacher education.

All of the above happens on a voluntary basis. The potential of this system for making external judgments remains to be tested. If standards and assessments are used to provide external accountability or as the basis for resource allocation at the institutional, local, or state level, then, certain changes have to be made.

Other questions need to be addressed: How good is good enough? Are any of the standards negotiable? A process targeted at supporting a resource or an accreditation decision might require a restructuring of levels, with the possible elimination of one level to facilitate decision-making.

In contrast, certain factors may make it easier for the PDS system to be used for external accountability. The importance of context is acknowledged in the standards and process. Field-test experience suggests that the standards and assessments can accommodate differences without compromise. This might ease their acceptance. The authenticity of the standards, derived from the way in which they were developed, could be a factor in their acceptance as a means of external accountability.

What, if anything, is likely to be lost in the shift from internal to external accountability? In many instances, accountability processes used for external purposes do little to build capacity; however, this system was designed to accomplish this objective. Furthermore, the system reflects core beliefs and practices valued in the PDS community, including the systematic examination of practices and helping students to learn. There is an important alignment between what is valued publicly and what is valued professionally. This alignment could smooth the transition, resulting in one system that is effective for both purposes.

Implications

The PDS Standards Project was complex. First, the Project sought to design standards that would bring rigor to the definition of Professional Development Schools, so that their potential would not be lost. Then, the standards could be used as a framework by PDS partnerships to guide their development and provide feedback to the partners about their work. Further, it was anticipated that local, state, and national policymakers might use the standards to shape policies intended to encourage the formation of PDS partnerships. Finally, the standards could be useful in framing research that addressed learning outcomes in PDS settings. Overall, this was accomplished. The standards and assessment processes are used by partnerships to shape their work, by states and local districts to encourage and support partnerships, and by designs for further PDS research. Thus, co-construction (another objective) is a useful approach that represents specific strategies for partnering in the field, and devising an interactive approach to developing standards and assessments.

Partnering

Engaging practitioners in the process of developing standards and assessments has benefits. Practitioners focus on work, in contrast to conceptual notions or theories about work. Standards and assessment processes need to focus on work because this is where change, improvement, and development take place. This does not mean they are defined by or limited to existing levels of practice. Rather, it means standards can be constructed to provide scaffolding to assist practitioners in seeing how they can move from where they are to where they need to go. Engaging practitioners elevates the probability that standards and assessment will be accepted and used.

Co-constructing Standards and Assessments

This strategy was driven by concerns of the PDS community. They insisted that the standards needed to address what was important in a PDS, and the assessment process needed to reflect or mirror those characteristics. Project participants created an interactive process designed to achieve this alignment.

Partnering and co-construction have resulted in an assessment process that is valuable. It is aligned with standards and reflects what is important in them. It can be used for developmental purposes because of its focus on work taking place in a partnership. And, for these same reasons, it should have strength as an evaluative process for external purposes.

References

Freeman, D. (1998). From here: A synthesis of the Chicago discussions on PDS standards. In M. Levine (Ed.), *Designing standards that work for professional development schools*, 111–129. Washington, DC: National Council for Accreditation of Teacher Education.

Goodlad, J. (1988). School-university partnerships for educational renewal: Rationale and concepts. In K. Sirotnik & J. Goodlad (Eds.), *School-university partnerships in action: Concepts, cases and concerns*, 3–31. New York: Teachers College Press.

Guyton, E. & McIntyre, D.J. (1990). Student teaching and school experiences. In W.R. Houston (Ed.), *Handbook of research in teacher education*, 514–534. New York: Macmillan.

Kroll, L., Bowyer, J., Rutherford, M., & Hauben, M. (1997). The effect of a school-university partnership on the student-teaching experience. *Teacher Education Quarterly*, 24 (1), 37–52.

National Council for Accreditation of Teacher Education. (2001a). *Standards for Professional Development Schools*. Washington, DC: Author.

National Council for Accreditation of Teacher Education. (2001b). *Handbook for the assessment of professional development schools*. Washington, DC: Author.

Sarason, S.B. (1972). *The creation of settings and the future societies*. San Francisco: Jossey-Bass.

Schlechty, P.C. (1988). Inventing professional development schools. *Educational Leadership, 46* (3), 28–31.

Sirotnik, K. & J. Goodlad (Eds.) (1988). *School-university partnerships in action*. New York: Teachers College Press.

Snyder, J. (1998). Finance and policy structures that support the sustenance of professional development schools. In M. Levine (Ed.). *Designing standards that work for professional development schools, 155-190.* Washington, DC: National Council for Accreditation of Teacher Education.

Stoddart, T. (1993). The professional development school: Building bridges between cultures. *Educational Policy, 7* (1), 5-23.

Sykes, G. (1997). Worthy of the name: Standards for professional development schools. In M. Levine & R. Trachtman (Eds.), *Making professional development schools work,* 159-181. New York: Teachers College Press.

Teitel, L. (2001). *How professional development schools make a difference: A review of research.* Washington, DC: National Council for Accreditation of Teacher Education.

Teitel, L. (1998). NCATE PDS Standards Project literature review. In M. Levine (Ed.), *Designing standards that work for professional development schools,* 33-80. Washington, DC: National Council for Accreditation of Teacher Education.

Trachtman, R. (1998). The NCATE professional development school study. In M. Levine (Ed.), *Designing standards that work for professional development schools,* 81-109. Washington, DC: National Council for Accreditation of Teacher Education.

Wilson, T.A. (1998). Accreditation standards and school improvement: Putting methodology in its proper place. In M. Levine (Ed.). *Designing standards that work for professional development schools,* 111-130. Washington, DC: National Council for Accreditation of Teacher Education.

Wilson, T.A. (1996). *Reaching for a better standard: English school inspection and the dilemma of accountability for American public schools.* NY: Teachers College Press.

Wise, A.E. & Levine, M. (February 27, 2002). The 10-step solution: Helping urban districts boost student achievement in low-performing schools. *Education Week, 56,* 38.

Zeichner, K. (1996). Designing educative practicum experiences for prospective teachers. In K. Zeichner, S. Melnick & M. Gomez (Eds.), *Currents of reform in pre-service teacher education,* 215-234. New York: Teachers College Press.

Zeichner, K. (1980). Myths and realities: Field experiences in pre-service teacher education. *Journal of Teacher Education, 31,* 45-55.

CHAPTER 10 *Mary Gendernalik Cooper*

Systematic Evaluation in PDS-Centered Educator Preparation
Turning State and National Accreditation Standards to Program Advantage

The adoption of the NCATE (National Council for Accreditation of Teacher Education) 2000 Standards has made comprehensive, systemic assessment an explicit requirement of nationally accredited educator-preparation units. As noted, "The unit has an assessment system that collects and analyzes data on the applicant qualifications, the candidate and graduate performance, and unit operations to evaluate and improve the unit and its programs" (NCATE 2002 Unit Standards, p. 1). The standard identifies interrelated categories for assessment: performance, processes, and programs. The elements of these categories are detailed in a reading of the other NCATE standards and the accompanying explanations contained in the standards document.

In terms of performance, data must be collected that include evidence about pre-admission applicants' abilities, admitted candidates' knowledge, skills, dispositions, and abilities to affect P–12 students' learning. Data about the faculty, in relation to program implementation and candidate learning and achievement, must also be collected and analyzed. This is a process assessment that has been developed to monitor and gauge the effect on and efficacy of activities and procedures pertaining to candidate performance, program implementation, and collaboration among PDS partners. These partnerships include: university-based teacher educators, arts and sciences faculty, and school-based P–12 practitioners including faculty and administrators. Program assessment has been developed in order to focus on the integration of content, the enactment of the curriculum, field experience, and the alignment of these elements with the program's standards. The assessment-related language of the NCATE 2000 Standards defies the inclination toward reductionism in current federal policy, which results in using a standardized test for judging a candidate unit's proficiencies in producing competent professionals. NCATE expects units to develop a system of multiple indicators of performance, program, and process effectiveness. This expectation reflects the substantiated conviction regarding the complex nature of teaching and the necessity of deliberate, coherent integration of the content, pedagogy, and application components of professional preparation programs.

As is evident in the series of papers commissioned by NCATE regarding Standard 2 ("The unit has an assessment system that collects and analyzes data on the applicant qualifications, candidate and graduate performance, and unit operations to evaluate and improve the unit and its programs.") (see Scannell, 2000; Stiggins, 2000; Stroble, 2000; Weisenbach, 2000), the processes and considerations inherent in developing an assessment system are complex, extensive and intensive, and challenge longstanding institutional and faculty traditions. Stiggins, for example, notes that assessment is often a neglected element of teacher-preparation programs in terms of programs having a coherent, comprehensive assessment system in place. Stiggins, Weisenbach, and Stroble each suggest that the culture of teaching in higher education is essentially autonomous and private. A system of assessment requires considerable faculty collaboration, across units within a university or college and with P–12 school-based colleagues. This requires articulating a common vision of expectations, a shared set of achievement standards for candidates. It also requires working simultaneously toward a vision of the program and a shared understanding of the contributions that distinct pieces make to program objectives. The range of stakeholders must be engaged in developing and implementing the assessment system, utilizing the evidence generated, and contributing to its ongoing improvement. A collaboratively generated Professional Development School Network (PDSN) is pivotal to the effectiveness of assessment. Weisenbach recommends building the assessment system around the unit's conceptual framework and standards. This forms the foundation of the assessment system, thus integrating performance, process, and program implementation. Weisenbach and Stroble note the potential that building and utilizing assessment systems might hold for cultivating communities of inquiry that involve candidates, university faculty, and school-based faculty. They further note that in addition to meeting NCATE 2000 Standards, assessment can provide substantive, valid, and reliable evidence about the complex responsibilities and challenges of teaching.

In this chapter, the development of a comprehensive assessment system within a PDS school–university educator-preparation collaborative is described. The assessment system is reviewed in relation to evaluation, inquiry, and informing and transforming practice.

The Assessment System

Program revisions, performance expectations and processes for decision-making, program implementation, and the assessment system are comprehended within a conceptual theme adapted from Project Zero at Harvard (Perkins, 1998; Perrone, 1991, 1998; Wiske, 1998) and a variety of standards. In addition to Interstate New Teacher Assessment and Support Consortium (INTASC) and NCATE standards, this work is informed by standards, principles, and guidelines promulgated by national professional societies such as Association for Childhood Education International, National Association for the Education of Young Children, National Middle School Association; content-specific professional societies, including National Council for the Social Studies, National Council of Teachers of Mathematics, National Council of Teaches of English, National Science Teachers Association, American Association for the Advancement of Science; the state certification agency's standards, and the university system's Regents' Principles and Guidelines for Educator Preparation. The NCATE PDS Standards—the 1997 Draft Standards and the 2001 adopted version—figure prominently in the design, implementation, and assessment of the PDSN as a process and program component.

There are currently 30 distinct evidence sources in this assessment system. Each category is identified in Table 10.1. Notations indicate the frequency of data collection from each source and the relative significance of each in the assessment of a category. The PDS Perceptual Survey has been in use since the first semester (Fall 1998) of implementation of the program, and now there exists eight semesters' worth of data from using this survey. By contrast, the Employer Satisfaction Survey was first piloted just over two years ago. A more extensive explanation of each category of the assessment system and its primary evidence sources is provided in Table 10.1.

Performance Assessments

The performance category includes evidence sources related to educator candidates and the university and P–12 faculty who participate in the educator-preparation programs, as well as P–12 students who attend the PDS sites. Fifteen of the 30 evidence sources relate to this category; nine relate to educator-preparation candidates. The first four—course performance assessment, lab assessment, professional qualities, and ISL (Impacting Student Learning)—encompass candidate performance in program coursework and integrated field experiences (labs). As noted previously, the ten INTASC Standards were adopted for all educator-preparation programs and as primary objectives in each course. Within each course, performance requirements are keyed to specific INTASC Standards. The faculty adopted a four-point scale that reflects a common evaluation rubric for scoring performances. Each course-performance assessment summarizes each candidate's performance score for each course objective. At the end of each semester, faculty members submit a course-performance assessment summary on each candidate to a secured electronic data file. Electronic files can be aggregated by course, by INTASC/Conceptual Framework Principle, by candidate cohorts, and by program to provide various representations of performance assessment.

TABLE 10.1. Comprehensive Assessment System Framework

NCATE/PSC STANDARDS	USG Board of Regents Principles	Performance Outcomes (INTASC)	Evidence Sources	Performance Frequency	Process Frequency	Program Frequency
1, 7	IIA, IIIBCDIKLM	1,2,10,11	Core GPA	C 1—Admission		1—Semester
1	IIA, III I	1	PRAXIS I	C 1—Admission		1—Semester
1,3,4,7,8	IIA, IIIBCDI	1-12	(see Detailed Program Matrices)	Course Performance Assessments	C 1—Semester	1—Annually
1,3,4,7	IA, IIA, IIIFGH	1-12	Field Assessments	C 1—Semester		1—Annually
3,4,7		9,10,11	Professional Qualities	C 1—Semester		1—Annually
1,3,4,7	IA, IIA	1-8	ISL	C 1—Semester		1—Annually
1,3,4	IIA	1-12	Intervention	C 2—As Needed	1—Annually	1—Annually
1,3,4,7,8	IIA	1-8, 12	Candidate Portfolio	C 1—Semester		2—Annually
1,3,4,7,8	IIA, IIIBCDI	1-8,12	GPA in Major & Prof. Ed. Courses	C 1—Semester		
1,3,4,7,8	IA, IIA, IIIFGH	1-12	Student Teaching Assessments	C 1—Semester		1—Annually
1,8	IIA,B-7, IIIBCD	1	PRAXIS II Scores	C 2—Annually		2—Annually
1,3,4	IA, IIB-5	1-12	Guarantee Referrals	C 2—Annually		1—Annually
5	IIB-8		Course Evaluations	F 2—Semester		
5	IIB-8		Tenure & Promotion	F 1—Annually		2—Annually
3,4,5	IIB-6		Master Teacher Evaluation	F 2—Semester	1—Annually	2—Annually
3,4,5	IIB-8		University Liaison Evaluation	F 1—Semester	1—Annually	1—Annually

TABLE 10.1. (continued)

NCATE/PSC STANDARDS	USG Board of Regents Principles	Performance Outcomes (INTASC)	Evidence Sources	Performance Frequency	Process Frequency	Program Frequency
3,4,5	IIB-6		Building Liaison Evaluation	F 2—Semester	1—Annually	2—Annually
1,3	IIB-5 & 9		P-12 State Report Card	S 2—Annually	2—Annually	2—Annually
3,4	IIB-6		PDS Perception Survey		1—Semester	2—Annually
1,3,4	IA	1-12	Candidate Satisfaction Survey (SoS)		2—Annually	2—Annually
1,3,4	IB	1-12	Graduate Satisfaction Survey (SoS)		2—Annually	2—Annually
1-6	IIB-5		Employment/Retention Rates			2—Annually
1,3,4	IB, IIB-9	1-12	Employer Satisfaction Survey		2—Annually	2—Annually
3,4,5	ID		Master Teacher Selection & Review		1—Annually	1—Annually
3,5	IIB-6 & 8		Prof. Development		1—Annually	1—Annually
3,5	IIB-6		PDSNI Meeting notes		1—Annually	1—Annually
3,5	ID, IIB-6		PDS continuation		1—Annually	2—Annually
3,5	ID, IIB-6		PDS Inquiry Year		1—Annually	2—Annually
3,5	ID, IIB-6 & 9		PDS Review & Renewal		1—Annually	2—Annually
	ALL		Regents' Annual Review		2—Annually	1—Annually
1,3,4,5	IIIA		Program Reviews		1—Every 5 years	1—Every 5 years
1-6			NCATE/PSC Visit		1—Every 5 years	1—Every 5 years
6	IIB-2 & 3		Enrollment Patterns		2—Biennially	2—Biennially

Key: C=educator preparation candidate; F=P-16 faculty; S=P-12 students; 1=primary significance; 2=secondary significance. Frequency indicates the time frame of data collection.

As candidates proceed through the program they can review their course-performance assessments with their advisors to clarify areas needing improvement, more attention, or fuller documentation. Candidates must include evidence from specific course performances in their portfolios, organized in terms of the INTASC/Conceptual Framework Principles. These become the evidentiary basis for evaluating candidates' programmatic progress and their proficiency on each standard/principle.

As part of the revision process that preceded the program's implementation in fall 1998, university and school-based faculty worked collaboratively to improve the integration of field experiences within courses, in part, through the alignment of performance tasks and course objectives. Course syllabi revisions reflected a commitment to lab experiences as the opportunity for candidates to apply classroom knowledge, strategies, and propositions regarding teaching and learning. The strategy, adopted across courses and programs, was to convey the significance of lab performance expectations and thereby ensure that students had to perform satisfactorily in the lab in order to pass a course. Faculty configured the relative weight of graded assignments to reflect this requirement. Through this strategy, school-based application and related reflection performances were more rigorously structured and gained considerable significance with candidates.

As of fall 2001, the introduction of the Impacting Student Learning component into each program further provided structure and focus to lab performance expectations. Through a series of workshops, university and PDS faculty developed a common set of ISL elements—a scoring rubric and an evaluation form. Each program tailored the distribution of ISL requirements to its structure and curriculum. Although candidates include evidence of student learning and achievement in their completed ISLs, the evaluation of the candidate's performance on an ISL is not reduced to specific evidence of gains documented in P–12 students. In designing the ISL, faculty were careful to avoid that kind of distortion-prone reductionism. The intent is to help candidates link their instructional planning and delivery to evidence of student progress and achievement, and then, to reflect on these integrated elements of instruction/learning to inform their self-evaluations and subsequent iterations of instructional planning and action. Reflections on the preliminary ISLs by candidates and faculty indicate that they enrich candidates' comprehension of each element of the complexity of teaching, their interactions, and their interdependence. Candidates are better prepared to integrate their efforts in clarifying instructional goals, understanding curriculum with sufficient depth and facility to select materials, strategies, and sequences of activities, while keeping in mind the goals and knowledge of students as learners, and planning assessments that align with these other elements. The anecdotal evidence accumulated from the first two semesters of implementation indicates the ISL shifts candidates' focus from themselves as students—meeting requirements and the expectations of others—to the students for whose learning they are responsible. Candidates are increasingly focused, even those in the first semester of the program, on the impact their efforts are having on their P–12 students' learning and achievement—a pivotal performance expectation of the program. The ISLs include evidence of P–12 student learning and achievement. Assessment of candidate performance and effectiveness has not, however, been reduced to this single measure.

The "lab" teacher with whom a candidate works during the intensive five-week field experience completes the Lab Assessment and Professional Qualities instruments. The Lab Assessment instrument provides a holistic rating of the candidates' performance in the classroom in relationship to the targeted INTASC/Conceptual Framework Principle. Also, it includes indicators of the candidate's oral and written language skills. These scores are notated in the course-performance assessment data set. The Professional Qualities data are maintained in the candidate's file, primarily for use by the candidate and his/her advisor.

The Apprentice Assessment instrument allows for summarizing the candidate's and his/her master teacher's evaluation of performances within the intensive culminating semester (formerly student teaching). This instrument's categories and items are keyed to the INTASC Standards, and the same four-point scale for scoring performances that is used in coursework is used here. Candidates and their master teachers each complete the form at mid-term and semester's end. The completed instrument reflects evidence of progress and proficiency. Intervention to enhance performance and proficiency can then occur. Interventions are formal procedures undertaken to encourage and support candidates identified with significant difficulties in professional qualities or course/lab performance. The intervention includes counseling with the candidate, a plan and timeline for addressing the difficulties, and indicators for determining successful resolution. Interventions are maintained in the candidate's file.

At the end of each semester, the department chair and the faculty summarize the status of each intervention. The data set indicates any patterns of difficulties, origins (class or lab), numbers of interventions and successful resolutions by candidate, cohort, and program. With regard to the performance assessment category, this data set reveals the candidate's relative success with owning, acting on, and resolving a difficulty that is perceived by faculty to warrant formal deliberate attention. Candidates are counseled about what to do to address and resolve an issue identified as needing attention.

In spring 2001, educator-preparation program faculty discussed the implementation of the university system's requirement of the "graduate guarantee." The performance expectations and rubric in the guarantee mirror the INTASC/Conceptual Framework Principles, and a set of procedures for referral by school principals also is spelled out in the guarantee document. There have been no referrals to date, which is one form of data. If referrals are made, the procedure will allow for collecting data on areas of deficiency that can be linked to program elements and to the individual's performance record while in the program.

Faculty have not relinquished fundamental course and instructional prerogatives. Individual faculty members continue to organize course content, set objectives, determine materials to be used, and plan performance tasks that will figure in the end-of-course summative evaluation of candidates. Each instructor continues to determine the weight each task will carry into the final calculation of a course grade and proficiency scores. A review of syllabi reveals a range of performance strategies, including tests, essays, research projects, as well as analyzing artifacts of varied application tasks. The adoption of the common elements—weighting lab experience requirements, the ISL outline, rubrics, inclusion patterns, the adoption of a common scoring scale, and the utilization of the course-performance assessment for data compilation—reflects a collegial effort to clarify and connect curriculum components of programs. These commonalities facilitate communication and comprehension among all participants: P–12 and university-based faculty and candidates. They are a consequence of deliberate faculty collaboration in pursuit of more transparent program coherence. This work reflects the type of transformation that Stiggins (2000) suggests is important in the development of an integrated assessment system. This has altered relationships between P–12 and university faculty but not in the detrimental way projected in some of the literature on school–university partnerships (Thom, 1998; Bullough et al., 1997; Stoddart, 1993).

The PRAXIS II exam is required by the state for certification. One difficulty with using PRAXIS II scores as a primary performance measure is that, in all but one program, the required exams focus exclusively on content preparation. The state does not require completion of the pedagogy/learning tests in the PRAXIS II series for certification, so those components of the educator-preparation programs are not considered in this high-stakes certification requirement. The most compelling limitation of using PRAXIS II scores as a performance measure is that it does not authentically reflect instructional practice. Nevertheless, a review of cohort performance and subtest scoring patterns on PRAXIS II can contribute to program review, particularly with regard to alignment between the exam and pertinent components of the curriculum—what each addresses and how it does so.

The evidentiary sources included for university-based faculty assessments include the annual departmental evaluation based on individual faculty reports of progress and achievement in the areas of teaching, service, and professional development. This evidence includes exemplars of scholarship, course and curriculum development, and course evaluations that are completed for every course taught during the academic year. It also includes documentation of work in the PDSN. These procedures comply with university-wide faculty performance evaluation policies. The university formally recognizes the collaborative work of faculty in the PDSN as well. This work includes university coordinator functions, school-based inquiry projects, participation on school-based committees, work with PDS faculty on particular professional development activities, and instruction with candidates during the five-week lab experiences each semester.

The university coordinator evaluation is used for faculty with formal liaison responsibilities in the PDSN. This evaluation instrument has a parallel version for PDS-based building coordinators. Items on the instrument reflect the jointly determined expectations for these roles. Educator preparation candidates and lab teachers, as well as role counterparts, complete this instrument each semester. They are collected and compiled by the department chair. For university-based faculty, the data from this evaluation are used in the annual performance evaluation. A procedure for formal and systematic review of the building coordinators, based on data generated from this instrument, has not yet been developed. Individual PDS building coordinators and their university-coordinator counterpart have informally reviewed the data and used it in refining their work in this role. Similarly, the department chair reviews the data for indicators of problems and concerns that might need to be addressed. This dimension of the performance assessment clearly requires further development.

The Master Teacher Evaluation is used to examine how the mentor performs along three dimensions: modeling research-informed best practices; ability to mentor, support, and evaluate the educator preparation candidate's performance; and ongoing engagement in professional development. The first cohort of master teachers initiated the master-teacher evaluation process in fall 1998. It has been tailored and refined within each program by master teachers in conjunction with university faculty (Thompson, 2001). This evaluation serves as the basis for teachers maintaining their master-teacher designation.

Currently, the data set related to P–12 student performance in the assessment framework is limited to the annual "State Report Card," and then only the section that reports criterion-referenced test data. The Criterion Reference Competency Test is an evaluation linked to the state's Quality Core Curriculum. This is the document in which achievement targets, by subject area and grade level, are outlined, and around which teachers/schools are required to build their instructional programs. The state requires and administers a commercially available norm-referenced test to all K–8 students. By nature, these are not tests that should be used to evaluate teacher performance or effectiveness. Furthermore, during academic years 1999–2000 and 2000–2001, neither the State Department of Education nor the test vendor could/would validate the test results. Classroom-specific documentation of instructional effectiveness constitutes the main source of data on student performance. For education preparation candidates, the Impacting Student Learning components that they complete each semester constitute their primary evidence of influencing student achievement.

Process Assessment

Developing comprehensive and coherent collaborative procedures, through which university and school-based faculty would equitably participate in educator preparation, has been as much a goal of this initiative as have been improvements in program content and candidate performance. Monitoring and gauging the extent to which processes and procedures effectively address the goals is the focus of the process category of the assessment system. With regard to the role-enactment evidence sources (master teacher, university, and building coordinators), the process assessment focus relates to how these roles serve to link the university- and school-based components of the programs; or, how well these roles facilitate substantive communication, problem-solving, and collaborative action centered on program implementation and candidate performance.

Perceptual and satisfaction-survey data sources provide indirect indicators of process effectiveness. In the first two semesters of PDSN implementation, for example, consistent negative responses by candidates and lab teachers to an item regarding whether or not everyone was adequately informed about course requirements prompted a review of communications by building and university coordinators. The review led to procedural changes that, in subsequent survey data, indicate that communication was enhanced.

Sources relating to PDSN operating procedures include the PDS Perception Survey, the Master Teacher Selection, Professional Development School Network meeting notes, and the comprehensive PDSN self-evaluation completed in spring 2000. In addition, the PDS Inquiry, Review and Renewal documents, and a number of satisfaction surveys were used. As these procedures are enacted, meetings and informal communications will afford participants opportunities to endorse continuation, identify difficulties and challenges, and suggest changes. One example in this area relates to the equitable representation of stakeholders on the university's primary policy body for educator-preparation programs. For two years after the PDSN began functioning, the Teacher Education Council included one teacher and an administrator from the PDSs. PDS university coordinators and building coordinators proposed that the Council should include teacher/administrator representation from elementary, middle, and secondary levels. The Council and university adopted the proposal in spring 2002, resulting in increased P–12 representation from the three grade level groupings and special education.

At the end of the second full year of implementation, spring 2000, each of the 28 PDSs undertook a self-evaluation. They used the NCATE Draft Standards to organize documentation of activities, strategies, and practices. Once compiled by the PDSN evaluator, these data served as the basis for an overall self-evaluation. This self-study provided data about the progress of the initiative against a relatively constant set of benchmarks. Also, it accommodated reviewing this work in relation to a broader national perspective on PDS work. Even at this early stage of implementation, the self-evaluation revealed considerable strength in the functional area of collaborative educator preparation. This was expected, as educator preparation was the primary focus of our collaborative work during this period. The professional development function emerged as the second strongest functional area in the self-evaluation. As faculty in the PDSN began working more closely with university faculty and educator-preparation candidates, they began to identify a professional-development agenda for themselves. The PDSN sponsored workshops, seminars, and meetings to address this agenda. PDSN faculty also began to connect other schools' system-based professional-development support to their PDS work. One of the dominant themes of the self-evaluation was the increased integration of educator preparation into the mainstream professional culture of each PDS.

While the PDS faculties acknowledged that students' academic achievement is their priority (and they could point to considerable evidence of effort in this regard), they noted that they had not directly connected it to their PDS roles. Many suggested that completing the self-evaluation had brought the connection between this function and the educator-preparation function into focus. The self-evaluation also revealed a consistent dearth of evidence related to the inquiry function of the PDS. Each PDS also provided evidence of work on each of the (then) five standards in the NCATE PDS Draft Standards framework. These data were compiled to create a PDSN status snapshot. Three individuals reviewed the evidence separately and generated a composite rating for each standard. They reviewed their ratings together and came to consensus. A narrative explaining the basis for each rating was generated and shared with the PDSN. From Network members' collective review, a follow-up agenda for the PDSN was formulated. A key element of the agenda was the creation of a formal four-year cycle of participation in the PDSN, which included an Inquiry Year, a Review, and Renewal Year. The Inquiry Year would result in each PDS pursuing a formal exploration of a topic or issue of interest to it, engaging faculty, administrators, university colleagues, and educator-preparation candidates in the process. This would formally encourage the inquiry function of PDS and situate it within the work and concerns of each PDS faculty. The Review Year and Renewal Year require each PDS to maintain evidence of its work in terms of the NCATE PDS Standards, with a formal review of evidence every four years to evaluate itself as a PDS. Based on this review, the PDS would determine if it wanted to continue in the PDSN and identify a self-improvement agenda for the next four-year cycle. During spring 2002, the PDSN generated a cycle to begin in fall 2002, with approximately one-quarter of the PDSs situated in each of the four years of the cycle.

Through process assessment, deliberate reflective attention is paid to effects of procedures and processes on candidate performance and program implementation. Process assessment also is used to illuminate the extent to which procedures and activities are supporting or inhibiting collaboration among P–12 and higher-education participants in the PDSN.

Program Assessment

Candidate-performance evidence sources constitute a primary basis for program assessment, linking candidates' course- and lab-performance evaluations to program quality and/or effect. Review of course-performance assessment data and candidates' portfolios figure prominently. In their portfolios, candidates are expected to include performance evidence (an essay, a lesson or unit plan, a presentation outline, a critical reflection on a lesson taught in lab) from graded course assignments, which the instructor has keyed to one or more of the INTASC/Conceptual Framework Principles. A challenge related to this component of program assessment is moving to a more direct examination of the course tasks and activities that form the basis for the candidates' performance evaluations. Such an exercise might exemplify the departure from the tradition that Stiggins (2000) asserts is embedded in authentic program assessment.

The various perception and satisfaction surveys provide a continuous stream of evidence regarding participants' views of program objectives, elements, and effects. The PDS Perception Survey includes a number of items related to integration of the class and field-experience components of courses, and to the integration of the programs overall. The data set, including eight successive administrations of the survey, indicates positive perceptions of integration across all participant groups. These items have been monitored closely, particularly in semesters when program refinements have been initiated. The employer satisfaction survey and the graduate satisfaction survey include items correlated to INTASC/Conceptual Framework Principles. The objective is to gauge program effects by exploring respondents' assessment of graduates' performance in relation to these principles. Data from the pilot survey of employers suggest above-average satisfaction with graduates' performance on items related to all ten INTASC/Conceptual Framework Principles. The strongest scores were on content knowledge and instruction (INTASC/CFP 1 & 7) and in meeting students' developmental needs (INTASC/CFP 2). Scores did not vary significantly across grade levels or school type. Over time, the data from these surveys should inform the assessment of the program's impact on the professional practices of graduates. The assessment of graduates' effectiveness, as a result of program preparation, is constrained by the extent to which the professional culture of the schools in which they are employed supports and nurtures practices that are grounded in that preparation. Additional strategies for investigating this alignment need to be developed.

Referrals (or the lack thereof) under the terms of the guarantee also can be used as evidence of program effectiveness. Still, more direct methods of assessing program impact on the teaching practices of graduates need to be developed, implemented, and integrated into the program.

Analysis

The assessment system is evolving in concert with ongoing refinements in the educator-preparation programs, cultivation of genuine university-school collaboration, and enhancements of candidate proficiencies in supporting student learning.

Each of these categories is inherently complex—their simultaneous pursuit can be overwhelming. Experience suggests complementary and mutually supporting momentum between and across the categories. The assessment system continues to emerge, prompted by questions, issues, concerns, and opportunities arising from program implementation. In this regard, the assessment system is an opportunity for inquiry and professional development as well as for evaluation, serving to inform and transform practice. The utility in transforming P-12 teaching practices, expanding teachers' participation in decision making, and enriching their professional-development agenda is becoming increasingly evident.

Assessment as Evaluation and as Inquiry

Traditionally, assessment is thought of as distinct and deliberate activities or events that are undertaken to provide evidence of accomplishment or achievement, and a basis for an evaluation of that evidence. In recent years, considerable professional attention has been paid to the form assessment activities take. Particular focus has been directed on the extent to which the assessment activity aligns with the type of learning and is an authentic demonstration of the learning. In educator preparation, this concern is evident in expectations (internal and external) that candidates demonstrate proficiency in instruction-related tasks and in affecting their students' learning and achievement.

Within the system just described, assessments of the candidates' performances to standards are embedded in courses/labs that comprise the program curriculum. Candidate performance evidence is summarized in course grades and is compiled in considerable detail in their portfolios. Similarly, the Impacting Student Learning component, strategically situated within designated courses in each program, provides evidence contributing to course grade determinations and to the candidate's portfolio. Different evaluative questions prompt an examination of different arrays of candidate performance evidence. The electronic database, for example, was created to compile and store individual candidate's INTASC related scores, lab performance, professional qualities, and ISL scores by course. The data can be aggregated in varied ways to represent class and cohort proficiencies, patterns related to the INTASC standards, and program quality. Individual portfolios provide detailed evidence of proficiencies, specific patterns of strengths and weaknesses, areas of growth and development within the program, and areas of stability. As Scannell (2000) notes, evidence compiled in assessment systems are of interest to different audiences and at varying levels of detail. The capacity to manipulate compiled evidence in varied ways enhances the utility of the assessment system.

The assessment system accommodates inferences from candidate performance evidence, program enrollment patterns, and graduates' employment rates in terms of program quality. The more direct evidence sources include various perception and satisfaction surveys as well as periodic formal program reviews by external approval and accrediting agencies. By administering varied perceptual surveys each semester, a continual source of data is provided through which the effects of program and personnel changes, as well as the impact of environmental forces, can be detected and tracked. For example, the PDSN Perception Survey has been sensitive to changes in participating university faculty, perceptions of candidates' preparedness relative to their cohort status (first, second, third semester), and external (particularly political) environmental forces affecting P–12 education.

Assessment-as-inquiry emphasizes linkages across processes, data, outcomes, and meaning. Within the context of the assessment system, this view of assessment encourages examination of processes and actions undertaken in pursuit of goals, within and across the categories of performance, processes, and program. When candidates' ISL reports are reviewed (rather than just the student achievement scores), evidence of their thinking, attention to students' learning, and their own questions and concerns as they worked through the instructional unit is illuminated. Assessment-as-inquiry requires looking within learning performances and summary scores in order to appreciate the dimensions and quality of learning outcomes. Candidates are encouraged to review these documents as a basis for examining their learning, how they are comprehending and applying it, and how it is shaping their professional identities. Within the "Teaching for Understanding" framework, this strategy reflects the ongoing and recursive qualities of assessment in the learning process (Wiske, 1998) and begins to approximate Delandshere's (2002) inquiry metaphor for assessment.

Assessment-as-inquiry serves a role in the program and process categories of assessment. In the process category, for example, the NCATE PDS Standards serve as a framework for undertaking, recording, and reviewing the quality of collaborative processes. The narratives generated by each PDS in the year-2000 self-evaluation are revealing of how faculty within each PDS understood and prioritized the standards, and how they categorized their work. The narratives reveal commonalities as well as distinctions across the PDSs. In turn, this provides a basis for systematic inquiry into how institutional climates and professional cultures influence participation in an inter-institutional partnership.

Assessment Informing and Transforming Practice

As Stiggins (2000), Weisenbach (2000), and Stroble (2000) note, the development, implementation, and utilization of a comprehensive assessment system are likely to challenge entrenched traditions. Stiggins suggests that deliberate, concerted attention to assessment of candidate performances would be a major innovation in educator preparation, and the introduction of an assessment system would signal a transformational threshold in higher education. Weisenbach and Stroble both suggest that by including all key stakeholders in developing the assessment system, individuals relinquish exclusive and private prerogatives in defining course expectations, teaching practices, standards, and performance requirements.

In this collective endeavor, for example, university faculty determined that field-experience performances had to carry substantial weight in the calculation of course grades in order to convey to candidates that field experiences were an integral component of program coursework. This determination necessitated more substantive collaboration between university- and PDS-based faculty regarding program/course content, candidate performance expectations, and opportunities for candidates to undertake required tasks in the PDS settings. This work prompted the PDS-based faculty to identify a professional development agenda so they could enrich their own understandings and skills. The self-assessment, much like the individual PDS self-evaluations in 2000, revealed much about the views of PDS partners regarding the collaborative partnership and program enactment. Over time, assessment has become an integrated component of the unit's work, informing, challenging, and bridging performance, process, and program-focused endeavors. Most significantly, assessment has fostered greater openness and more substantive engagement of participants in the educator-preparation partnership.

The NCATE 2000 Unit Standards challenge educator-preparation program personnel to enrich their curriculum by integrating theory and practice, to collaborate substantively with P–12 colleagues, and to provide extensive evidence of the quality of their graduates and the positive effects their programs have on education practitioners and P–12 student learning and achievement. Through this assessment system, data from multiple sources affirm and substantiate evaluative judgments regarding candidates' performances, program quality, and process effectiveness. The assessment system facilitates critical review of the unit's work, in reference to articulated standards and in terms of performance-based evidence. It is complex and demanding of time, resources, and commitment, but the system holds promise for contributing to the quality of education practitioners and ultimately to the enrichment of P–12 student learning and achievement.

References

Bullough, R.V. Jr., Hobbs, S.F., Kauchak, D.P., Crow, N.A., & Stokes, D. (1997). Long-term PDS development in research universities and the clinicalization of teacher education. *Journal of Teacher Education, 48* (2), 85–95.

Delandshere, G. (2002). Assessment as inquiry. *Teachers College Record, 104* (7), 1461–1485.

National Council for Accreditation of Teacher Education (2002). *Professional Standards for the Accreditation of Schools, Colleges, and Departments of Education.* Washington, DC: Author.

Perkins, D. (1998). What is understanding? In M.S. Wiske (Ed.), *Teaching for understanding: Linking research with practice* (pp. 39–59). San Francisco: Jossey-Bass.

Perrone, V. (1998). Why do we need a pedagogy of understanding? In M.S. Wiske (Ed.), *Teaching for understanding: Linking research with practice* (pp. 13–38). San Francisco: Jossey-Bass.

Perrone, V. (Ed.). (1991). *Expanding student assessment*. Alexandria, VA.: Association for Supervision and Curriculum Development.

Scannell, D.P. (2000). Aggregating data for NCATE 2000. Washington, DC: NCATE.

Stiggins, R.J. (2000). *Specifications for a performance-based assessment system for teacher preparation*. Washington, DC: NCATE.

Stroble, B. (2000). *Unit assessment systems*. Washington, DC: NCATE.

Stoddart, T. (1993). The professional development school: Building bridges between cultures. *Educational Policy, 7* (1), 5–23.

Thom, A.R. (1998). *Professional development schools and the destabilization of faculty work*. ERIC Document: ED 420297.

Thompson, S. (2001). Master teacher selection. *Georgia P–16 in Action, 3* (1), 6–7.

Weisenbach, E.L. (2000). *Making the case: Marshaling evidence about candidate proficiency*. Washington, DC: NCATE.

Wiske, M.S. (Ed.). (1998). *Teaching for understanding: Linking research with practice*. San Francisco: Jossey-Bass.

CHAPTER 11   *Dennis R. King & Cherie L. Roy*

Teacher Candidates Document Professional Growth by Connecting Theory to Practice in a Rural Clinical Setting

Background

Traditionally, university students aspiring to make a significant contribution to society and make a difference in the lives of others will consider becoming teachers. Since these students have spent the last 13 years of their lives as students in a classroom, usually they feel as if they know what they are getting into when they make this important career decision. But do they know of the multiple aspects of the role of being a classroom teacher? Or, do they understand the specific demands placed on teachers by parents and others? And how can they know of the complexities of school culture?

University coursework, with general-education requirements, an area of specialization, and electives, does provide students with a well-rounded introduction to the knowledge and concepts of being an educated person. Required professional education courses will introduce students to educational foundations, child and human development, curriculum design, student diversity, assessment, classroom management, instructional technology, and the teaching methods necessary to become a successful teacher candidate and beginning classroom teacher. The content (subject-matter knowledge) and pedagogy (creation of learning experiences designed to make content meaningful to students), though, still needs to be connected to the classroom setting in schools. This is an important part of all teacher candidates' personal and professional development, with theory being connected to practice in the classroom so all of this can be internalized and processed by the candidates themselves.

At the PREP/PDN (Penobscot River Educational Partnership/Professional Development Network), a collaborative composed of the University of Maine's College of Education and Human Development and seven local educational administrative units within a 35-mile radius of the campus, a professional skill-building experience is provided for students who are on the pathway to becoming teachers. This allows for the kind of practical and reflection opportunities necessary in a professional teacher preparation program.

Founded in 1865, the University of Maine is the land-grant university for the state of Maine. The largest institution in the statewide University system, Maine's five undergraduate colleges have a combined enrollment of about 9,000 students and its graduate school enrolls about 2,400. The Orono campus, with approximately 800 faculty members, is also the state's center for research and graduate education. The College of Education and Human Development is the state's primary provider of undergraduate and graduate education programs and educational policy research. Here, teachers and other specialists are prepared with the skills necessary to apply research-based knowledge, field-tested experience, and the latest technology to help address the changing needs of schools, children, and families. The College's education programs are accredited by the National Council for the Accreditation of Teacher Education and approved by the Maine State Department of Education.

PREP/PDN is a critical part of Maine's NCATE accreditation and state approval, as it helps shape the conceptual framework for developing curriculum and guiding field experiences. The partnership's development was based upon a standards foundation, and it has kept evolving in response to a systematic analysis of program assessment data. The mission of PREP/PDN is to improve the academic achievement of K–12 public-school students, to provide a clinical opportunity for teacher candidates to link theory to practice while reflecting on their teaching, to increase the number and quality of professional development opportunities for classroom teachers and administrators, and to promote school improvement within partnership schools (PREP/PDN, 2003).

In this chapter, the experiences of PREP/PDN teacher candidates assigned to one of the local educational administrative units, School Union 90 (Alton, Bradley, Greenbush, and Milford) are highlighted. The population of these four towns is 6,429 citizens (Alton, 816; Bradley, 1,242; Greenbush, 1421; and, Milford, 2950). In Union 90, schools are located in a rural area in the middle of the state. All of the Union 90 schools are within a 15-mile radius of the University. Further, Union 90 is composed of the four towns and an unorganized territory with a student population of 706. Each of the four towns has an elementary school. The students in the unorganized territory, Greenfield, attend the school in Milford. Approximately 98 percent of the population is Caucasian, and the remaining 2 percent are either African-American or Native American, depending upon the school. Union 90 provides special-education support to 23 percent of the students, and from 25 percent to 65 percent of the students at the various schools qualify for free and reduced meals.

The PDS Field Experience and the Portfolio

As part of the teacher-preparation program experience, each teacher in the Union 90 schools designs a professional development plan delineating goals for short- and long-term objectives for professional growth. These goals are aligned with the performance standards identified by the school system (Costantino & De Lorenzo, 2002). Each teacher candidate also is expected to produce the same kind of plan as evidence of his or her professional growth, and this plan needs to be aligned with standards identified by the school district and the University. Prior to gaining approval for the plan, each teacher candidate must file a preliminary professional development plan (called Strategic Improvement Plan, see Appendix A) to School Union 90 at the beginning of each of two field-based opportunities. The first opportunity requires a minimum of 100 hours for elementary-level teacher candidates in the schools, taken concurrently with five content-specific methods courses. The second experience is an internship that lasts at least 15 weeks. At the end of these opportunities, each teacher candidate submits a working portfolio based on Maine's Beginning Teacher Standards (MBTS) and an overall reflective statement of his or her professional growth to date. This is presented at an exit interview with a four- or five-member support team, including the assigned mentor-teacher, building principal, team facilitator, and PDS university liaison.

The introduction of the portfolio, as the product to document one's individual professional growth, is a logical medium for teacher candidates to present a reflective summary grounded in the MBTS. It is also important to stress that NEASC (New England Accreditation of Schools and Colleges), NCATE, NBPTS (National Board for Professional Teaching Standards), and the MBTS require more than just performance-based assessments. Rather, the portfolio and overall reflective summaries presented during exit interviews are scored on rubrics designed to meet program criteria.

The process of portfolio development is deliberative. Teacher candidates are carefully presented with the expectations of each field-based opportunity and how to create their own developmental statement and preliminary professional development plan. The developmental statement is introduced as being a descriptive paragraph with baseline information to identify prior experiences and knowledge of each of the ten MBTS standards. (Note: during the first field experience, only five standards—Content Knowledge, Planning, Assessment, Classroom Management, and Professional Development—are selected to avoid overwhelming the teacher candidates during their initial field experience.)

Each statement sets the stage for creating the professional development plan by suggesting the logical next step. For example: Standard #4: *Plans instruction based upon knowledge of subject matter, students, and curriculum goals.* (MDOE, 2002):

Developmental Statement: "I have been exposed to a variety of lesson design formats, created a number of lesson plans for university professors to critique, revised those lesson plans which did not meet the adequate level criteria, and taught one of those lessons during a microteaching experience with some of my peers. I have yet to plan, implement, and self-evaluate one of my lessons with real kids."

The next step, then, would be to teach the lesson to children.

Professional Development Plans (or Strategic Improvement Plans) are introduced to the teacher candidates in order to highlight MBTS goals and other related areas such as "to improve learning opportunities for K–8 students," "to improve teacher effectiveness," and "to promote positive school climate." Teacher candidates may design other goals if they have another competency they wish to work on, such as "to understand how to communicate effectively with parents." Each goal, though, is keyed to one of the MBTS standards, and the teacher candidate will design related objectives under each goal, such as "to observe and identify how my mentor-teacher sets up and conducts a parent-teacher conference," or "to conduct, self-assess, and receive mentor-teacher feedback about a parent–teacher-candidate conference designed to discuss social issues and the academic progress of a student." In addition, the teacher candidates need to link their objectives to indicators of success or documentation, such as "summarize how the teacher reacts to the various situations one is faced with when meeting with a parent during the parent-teacher conference." The final required component for each section of the professional development plan is the timeline, for example, "by the end of the semester."

During the exit interview, each teacher candidate brings in the working portfolio, which includes the developmental statements, professional development plan, documentation for all objectives of each MBTS, an overall reflective statement, and letters of support. The self-evaluative reflective statement usually contains enough information to easily write the next phase of developmental statements. With this experience, a teacher candidate is ready to meet the requirements for initial certification as a new teacher during the period of induction in a new school system.

What are the advantages of using developmental statements and professional development plans with pre-service teacher candidates? The PDS faculty feels that:

- each teacher candidate takes responsibility for his or her own professional growth
- this is an authentic activity since teachers are expected to file a professional development plan
- there is a common language developed between the teacher candidate and mentor-teacher on MBTS, theory to practice, and practice to theory
- teacher candidates show they are effective teachers and lifelong learners, and good/best practice comes with implementing theory effectively and linking that with student academic achievement

- teacher candidates are empowered to make an informed career decision based upon experience with the various roles of a classroom teacher

What are the limitations of using developmental statements and professional development plans with pre-service teacher candidates? It is felt that:

- teacher candidates need their own group of students in their own classroom in order to be in the most authentic situation
- there is no assurance that a period of induction will provide the same level of support with complementary expectations for professional growth
- specific need exists for the development of a holistic scoring criteria for portfolios keyed to the MBTS
- training a cadre of mentor-teachers is necessary in order to prepare teacher candidates and new teachers for success as an effective classroom teacher

Summary

After four years of PDS effort based upon PDS faculty perspectives, it has been found that the teacher candidates assigned to School Union 90 have successfully implemented the professional growth process of writing Developmental Statements and Professional Developmental Plans that provide documentation of their own professional growth. Further, each teacher candidate has had an opportunity to make specific meaningful connections between theory and practice in order to assist K–8 students in the pursuit of academic achievement. With the culminating activities of an exit interview, presentation of a working portfolio, and an overall reflective summary of individual professional growth, each teacher candidate has been held accountable by linking this effort to experience. This combination of training and experience provides an authentic introduction to the world of a regular classroom teacher and the school culture that all teachers must work in daily.

Teacher candidates report a high level of satisfaction by having realistic experiences consisting of challenging, yet reasonable expectations. As each teacher candidate takes on more responsibilities with greater levels of preparation, she indicates that her level of commitment in becoming a classroom teacher is stronger. It is interesting to note that the teacher candidates see the MBTS as important, and list these "first-time" experiences (supervising students on recess duty, attending to a student with a bloody nose, or speaking with a parent about her child's misbehavior) as being important to his professional growth.

There are questions about the need for further investigation into whether or not a teacher candidate's knowledge of theory influences his practice in his assigned classrooms. Also, what criteria should be used to evaluate his working portfolio? Do teacher candidates improve student academic achievement? And, what training do mentor teachers need in order to support teacher candidates during field experiences and internships?

References

Costantino, P.M. & De Lorenzo, M.N. (2002). *Developing a professional teaching portfolio: A guide for success*. Boston: Allyn & Bacon.

MDOE (Maine Department of Education). (2002). *Maine's Beginning Teacher Standards Chapter 114*. Augusta, Maine. Retrieved on September 12, 2004, from www.maine.gov/education/aarbec/ Teaching_Standards/TenStandards.htm.

PREP/PDN (Penobscot River Educational Partnership/Professional Development Network). (2003). Orono, Maine. Retrieved on September 12, 2004, from www.preppdn.org.

Appendix 11.A.

Strategic Improvement Plan
Dr. Lewis Libby School
Union #90

Name: _____   Date: _____

Goals of the SIP

- to improve learning opportunities for students
- to improve teaching effectiveness
- to improve positive school climate

Category
Place corresponding box # on the line

_____ Professional

_____ Communications

_____ Teamwork

_____ Management

_____ Teaching

Objectives	Activities	Indicators/Documentation
to increase, develop, create, review, enhance, strengthen, etc.	course, workshops, visitations, readings, observations, participation, etc.	journals, portfolios, reports, artifacts, log sheets, articles, units, etc.

PART IV

Determining the Impacts of Professional Development Schools through Research

CHAPTER 12

Diane Davis, RaeAnn T. Wuestman, Betty Kansler, & Linda Williams

Service Learning
Where the Action Is!

Introduction

In this chapter, we describe the collaborative efforts of College of Notre Dame of Maryland Education Department (CND) faculty members and their professional development school partners to create school-based learning communities that engage in action research/inquiry projects related to school-improvement plans. The collaboration within the PDS and the communication among the supervisors, mentors, and interns serves as a catalyst for continuous reform and renewal.

In particular, we present three approaches to implementing service learning, through the action research described by the persons responsible for implementing these efforts. Although different in design, each approach addresses the needs of the school as identified in the school's strategic plans.

The first model emphasizes the role of CND in conducting a course in research that requires interns to investigate an issue aligned with strategies for improved student achievement, as stated in the school improvement plan. Within this framework, the interns provide a service to the school while they gain guided experience in the role of a reflective practitioner.

The second model approach is how the PDS partnership provided the opportunity to initiate classroom action research at Kenwood High School, Maryland, as an option in the ongoing school staff development program. The program itself, as well as the topics the teachers selected for action research, was aligned with the school's improvement plan.

In the third approach, the focus is on facilitating the engagement of PDS teachers in an action research project in order to align coursework with the promise of change within the school. Interested teachers developed projects to test the effectiveness of recognition and praise as presented in *Classroom Instruction That Works* by Marzano, Pickering, and Pollack (2001).

Background

The CND Commitment to Service-Learning & Education Department Efforts

The mission of CND regards education as a means of transforming the world. Therefore, service learning, as a philosophy and pedagogy, provides a curricular framework for accomplishing this mission. A component of the College's strategic planning is the implementation of service learning within all academic and service areas of the campus. The members of the Education Department have been involved in service learning initiatives from their inception on campus.

The Conceptual Framework of the Education Department is entitled "Research, Self-Reflection, Vocation and Practice" (RSVP) and mirrors the College's commitment to prepare teachers who are research-oriented, reflective practitioners. As a result, these teachers value teaching as a commitment to support the human impulse to grow and learn, and they seek best practices to inform daily decision-making. Service learning intentionally involves experiential activities within the academic curriculum, designed to address community needs. Teacher candidates and interns are encouraged to integrate what they know from a theoretical frame of reference with what they are practicing in the school environment, while providing a service to the school. Service learning has been established as pedagogy that is linked to important educational outcomes, including improved academic performance, higher achievement-test scores, higher grades, and increased academic engagement of CND students.

As a parallel activity, action research can be conducted through a variety of methods or approaches. However, for the researchers, interns, or practicing teachers to provide service to the local school, action research needs to be aligned with the school improvement plan. Within the call for No Child Left Behind, implementing action research within a PDS model provides a venue for collaborative engagement and problem solving, leading to improved student achievement. Thus, action research within a Pre-K–16 PDS partnership is the cornerstone for the school's restructuring and attainment of goals within the framework of the school's improvement plan.

Differentiated Action Research

There follows a description of each model of action research implemented within the PDS partnerships, with examples of the various action projects and the results obtained included in the descriptions.

Model One: A Curriculum Approach to Action Research in Service Learning
There are various approaches to action research. In general, action research should be systematic and organized to examine assumptions about learning, and it should be relevant to policy and practice. Therefore, the decision to include action research in service learning as a component of an internship required a conceptual shift in the Master of Arts in Teaching (MAT) program. The traditional research seminar would no longer be considered a capstone course taken after the internship. Instead, service learning would be integrated as a collaborative experience. Interns would learn about educational research and actively engage in it. In this approach, interns participated in the following seminars throughout the year:

Orientation Sessions. In August, four two-hour sessions with a focus on the foundations of educational research and service learning.

Seminar 1. In October, a session focused on qualitative data collection methods.

Seminar 2. In November, interns prepared a review of the literature based upon a school's issue for investigation.

Seminar 3. In December, there was discussion about qualitative data analysis.

Seminar 4. In January, the learning environment was the area given attention.

Seminar 5. In April, interns presented their collaborative action-research projects to the School Improvement Team.

This process has caused a revision in the MAT curriculum. Now, interns are required to participate in the action research seminars while fulfilling the demands of the fall weekly observational phase and the intensive spring daily student-teaching internship phase. The goal is to guide the interns through the action research process while they develop an understanding of service-learning philosophy and pedagogy. Interns learn the process of inquiry as a means of becoming critical and reflective practitioners who have an enhanced sense of social responsibility. Additionally, there is an intent that this action-research/service-learning effort will provide a forum for teachers and administrators to engage in conversation about classroom and/or school-based issues of concern. The following is a list of the questions investigated by the interns during the 2002–2003 academic year:

- What are the benefits and concerns associated with tracking children in math and science?

- What are the most effective artifacts for students to include in their portfolio to document growth and improvement?
- What variables have an impact on closing the achievement gap among underachievers?

The faculty providing guidance to the interns recognized that the pre-service MAT program is demanding, as is the profession of teaching. When initiating this program in August 2002, they had high expectations but an awareness of the limitations imposed by variables having an impact on the implementation of the ambitious curriculum change. A review of the data from the project indicated a direct relationship between the interns' ability to complete successfully the action research and the administrative and faculty support for them in the schools. Although the sample was too small for statistical analysis, a content analysis showed that presenting projects to the School Improvement Team was an empowering experience for the interns. In written reflections collected at the end of the experience, the interns viewed their action research projects as service learning; and they felt they provided a service to the school and learned from reflecting on that experience.

As the CND faculty reflected on the project and considered revisions for academic year 2003–2004, the question that emerged was: What impact, if any, does the CND model have for service learning through action research on teacher education?

Model Two: Action Research as Ongoing Professional Development
As a Challenge Grant School and PDS, the faculty members at Kenwood High School have learned to guide their school improvement planning by using research data. They identify problems, collect information about them, develop strategies to solve them, and then collect more data on how implemented strategies are working. Because professional development is an integral part of the school improvement process, as well as a primary concern of the PDS, the process of professional development planning at Kenwood is also data driven.

Over the years, needs assessments have been conducted at Kenwood, leading to the development of a program of professional development differentiated according to the experience and needs of the teachers and their academic or subject-area departments. New teachers choose from workshops in five strands: technology, improving student achievement in reading and writing, classroom management, integrating testing formats into instruction, and improving human-relations skills. The interns are invited to participate in these workshops with the Kenwood teachers. Veteran teachers may participate in the workshops or undertake departmental projects under the guidance of their subject-area chairperson, or combine the two options. It is important that the principal make professional development a priority in the teacher appraisal process, and guide all teachers in reflecting on what they have learned and need to learn as part of the yearly evaluation conference.

During the 2002–2003 academic year, the addition of independent, classroom-level action research to the program was a logical next step. The reflection-research-action-reflection cycle has long been a part of the process of school improvement. As a result, action research options were extended into classrooms, particularly for experienced teachers who are site-based PDS coordinating council members, or PDS mentors or potential mentors. Funding for this effort was obtained from Baltimore County's Office of Professional Development as part of the summer strategic planning for Kenwood's PDS. Six teachers participated in the summer training and continued to meet throughout the school year on a monthly basis. The teachers pursued classroom-based inquiry that developed from their own questions and concerns about how to raise the level of achievement among students. The inquiries were as varied as the teachers and students themselves, and included a focus on the following:

- An English teacher, a veteran mentor, investigated how to increase the level of engagement among her twelfth-grade students.
- Another English teacher, a member of PDS coordinating council, inquired if a writers' workshop can produce better attitudes toward writing, and thus, better results in writing assessments than more test-driven methods.
- An algebra teacher worked with ways in which format training can improve achievement on brief constructed response items on tests and final examinations.
- A family-studies teacher and member of the PDS coordinating council investigated the effects on achievement of improved notebook organization and note-taking methods among students in the child-development class.
- A social studies teacher examined the relationship between higher-level thinking skills and the ability to write, as well as what instructional strategies help students to improve both skills.
- Another social studies teacher, a veteran mentor and PDS coordinating council member, investigated the relationship between homework compliance and achievement on tests; and how the rate of homework compliance relates to the type of homework given.

Because it is problem focused, classroom action research inquiries such as these are highly individualized to the teachers, students, and classrooms involved. At the same time, however, this encourages teachers to compare methods and collaborate to help each other solve problems of common concern. Each of the teachers has shared findings at department meetings as well as within the action research group meetings. This has created an increased sense of collegiality among the staff, and good news is disseminated about the PDS and its benefits among the faculty as a whole. Thus, the participating teachers have developed a sense of empowerment in being able to do something about obstacles to achievement that they and their students face. They report being more open to change, more reflective, and better informed as a result of this process.

In sum, this project has helped support the PDS in creating learning communities and increasing collaboration through action research. It has supported the program of professional development driven by the school improvement plan. And, it has put ideas to work to encourage self-improvement; helping teachers grow by becoming better learners in their own classroom laboratories. All of these efforts are aimed at increasing student achievement.

Table 12.1 describes several of the action research questions, results, and impact on "improved practices":

Model Three: Theoretical and Practical Considerations for Action Research Applied to Classroom Instruction That Works
Action research is a way of applying a scientific method of inquiry to educational practice. Teachers grow professionally by engaging in action research and using the findings to improve student achievement. Although the methodology may vary, most teacher-researchers follow a standard process, including identifying a problem or question, reviewing the research, establishing a plan to answer the question, and testing. The sense of accomplishment and the practical value to the school community make the investment of time and energy worthwhile. Most teacher-researchers commit to more action research as one question leads to another.

In *Classroom Instruction That Works* (Marzano, Pickering & Pollack, 2001), instructional strategies are described indicating that there can be a major impact on student achievement. Nine strategies are explored with summaries of research for each strategy. The Maryland Association for Supervision and Curriculum Development (MASCD) has undertaken a project in which several colleges and universities have paired with local schools or school systems in order to use an action research approach to test the research regarding the strategies.

Among the research-based strategies in this work are ways to reinforce effort and provide recognition. These techniques refer to attitudes and beliefs with an understanding that not all students understand the positive relationship between effort and achievement. Further, students can be taught the importance of effort by the teacher's use of rubrics and literature.

Recognition takes many forms in schools. Rewards and praise are used often. However, it has been shown that rewards do not always have a positive effect on recognition. Abstract recognition, including praise, often is more effective than tangible rewards.

At Baltimore Highlands Elementary School in Baltimore County, a PDS aligned with the College of Notre Dame, ten teachers explored ways to reinforce effort and provide recognition by engaging in a graduate course that included opportunities for experimentation. The teachers met to discuss research findings and to formulate questions meaningful to their classrooms. Classes of students or selected individuals were

TABLE 12.1.

Area	Question Investigated	Data Collected	Data Results	What Learned	Changed Practices
Algebra	Can direct instruction on test-taking strategies improve performance on HSA assessments?	Baseline: 2002 final-exam scores, this year's Unit A test scores. Milestone: test scores from Units B – F to date	Marked improvement in completion and quality of BCR from previous year; now looking at multiple-choice strategy training	Results of test format/writing instruction is well worth the time taken away from content instruction	Instructor will continue to integrate the test format instruction into daily content instruction.
American Government	Does the type of homework given affect completion rates? Does increased homework completion improve unit test scores?	Homework completion rates from quarters 1–3; Unit test scores	Homework given on ditto sheets is completed most often regardless of type of assignment; homework aligned to assessment increases success in those who complete the homework	Homework does not need to be assigned each night to make a difference, and should be given in the form of handout sheets. Assignments need to align with assessments	Instructor plans to reduce homework assignments and align effectively to assessment.

TABLE 12.1. (continued)

Area	Question Investigated	Data Collected	Data Results	What Learned	Changed Practices
Family Studies, Child Care	Does direct instruction on the organization and maintenance of a notebook enhance student success?	Notebooks checks, drill checks, test scores	Every student passed the required safety exam. (First time while teaching the course)	Students have a sense of pride and ownership about their notebooks and are more accountable for their work.	Instructor will continue the notebook instruction and checks, will add training in other notebook requirements
English	How do motivational activities affect long-term learning and retention?	Student surveys, student writing samples	Student engagement does have a positive effect on student learning and retention. This was especially evident when students could tie what was going on in class with their own prior knowledge or interest.	Motivational activities that have the greatest affect on engagement and learning are ones that are more than just "fun." The most effective ones relate student interests clearly to the learning goals.	Instructor will clarify her long-term goals and make sure that students are aware of them. For example, students responded better, learned more about literary criticism when they knew that their senior project would relate to it.

TABLE 12.1. (continued)

Content Area	Question Investigated	Data Collected	Data Results	What Learned	Changed Practices
English	What is the effect of portfolios, Writers' Workshop, and direct instruction on student's writing and attitudes as indicated by standard assessments? (HSA and BCRs)	Student surveys, writing samples, observation of students	Students showed improvement in attitude and performance	There is a lot more to writing instruction than teaching "formulas."	Instructor will bring "Writers' Workshop" to all classes.
Pre IB American Government	How can the instructor help students become better critical thinkers?	Student surveys, student essays	Students rated themselves as good critical thinkers, but essays did not bear this out. Students did not know what critical thinking meant nor how to do it.	Reading, writing, and thinking are interconnected. Questioning techniques are essential to helping students learn to think.	Instructor will reinforce good critical thinking when she sees it, concentrate on her ability to ask higher-level questions and teach student to do the same. Instructor will integrate instruction on how to read, think, and write critically into all content instruction.

studied in order to answer questions posed by the teachers. Results were shared with the faculty at the school, and the results will be shared with the larger community at the 2004 MASCD conference.

The following are the research questions each group explored and the results of their investigations. The results were positive and provided natural opportunities for extended research during the next school year:

1. A kindergarten team asked: "How can there be an improvement in the consistent recognition of sight words over time?" Team members found that by practicing words daily, meeting with the language-resource teacher for praise, and promising a party for those who mastered 20 words over a four-week period, 16 of 20 students mastered 20 words.
2. Three first- and second-grade teachers asked: "Will students select a more challenging spelling task based upon the promise of a greater reward?" They found students showed a gain in spelling ability. Lower-achieving students demonstrated more effort when choosing a more difficult set of words. Students worked for praise and rewards if they chose the more difficult sets of words during the four-week experiment.
3. Two second-grade teachers used tape recorders as a prewriting strategy to see if that would improve children's expository writing. They noted dramatic differences in the quality of the writing by having children "talk" their paragraphs into the recorder, and then with the help of an adult, transcribe the paragraph.
4. The school nurse chose to focus on a third-grade class with low attendance to determine if individual goal setting with rewards would boost attendance. The nurse found that when individuals could set goals, their attendance improved.

Conclusion

The College of Notre Dame and PDS partners use multiple approaches to conduct action research as service learning. Each form or approach to inquiry has provided an opportunity to learn from the experience, and has been a service for the school. The investigations ranged from curricular focus, to strategy-based issues, and to the concerns found in individual classrooms. The organizational patterns of this work vary from individual classrooms to the entire school, leading to a broader system-wide understanding. Across all these variations, the goal is the same—to improve student achievement in collegial learning communities where all participants teach and learn from each other.

Reference

Marzano, R., Pickering, J., & Pollack, D. (2001). *Classroom instruction that works: Research-based strategies for increasing student achievement.* Alexandria, VA: Association for Supervision and Curriculum Development.

CHAPTER 13

Marybeth P. Miller, Patricia Rawson, & Carl Holmes

Measuring the Perceived Competency of Physical Education Interns
A Two-Year Analysis of the Physical Education Professional Development School

Across the nation, teacher preparation programs, including those in physical education, are undergoing reforms intended to improve the knowledge and teaching competencies of pre-service teachers. Attempting to address national standards, state regulations, and evolving professional practice in teacher preparation, colleges and universities are at a crossroads for program and curriculum revision (Guyton & Byrd, 2000). In their 1990 report, *Tomorrow's Schools: Principles for the Design of Professional Development Schools,* the Holmes Group provided an early blueprint of a collaboration field experience where teacher preparation, in part, occurs in community schools.

In the mid-1980s, education reform efforts led to a movement toward school restructuring and a redesign of teacher education to prepare teachers for restructured schools (Abdal-Haqq, 1998). At this time there was the emergence of Professional Development Schools. The National Commission on Excellence in Education (1983) and the Holmes Group (1990) promoted a new understanding of how universities and schools could do business with each other. The development and implementation of a PDS at St. Bonaventure University has expanded the university-school partnership from a model of cooperation to a model of collaboration. The partnership now meets each other's needs through shared decision making and responsibility, with outcomes affecting each program's goals, purpose, and structure.

Colleges and universities are examining their pedagogical practice and moving toward comprehensive field experiences in support of effective university-school collaboration (Fiorentino, Kowalski & Barrette, 1993; Graham, 1988). By connecting communities of practice (Grisham et al., 1999), the partnership promotes change benefiting the school and the university (Hobbs et al., 1998). The belief that faculty and teachers contribute equally (Sharpe, 1992) is essential to the PDS. The strength of collaborative university-school partnerships needs to be built on a base of knowledge generated from research in the formation of collaborative research (Martinek & Schempp, 1988).

Background

Physical Education PDS models may be considered unique to teacher education. However, it should not necessarily be considered a new model. Sharpe (1992) wrote about the University of Nebraska-Lincoln's PDS created within the School of Health, Physical Education, and Recreation. This model involved 49 partner schools in the surrounding Lincoln Public School System. The PDS hierarchy "comprised observation, teacher assistance, mini-teaching episodes, supervised large-group teaching, and the student teaching experience which occurs in concert with all pedagogical classroom experiences" (p. 83). University faculty and teachers and administrators from two laboratory schools, along with teachers and administrators from other partner schools, helped to create positive collaboration. Summary results from formal interviews about the perceptions of faculty, practitioners, graduate students, and pre-service teachers, indicated the benefits outweighed the disadvantages.

In 1993, Adelphi University created SUPPORT-PE, a school-university collaboration involving 20 schools on Long Island, New York. This field-based teacher preparation model includes a full-year junior-level field experience in the schools. The mutual reciprocity of "teachers helping university students learn more about teaching, and students helping teachers teach children" (Fiorentino, Kowalski & Barrette, 1993, p. 78) is vital to the junior year experience and the transitional journey from student to professional. Indicators related to the success of the program support this as a beneficial way to strengthen the school-university partnership to better prepare teachers, while lending further support to the positive impact of PDS training.

The Western Kentucky University (WKU) Physical Education PDS, the mentor for the physical education PDS at St. Bonaventure University, is a junior-year, half-day, five-days-per-week program involving elementary (Elementary Block) and middle/high partner schools (Secondary Block) in Bowling Green, Kentucky. Campus-based teacher-educators work in the schools collaborating with the school-based teacher-educators for planning, teaching, and supervising interns. At the elementary-school sites, each intern teaches classes three to four times per week, twice daily, for eleven weeks, for a total of 66 instructions. At the middle school and high-school sites, each intern accrues a total of 24 instructions. WKU has provided data showing improved outcomes in individual and group use of time for pre-service teacher candidates in their sixth year of training in a PDS model, when comparing the first to last lessons in the elementary block on measures of Academic Learning Time-Physical Education (Askins et al., 1999). Interns' perceptions about the success of the PDS in their preparation indicate that for all variables measured (curriculum development, instruction and methods, and professionalism), the majority of interns responding (12 out of 13) felt either adequately prepared or strongly prepared (Daniel et al., 2000). The examples provided in their models support the notion that university-school collaborative field experiences have a positive effect on (student) teacher development.

St. Bonaventure University Professional Development School

At St. Bonaventure University in 1998, there was a redirection of traditional practica connected with methods courses. Supporting a greater commitment to applied school-based teaching and learning experiences, the St. Bonaventure School of Education adopted the PDS model. The PDS model has become integrated with programs in Childhood Education and Physical Education. Expansion is currently underway for a new graduate-level PDS program.

The School of Education established a network of six partner schools extending throughout southwestern New York and northwestern Pennsylvania. In each school, tenured teachers are recruited and incorporated into the model clinical faculty. There are 70 clinical faculty in the Childhood Education PDS and five in Physical Education. In exchange for their mentorship of pre-service teacher candidates, clinical faculty have access to university resources, network with colleagues, and have a direct impact on teacher-preparation programs at the university.

The Elementary Physical Education PDS Program Experience

One of the Physical Education PDS models at St. Bonaventure University is the Elementary Physical Education Field Block. Two physical education teachers who are full-time employees of Cuba Elementary School in the Cuba-Rushford School District, Cuba, New York, serve as clinical faculty. There are two campus-based teacher-educators on site to work with the clinical faculty, assist interns with planning units and lessons, observe teaching, provide feedback, and assist with lesson reflection and revisions. The university supervisors also teach two university courses: PHED 303 Elementary School Physical Education Methods, and PHED 311 Physical Education for Children with Exceptionalities. Clinical faculty and university supervisors collaborate to plan the program, provide unit and lesson input, conduct observations, provide post-lesson feedback, and complete mid-semester and end-of-semester intern evaluations. The school provides two classrooms for planning and post-lesson reflecting and evaluations. The University equips each room with technology support and other materials for this to occur.

The semester is organized into three, four-week rounds. Interns are assigned to small groups, and within each group they are assigned a teaching partner. Each intern is assigned to a clinical faculty member and a university supervisor.

Interns and university supervisors go to the elementary school twice a week. Arriving at the school by 7:30 a.m., everyone reports to the classroom for morning briefing, and then they set up their instructional materials in the gymnasium. From 7:45 to 9:10, the courses are taught in the classroom by the university supervisors while the clinical faculty teaches the first class of learners during a first period. At the beginning of the second period, all interns report to their assigned placement, workroom, or classroom for observation. For every period, two classes are taught simultaneously. An intern is assigned to teach while his/her partner is responsible for videotaping the lesson. When the second period ends, the intern who taught has a conference with the mentor who supervised the lesson, and then switches roles with his or her partner. The same process is followed for the third period. At the end of the third period, after post-lesson conferencing, interns go to the workroom to view their lesson for their own systematic evaluation, guidance, and reflection and revision. Meanwhile, lessons continue in the gymnasium with a new group of interns rotating with clinical faculty and university supervisors. This procedure continues through the morning and afternoon, with an additional teaching station of aquatics instruction at the swimming pool two afternoons per week. All interns are certified lifeguards and water-safety instructors.

The development of the physical education PDS at St. Bonaventure University includes a goal of determining if the experience is meeting the needs of the interns. As Williams (2001) studied student teachers' perceptions of a teacher-training program, his basis for inquiry rested with the pre-service teacher candidates analyzing and describing their received service in order to determine perceived teacher-training program effectiveness.

Measuring the perceived competency or self-efficacy of pre-service teacher candidates is related to the type and extent of experience during the four-year training. For example, this includes the relationship between pre-service teachers' self-efficacy, task analysis, and classroom management beliefs (Henson, 2001), novice teachers' self-efficacy change and their beliefs about teaching (Ginns & Watters, 1996), or investigating components of pre-service teacher training likely to influence teachers' expertise development (Jablonski, 1995). The pre-service teachers' perceptions of their ability to become effective teachers and succeed can be explained by expected action-outcome contingencies gained through experiences; then valuable information may be obtained to identify the effectiveness of the physical education PDS.

Method

Participants

Thirteen third-year pre-service teacher candidates (eight women and five men), and 18 third-year pre-service teacher candidates (seven women and 11 men) participated during the fall 2000 and fall 2001 semesters. The students were enrolled in the Department of Physical Education's Elementary Physical Education Field Block, having two university professional-methods courses (three credit hours each). The pre-service teacher candidates (interns), were mentored by two tenured physical education teachers (clinical faculty), and taught one 40-minute lesson at least twice per week to learners in kindergarten through fifth grade.

Materials

A survey was used consisting of 21 Likert-scale items with values of one (strongly disagree) to five (strongly agree), and one open-ended question in which comments and suggestions for improvement were solicited about the program (see Appendix 13.A). (Note: No measure of validity or reliability is available at this time.)

Design and Procedure

The survey replaced the traditional required course evaluation instrument used at St. Bonaventure University. At the end of the fall 2000 and fall 2001 semesters, immediately following the PHED 303 Elementary School Methods final examination, interns were administered the survey to measure their perceived competency based upon their experience in the elementary physical education PDS.

Results

The results of the survey are central to the type of information considered most important to university supervisors, clinical faculty, and school administrators regarding PDS efficacy. The interns' perceived competency across the first two years of PDS implementation has been extrapolated to specific questions about five themes: organization, planning, teaching, supervision, and comfort level. Mean scores and standard deviations were calculated for the questions (see Table 13.1).

The outcomes for the questions of Table 13.1 imply that short-term feedback aided in promoting the interns' confidence and competence to know how to plan, and that the volume of assigned work was appropriate. These data improved for the second year. When provided, interns took advantage of the workroom resource, but felt the

TABLE 13.1. **Mean Responses by Interns about Program Organization**

Question	2000		2001	
	M	SD	M	SD
1	3.846	0.532	4.111	1.048
6	3.923	0.828	4.166	0.957
13	3.846	0.661	3.833	0.897
	n = 13		n = 18	

time in the workroom could be reduced so that they would be provided more teaching opportunities. However, at this developmental level, interns function best with structure and require more guidance by the university supervisors and clinical faculty. For fall 2000, the structure of the model was weak in the area of time for university personnel to contact and assist interns with planning, resource development, and post-lesson reflection.

While interns in both years agreed the PDS program was well organized, the tendency for a stronger agreement for the second year may be contributed to the correction of mistakes made during the first year, and the addition of one additional university supervisor in 2001 to assist interns in the workroom. During fall 2000, there was one university supervisor on site who spent the entire day supervising in the gymnasium, with no time to assist interns in the workroom.

Immediate feedback following unit and lesson plan submission was valued as important and relevant, and therefore it was retained to reflect upon post-lesson changes. While more than half of the interns for both years believed that the feedback provided after teaching, planning units in a more formative manner, and self-critiquing their teaching by video analysis aided in the planning process, the second year's marginal improvement may be attributed to a focus on working out the mistakes made in the start-up year, and a change in one clinical faculty member. The minimal change in response for question 12 may be due to the addition of the second university supervisor for fall 2001. This change led to assistance with lesson critiques, reflection, and revisions done in the workroom; yet post-lesson critique is a weakness needing to be addressed.

TABLE 13.2. **Mean Responses by Interns about Planning**

Question	12		2001	
	M	SD	M	SD
4	4.230	0.575	4.444	0.598
9	4.000	0.544	4.444	0.598
12	3.666	1.027*	3.777	0.711
	n = 13		n = 18	

* one intern did not respond

TABLE 13.3. **Mean Responses by Interns about Teaching**

Question	2000		2001	
	M	SD	M	SD
14	4.230	0.799	4.611	0.755
15	4.538	0.498	4.500	0.600
17	4.615	0.486	4.777	0.415
18	3.615	0.737	4.222	0.628
	n = 13		n = 18	

During the fall 2000 semester, the interns' discovery of their ability to more easily gain and sustain attention in the upper grades resulted in their perception that they were more effective teachers, because they taught more complete lessons with skill and competency (with less communication and management struggles). Thus, they felt more like teachers by receiving more immediate responses from the older learners (question 15).

Throughout fall 2001, interns perceived themselves as more effective teachers for grades K–2 than for grades 3–5 (questions 14 and 15). Interns experienced a greater success rate in teaching lessons to students in the younger grades (question 14) by completing these lessons with skill and less need for behavior management. The provision of an additional university supervisor, along with a change toward improved quantity and quality of post-lesson feedback and support, has had a positive effect on developmentally appropriate lesson planning.

The goal of the Elementary Physical Education Field Block was attained—the university-school collaborative PDS experience helped pre-service teacher candidates learn the profession. While model lesson plans provided to interns (question 18) were not different across the two years, the attitude of interns differed from fall 2000 to fall 2001. Interns in the first-year PDS were excited yet resistant to change, while the fall 2001 interns began the PDS program knowing what to anticipate and expect, possibly passed on by word of mouth by the fall 2000 interns. Further, interns were more receptive to models that may have indicated a greater willingness to try new techniques. A second explanation may exist: the consultation and guidance provided by the clinical faculty was of higher quality due to an increased comfort level created by clinical faculty providing methods-level mentoring in the PDS.

TABLE 13.4. **Mean Responses by Interns about Supervision**

Question	2000		2001	
	M	SD	M	SD
16	3.923	0.474	4.222	0.974
19	3.796	0.799	4.055	0.704
21	3.615	0.737	4.055	0.848
	n = 13		n = 18	

Question 19 had a focus on agreement with post-lesson feedback. The feedback may also include the intern's discussions with clinical faculty at other times. Overall, interns agreed that the quality of supervision was satisfactory. The model for the process of supervision is effective but with some stronger agreement made in the second year. This may be due to clinical faculty being more familiar with feedback delivery based on the Systematic Lesson Observation Form that they used.

The feedback process was new to clinical faculty. The rigors of formally observing each lesson two days per week in the fall 2000 semester appeared to be too much of a demand on the clinical faculty. At times, in the first year, the clinical faculty was unsure of what to look for in lessons, or not initially clear on the language. Also, clinical faculty had a difficult time separating the developmental levels between methods-level interns and student teachers. They were not involved in methods-level training, where the constant supervision and pedagogical nurturing was more intense. In this regard, clinical faculty had been transformed from an active participant in their daily teaching behavior to a passive observer with the task of writing and recording systematic observation data. The supervisory procedure was changed for the fall 2001 semester, and this may explain the increase in mean scores from 2000 to 2001.

The results from question 5 (see Table 13.5) support the belief that interns felt accepted by and important in the school community. This meant that they felt comfortable in the school culture. This feeling assisted their ability to recognize that the PDS experience is important to the elementary school personnel *and* the university community.

The results from question 10 may be interpreted as the interns' perception of the clinical faculty as not being overly demanding, yet respectful of the developmental level of the interns. This is an important feature for methods instruction. This improved mean score for fall 2001 may be due to a change in clinical faculty coupled with program refinements. Regarding the overall agreement of respect of interns by clinical faculty, the feeling was found to be mutual.

TABLE 13.5. **Mean Responses by Interns about Comfort Level**

Question	2000		2001	
	M	SD	M	SD
5	4.796	0.421	4.833	0.372
10	4.384	0.624	4.777	0.415
	n = 13		n = 18	

Open-Ended Question

Interns were asked to provide comments and suggestions for program improvement. Responses common across the fall 2000 and fall 2001 field block experiences include, "enjoyable, beneficial, valuable"; "a learning experience for all"; "felt very prepared—it did make a difference"; "great program—learned more than staying at the university"; "well organized—taught us how to be organized"; "gained a lot of confidence about teaching"; "instilled professionalism early on"; and, "I would never want to student teach without having done field block!"

These comments support the goal of a PDS: university-school collaboration allows for better preparation of teachers. Program revisions and refinements have been made as a result of information derived from this study. Further, in the Elementary Physical Education Field Block, advances toward integrating technology to have an impact on learners have occurred, as well as an extension of the development of intern's electronic portfolio training in order to link to the NASPE National Standards for Beginning Physical Education Teachers (National Association for Sport and Physical Education, 1995).

Discussion

The data presented in this two-year analysis indicate support for the physical education PDS model by the pre-service teacher candidates. Outcomes central to each of the five themes provide university supervisors and clinical faculty with the necessary data for enhancing PDS program effectiveness. It is believed that the interns' perceived competency at this developmental level provides a measure of the physical education PDS model meeting its goal.

The perceived competencies of the pre-service teacher candidates indicate that the PDS experience is a positive attribute in professional training. The feelings of candidates about being competent teachers for all grades, along with their satisfaction with clinical faculty mentoring, are worthwhile and necessary. Their expression of greater readiness for planning and teaching through the PDS model is a valued quality. From this study, it appears that the pre-service teachers participating in the PDS model perceive themselves as competent. These outcomes correspond with similar findings of studies involved with comprehensive field experiences where self-efficacy was examined as an outcome of intensive pre-service teacher training (Ginns & Watters, 1996; Henson, 2001).

The pre-service teachers who have been moving through the PDS model over the past two years recognize the field experiences to be valuable. Their early and frequent field experiences made sense to them because these experiences helped to strengthen the connection between theory and practice. Finally, the interns' perceptions of the PDS experience as it relates to the importance of their training can foster a stronger perceived competence toward becoming more effective teachers.

References

Abdal-Haqq, I. (1998). *Professional development schools: Weighing the evidence.* Thousand Oaks, CA: Corwin.

Askins, J, Jacobchik, C., Seabolt, C., Ward, C., Winders, C., Arnold, R. (1999). *A study of pre-service teachers' "use of time" during a physical education (P–6) block experience utilizing a school-based model.* Unpublished manuscript, Western Kentucky University.

Daniel, C., Arnold, R., Whitlock, S., Meadors, W., Crews, T., Deere, R. (2000). *The 21st-century classroom: A collaborative PDS model.* Paper presented at the National Association for Physical Education in Higher Education National Conference, Austin, TX.

Fiorentino, L., Kowalski, E.M. & Barrette, G.T. (1993). SUPPORT-PE: Moving towards collaborative teacher preparation. *Journal of Physical Education, Recreation and Dance,* 76–83.

Ginns, I.S. & Watters, J.J. (1996). *Experiences of novice teachers: Changes in self-efficacy and their beliefs about teaching.* Paper presented at the Annual Meeting of the American Educational Research Association. Retrieved February 11, 2003, from http://www.ericir.syr.edu.

Graham, G. (1988). Collaboration in physical education: A lot like marriage? *Journal of Teaching in Physical Education, 7,* 165–174.

Grisham, D.L., Bergeron, B., Brink, B., Farnan, N., Lenski, S.D., & Meyerson, M.J. (1999). Connecting communities of practice thorough professional development school activities. *Journal of Teacher Education, 50* (3), 182–191.

Guyton, E. & Byrd, D. (Eds.). (2000). *Standards for field experiences in teacher education. Task force on field experience standards.* Reston, VA: Association of Teacher Educators.

Henson, R.K. (2001). *Relationships between preservice teachers' self-efficacy, task analysis, and classroom management belief.* Paper presented at the Annual Meeting of the Southwest Educational Research Association. Retrieved February 11, 2003, from http://www.ericir.syr.edu

Hobbs, S.F., Bullough, R.V., Kauchak, D.P., Crow, N.A., & Stokes, D. (1998). Professional development schools: Catalysts for collaboration and change. *The Clearning House, 72* (1), 47–50.

Holmes Group (1990). *Tomorrow's schools: Principles for the design of professional development schools.* East Lansing, MI: Holmes Group, Inc.

Jablonski, A.M. (1995). *Factors influencing pre-service teachers' end-of-training teaching performance.* Paper presented at the Annual Meeting of the American Educational Research Association. Retrieved February 11, 2003 from http://www.ericir.syr.edu.

Martinek, T.J. & Schempp, P.G. (1988). An introduction to models for collaboration. *Journal of Teaching in Physical Educaton, 7,* 160–164.

National Association for Sport and Physical Education (1995). *National standards for beginning physical education teachers.* Reston, VA: Author.

National Commission on Excellence in Education (1983). *A nation at risk: The imperative for education reform.* Washington, D.C.: U.S. Government Printing Office.

Sharpe, T. (1992). Teacher preparation: A professional development school approach. *Journal of Physical Education, Recreation and Dance, 63,* 82–87.

Williams, H.S. (2001). Student teachers' perceptions of a teacher-training program. *College Student Journal.* Retrieved February 10, 2003 from http:// www.findarticles.com/cf_0/mOFCR/ 1_35/ 74221514/print.jhtml.

Appendix 13.A.

Field Block 1 Survey
Program Feedback by Interns

The purpose of this survey is to gather your thoughts and ideas on your experience in Field Block 1. While I recognize there are changes that will be made to various facets of the program that affect both its structure and function, your feedback will assist me in making program improvements. Please **do not put your name** on this survey, as they are anonymous. Clinical faculty and physical education faculty for future program improvements will review this feedback. *I will not look at these until your final grades are submitted to the Records Office.*

Directions: Please circle only 1 response.

1. Organizing the semester in Rounds 1, 2, and 3 permitted an adequate length of time to see change and progress in the students' skills and my teaching.

1	2	3	4	5
Strongly Disagree	Disagree	Undecided	Agree	Strongly Agree

2. I perceived solo teaching throughout Field Block 1 to positively affect my competence to begin teaching.

1	2	3	4	5
Strongly Disagree	Disagree	Undecided	Agree	Strongly Agree

3. To what extent were university-based learning experiences in your freshmen, sophomore and junior year (i.e. coursework, labs, projects) necessary for your participation in the field block experience?

1	2	3	4	5
Strongly Disagree	Disagree	Undecided	Agree	Strongly Agree

4. To what extent did you feel observation comments from the lessons observed helped you to plan more effective lessons?

1	2	3	4	5
Strongly Disagree	Disagree	Undecided	Agree	Strongly Agree

5. To what extent did you feel accepted by school personnel?

1	2	3	4	5
Strongly Disagree	Disagree	Undecided	Agree	Strongly Agree

6. In your perception, the workroom was useful for your instructional preparation.

1	2	3	4	5
Strongly Disagree	Disagree	Undecided	Agree	Strongly Agree

7. In your perception, the workroom was a valued resource among students in the teaching block.

1	2	3	4	5
Strongly Disagree	Disagree	Undecided	Agree	Strongly Agree

8. The feedback provided by my university supervisor inspired confidence in my teaching.

1	2	3	4	5
Strongly Disagree	Disagree	Undecided	Agree	Strongly Agree

9. To what extent did you find receiving feedback to each stage of the unit plan development process useful when constructing your final unit plan?

1	2	3	4	5
Very Non-useful	Non-useful	Undecided	Useful	Very Useful

10. To what extent did you feel that the clinical faculty respected your stage of development in teacher preparation?

1	2	3	4	5
Very Non-respected	Non-respected	Undecided	Respected	Very Respected

11. To what extent did you find the clinical faculty's feedback helpful?

1	2	3	4	5
Very Non-helpful	Non-helpful	Undecided	Helpful	Very Helpful

12. I found that watching my teaching videotape led to improvements in my instruction.

1	2	3	4	5
Strongly Disagree	Disagree	Undecided	Agree	Strongly Agree

13. The length of time for planning lessons between Tuesday and Thursday was adequate.

1	2	3	4	5
Strongly Disagree	Disagree	Undecided	Agree	Strongly Agree

14. In your perception, to what extent did you feel competent in teaching students in grades K, 1, and 2?

1	2	3	4	5
Very Incompetent	Incompetent	Undecided	Competent	Very Competent

15. In your perception, to what extent did you feel competent teaching students in grades 3, 4, and 5?

1	2	3	4	5
Very Incompetent	Incompetent	Undecided	Competent	Very Competent

16. I felt the university supervisor and clinical faculty member were clear when providing feedback from the Systematic Lesson Observation Form following my teaching.

1	2	3	4	5
Strongly Disagree	Disagree	Undecided	Agree	Strongly Agree

17. Field Bock 1 effectively prepared me to teach elementary physical education.

1	2	3	4	5
Strongly Disagree	Disagree	Undecided	Agree	Strongly Agree

18. The university supervisor's model lessons had a positive impact on my confidence as a pre-service teacher to try a new teaching style.

1	2	3	4	5
Strongly Disagree	Disagree	Undecided	Agree	Strongly Agree

19. To what extent did you agree with the university supervisor or clinical faculty member's post-lesson feedback?

1	2	3	4	5
Strongly Disagree	Disagree	Undecided	Agree	Strongly Agree

20. The university supervisor's model lessons had a positive impact on my confidence as a teacher to implement new activities.

1	2	3	4	5
Strongly Disagree	Disagree	Undecided	Agree	Strongly Agree

21. To what extent were my post-lesson observation conferences based on undisturbed observations (free of distractions) of my teaching presentations.

1	2	3	4	5
Strongly Disagree	Disagree	Undecided	Agree	Strongly Agree

22. Please provide any comments/ suggestions that may be helpful for program improvement:

CHAPTER 14 *Jane E. Neapolitan & Terry R. Berkeley*

Inquiry in Professional Development Schools
The "Misunderstood" Component

In *Tomorrow's Schools of Education* (1995), the Holmes Group emphasized *improvement-oriented inquiry* as one of the basic commitments for establishing Professional Development Schools. Schools of education "should (1) integrate faculty from schools, school districts, and other educational settings into the research and development activities of the school of education; (2) create opportunities for faculty research in a variety of field settings affiliated with the school of education; and (3) create opportunities for faculty research in collaboration with field-based practitioners" (p. 82). PDS research embodies, by its complex nature, multiple purposes, multiple outcomes, and multiple experiences. Although PDS partnerships have been in existence for about 15 years, collaborative inquiry or "impact research" (Teitel, 2000) has remained the least understood and utilized function of PDS.

The Standards for Professional Development Schools (NCATE, 2001) uphold that inquiry "is the process through which professional and student learning are integrated" (p. 4). This key concept is imbedded in the standards. Inquiry helps sustain the other PDS functions of teacher preparation, professional development, and student learning. At standard, "inquiry is used routinely at an individual classroom, departmental, and school-wide level (at school and university) to inform decisions about which approaches to teaching and learning work best" (p. 17). In a "leading" PDS, "sustained collaborative inquiry into improved learning for P–12 students is at the center of the partnership's vision and practices" (p. 17).

However, the road to *creating mutual understanding and capacity for inquiry* in a PDS can stretch the limits of a partnership. In his role as a department chair and faculty member, Terry Berkeley, co-author of this chapter, has seen how the form and context of PDS is constantly appearing and disappearing. In her role as a research liaison and university supervisor of teacher candidates, co-author Jane Neapolitan has experienced some of the shortcomings of conducting research in a PDS. These include limited knowledge and experience for using multiple research methods, paradigms, and traditions; lack of clarity about the purpose, goals, and outcomes of PDS research; and control over findings and their dissemination. Because these are considered "back-stage" issues about doing PDS work, it is not surprising that NCATE views inquiry as "the function to get least attention" (NCATE, 2001, p. 4). In a PDS, the professional roles of university faculty are transformed into work that is countercultural. This work "asks participants to let go of important beliefs, significant allegiances, and deeply ingrained practices" (Trachtman, 1997, p. 190). Thus, the extent to which players in a PDS relationship can become "insiders" is critical to implementing and sustaining the depth of inquiry suggested in the PDS standards. Without the resources of time, space, people, and money (National Commission on Teaching & America's Future, 1996), implementing and sustaining inquiry may be only an illusion.

In this chapter, a case of an elementary school that participated in the NCATE PDS Standards Field Test Project (1999–2001) is presented. Jane served as the principal investigator and NCATE research liaison for an inquiry project that examined the school's understanding of performance-based assessment (the school's focus). The project is described from "front-stage" and "back-stage" perspectives, weaving together documentation from the project's report with personal reflections made during the experience. Next, the case is discussed against broader issues for implementing and sustaining inquiry in PDS. These include the commitment of participants within a system of appearing and disappearing variables, conflicting priorities in a climate of national testing and accountability, and the role of leadership in a complex relationship.

Tying Together Teacher Education and Student Learning

Front-Stage Story

In October 1999, Jane began working with a school-university team at the PDS to explore the viability of conducting systematic inquiry for the NCATE PDS Standards Field Test Project (1998–2001). The NCATE project included 20 PDS sites in the United States, representing a variety of partnerships at different stages of development. Participation in the project included a self-study conducted by the PDS, an inquiry project that reflected the goals of the partnership, and a site visit to the PDS by a team of national experts.

The PDS was a large suburban elementary school on a commercial corridor in northwest Baltimore County, Maryland. The PDS was a Title I school with an enrollment of approximately 700 racially and ethnically diverse students, in preschool through fifth grade. During its partnership with Towson University, the PDS consistently improved its scores on the Maryland School Performance Assessment Program (MSPAP). (MSPAP was administered for the last time in May 2002, and was replaced by the Maryland State Assessment).

As part of its school improvement plan, the PDS had concentrated all of its professional development for in-service and pre-service teachers on designing and implementing performance-based assessment (PBA) in reading and writing. Because the school had devoted so much of its new energies on PBA, the school-university team (consisting of the assistant principal, several mentor-teachers, the university department chair and the associate dean) agreed that the inquiry project for NCATE should focus on some aspect of performance assessment as well.

The inquiry project entitled, "Tying Together Teacher Education and Student Learning," was an examination of how some of the partnership's performance assessment activities "impacted" children, teacher candidates, and mentor-teachers in the school. The inquiry focused more on the understanding of performance assessment and less on the technical aspects of it. It was a micro-ethnographic study in which multiple and varied sources of data for qualitative analyses were used, including written reflections and focus groups with teacher candidates and mentors, and interviews with children. The following were examined: (1) the level of understanding about performance assessment held by teacher candidates; (2) the ways in which collaboration on performance assessment and instruction affect the knowledge, skills, and attitudes (KSAs) of both mentor-teachers and teacher candidates; and (3) the effects on students resulting from collaboration between mentor-teachers and teacher candidates.

Participants in the study consisted of three convenience samples in spring 2000. These included 15 undergraduate interns (white females, ages ranging from 20 to 35), five mentor-teachers (two minority females and three white females with a range of 10 to 20 years teaching experience), five students from Grade 3 (three minority males, one minority female, and one white female), and four students from Grade 5 (one white male, two minority females and one white female).

Findings from the inquiry project suggested that teacher candidates developed their understandings of performance assessment through co-learning experiences with other candidates, mentor-teachers, university professors, and children. The strong emphasis on staff development for designing and implementing performance assessments was clear. The teacher candidates viewed their learning as meta-cognition, in which they were "weaned from their teachers" in order to perform independently. They understood why they implemented certain technical aspects of performance assessment, and related those "whys" to broader issues of instruction, classroom management, and developing a personal teaching style. The underlying impetus for these understandings was the preparation of children to perform well on MSPAP.

Back-Stage Story

Having the chance to carry out a micro-ethnographic study in a PDS (with funding to support it, no less!) was a qualitative researcher's dream come true. Jane's wish list for transcription costs, qualitative-data analysis software, a graduate research assistant, and course release time had all been granted. Little did she know, however, that coming into the PDS in the middle of the school year as an outsider would bring complications for getting the project started.

In her e-mail journal, Jane wrote to a researcher friend:

I wondered if any of the other sites were having difficulty getting their mentor-teachers to participate in their inquiry projects? As of last week, I had only three out of 15 mentors give their consent. Apparently, most of them objected to writing a one-page weekly reflection on their teaching. Same old excuse of "not having enough time" was given. I went back to them and said, one paragraph, if that would make it better. I haven't checked yet to see if any more have agreed to participate.

Because I'm new I realize that I haven't had a chance to establish "trust and rapport" with the mentors yet. I also have a hunch that this new focus on THEIR teaching (and by a newcomer, no less) is making them uneasy. Your suggestions or comments on this would be appreciated. (March 6, 2000)

The researcher friend replied:

It seems to me that you and your colleagues are experiencing some of the "challenges" associated with conducting inquiry. It takes a while for practitioners to agree to collect information. And then it might take even longer for them to use the results of their data collections and analysis. My guess is that this activity becomes especially tricky when participants feel as though the decision to "collect information" about a new initiative is not part of the initial agreement to try something new. At your PDS, mentors may feel as though your request related to this inquiry represent additional work that was not part of their Summer Institute planning process (the June 1999 Institute described in your proposal).

It may be prudent to scale back your inquiry and focus on the ways in which participants are engaging in the assessment of teacher candidates with the new performance-based instruments. Since the mentors agreed to assess the candidates in this way, you would not be asking them to do additional work. Further, you would not be asking them to examine the ways in which they are using performance-based assessment with the children in their classes. In this way, you would be asking the teachers to participate in an inquiry process that for them is less risky, less time-consuming, and more connected to what they believe is their role. (March 9, 2000)

After reading these comments, Jane realized she could no longer operate in a bubble when she was at the PDS. One of her key challenges for becoming an insider was to learn to take the perspective of a classroom teacher again—something she had not done in 25 years. She had to re-examine her expectations and focus more on the process of the work rather than on the final product. Making decisions jointly and collaboratively was key to becoming an insider.

Jane wrote back:

Regarding your comments about how the mentor-teachers might be feeling right now— I think you're right about the part of their possibly feeling threatened. Until now, the focus at [the PDS] has been on the teacher candidates. As you said, it's part of the PDS agreement. However, what was proposed for our inquiry project goes beyond that. Only a couple of teachers were included in the steering committee's discussion of what our focus should be. . . . What confounds the situation is that I'm new at [the school]. Due to my involvement with the NCATE project, I'm now supervising interns there (along with a colleague from my department who has worked there for the past year and is "easing me" into the new context.) I think if I had already established some previous track record of trust and rapport with the mentors, things may have turned out differently.

Good news, though, is that three more mentors gave their consent today! The principal also told me that he's "talking it up" with them and that some more will come around. As a newcomer to [the PDS], it seems to me that that is the culture of the place, and if I'm patient and we all get to know each other better, things will begin to play out differently. (March 9, 2000)

A couple of weeks later, Jane wrote to her researcher friend:

Although only six out of the 15 mentor teachers decided to participate in the project, I'm feeling better about it now. By having a dialogue with the teachers, I hope to give them a chance to think more deeply about their teaching and experience as a mentor.

My colleague who has been the university supervisor at [the PDS] for the past year (my "key informant") pointed out that many of the veteran teachers have not experienced the "reflective practitioner" model that new teachers have experienced. My guess is that having to write something about their teaching may be pretty scary for the older teachers. With that in mind, I'm going to take the time to write back to them every week in order to provide additional support. (March 17, 2000)

The researcher replied:

After reading your note a second time this morning what struck me was the part where you indicated that you will be "writing back" to the teachers weekly. I believe that the teachers will welcome your engagement; in fact, given the minimal feedback that most teachers receive, your input may be critical to them. I know that PDS participants sometimes provide this kind of feedback to each other, but that is not always the case in busy schools. Further, most folks continue to be reluctant to exchange ideas with each other in a regular and systematic way. (March 20, 2000)

Front-Stage Story

Mentor-teachers at the PDS had a slightly different take on performance assessment than did their less-experienced teacher-candidate partners. Although they praised the process of learning how to use performance assessments side-by-side with the teacher candidates, they did not focus so much on technical aspects. Instead, the mentor-teachers were more concerned about learner differences when using performance assessments. Like the master teachers they were, the mentors analyzed their experience with performance assessments more critically, and with an eye toward helping *all* children learn. In addition, the mentor-teachers were concerned about the resources needed to effectively implement performance assessments. Obtaining and purchasing materials for activities such as making pancakes or carving pumpkins required resources that went beyond buying typical school supplies. Finally, mentor-teachers took ownership of learning how to use performance assessments. They felt responsible for the real-world effects of the assessments on their students, especially children with diverse backgrounds and needs.

Back-Stage Story

Jane's position in the PDS as a researcher was endorsed at the political level by virtue of the school's agreement to participate in the NCATE project. However, her acceptance as an insider at the personal and professional levels still had a long way to go. After several months of planning the inquiry project, partly with others in the PDS and partly alone, she was still uneasy in her relationships with the teachers. During the data-collection phase of the research project, she learned she would become the university supervisor of the teacher candidates for the following year. The success of this new role would be predicated upon her becoming an insider (or not) over the next few months. In order to do a good job of supervising teacher candidates in the next phase of her PDS work, Jane first had to make sure that teachers found her to be a trustworthy colleague in their eyes.

Jane wrote to her researcher friend:

> Things are going better now for me at [the PDS]. Although there are only five mentor-teachers doing the weekly reflections for the inquiry project, I think people are beginning to see me as an ally and a support for them. I think part of what I'm experiencing is that the university supervisors have never really worked with the mentor-teachers in a supervisory or consultative way. In other words, mentor-teachers may take a grad course taught by a university supervisor, but they do not necessarily look upon the university person as one who would be a friendly critic or consultant to them.
>
> There are two modes, I think at [the school]: university supervisors supervise [teacher candidates] and teach graduate courses. That's it. Three-way conversations with the mentor-teachers, teacher candidates, and university faculty only occur when there is

a problem with the student teacher—it is not part of the standard procedure. Thus, my "intervention" as friendly critic or consultant has now changed that dynamic, at least for a few. (April 11, 2000)

A turning point occurred when Jane obtained permission to interview some children for the inquiry project. It was a collaborative effort on the part of the site coordinator (assistant principal), the third- and fifth-grade teachers, and the district's director of assessment and accountability. Within a few days, the teachers had obtained the necessary permissions from parents, and the district office supported the project.

Jane shared her feeling of triumph with her researcher friend:

Last week I conducted two focus groups for the project. One with third graders and one with fifth graders. Both groups had recently taken the MSPAP tests (performance assessments). With the help of the PDS coordinator, I devised some questions that basically asked the children to tell me what they had learned about doing certain performances in reading and writing. Frankly, neither she nor I are experts on the topic because we don't teach it, but we put the questions together as best we could. Also, the Director of Assessment and Accountability for [the county] wanted to see the questions in writing. The questions were approved post haste.

The interesting thing that happened during the actual focus groups was that the mentor-teacher [who worked with non-tenured teachers in the building] agreed to be with me while I interviewed the children. . . . As I started interviewing the third graders, it was apparent that my questions to them were not clear because they asked me for clarification. I deferred to the mentor-teacher, who in turn, did an excellent job of interviewing the children! She skillfully reworded the questions which the PDS coordinator and I had so crudely put together! It was amazing to witness because, suddenly, the research was really becoming COLLABORATIVE!!!

In addition, the PDS coordinator popped in to observe the conversation and added some of her questions and comments. Because both of them know the children and the kinds of activities that were done this year, they did a good job of using "kid friendly" terminology that elicited fuller responses from the children.

My wish is that the teachers will engage in some form of action research that will help open their eyes to the cultural aspects of performance assessment. . . . Because there is so much emphasis on how to design and implement a PBA, emphasis on child development, learning and motivation is often overlooked. I know that this is especially true for the teacher candidates. Although they are very skilled in writing the assessments as beginning teachers, their implementation of the assessments belies their lack of expertise in motivating the children and sustaining that motivation for a long period of time (which the assessments require). (June 5, 2000)

Front-Stage Story

Overall, the NCATE inquiry project work suggested there was interdependency for learning within and among the three groups of mentor-teachers, teacher candidates, and students at the PDS. Teacher candidates (referred to by the children as "the Towson teachers") enabled the students to recover their learning through one-on-one assistance in classrooms. Students, like their adult counterparts in the school, learned that if they "messed up," they would be given multiple opportunities to re-learn and re-do important information and skills. Thus, there was substantial evidence that a synergy existed between the high level of collaboration and learning at the PDS. The question remained, however, as to what resources would sustain the synergy, especially in a context of diverse learners.

Back-Stage Story

In her third year at the PDS, the excitement of the NCATE Project had passed and Jane settled into her teaching and supervision duties. During that summer, the principal's mother died, and Jane attended the funeral services with the other teachers and staff. There was a feeling of closeness as everyone shared in the principal's loss. On that occasion, Jane realized she had become a "true" member of the school's staff because she saw herself and the others saw her in a new light. This had nothing to do with joint decision-making, collaboration, or inquiry. Rather, it was a moment in time when respect and caring for each other was manifested publicly and was carried beyond the schoolhouse.

When she returned to the PDS in the fall, Jane felt that she had become an insider at a very personal level. On a professional level, she was also becoming more of an insider. By working with the site coordinator to schedule a series of meetings held during school hours, the teachers and administrators began to take a more active role in planning collaborative activities. These included the teacher candidates' portfolio review, a service-learning project, and an action-research project. Teachers' participation in the action research, however, would remain peripheral for the foreseeable future.

Discussion

The front-stage and back-stage stories of the PDS inquiry project presented here demonstrate how the form and context of PDS is based upon a system of variables. These include understanding schools, spending time in schools, and determining the professional development needs of teachers, administrators, and staff. While addressing the challenge of providing the means to meet those needs, the PDS is systematically preparing new teachers for initial certification and, finally, meeting PDS standards. This state of affairs is what Bullough and his colleagues (1996) have deemed as the "messy, context-sensitive, and dynamic and unpredictable nature of PDS work" (as cited in Berry & Boles, 1998, p. 122).

PDS work is labor intensive. This is work requiring a significant commitment on the part of school personnel. The main returns for their efforts are the tangibility and intangibility of expanded professional development opportunities, and their satisfaction with "seeing" that teachers newly entering the field are trained well. They gain satisfaction from taking on responsibilities for the mentoring of those students in addition to the teaching they do. This work is made even more difficult given the current environment of accountability, the introduction and adoption of new curricula, methods, and philosophical approaches to teaching a variety of subjects, and other pressures brought on by higher-level administrators, parents, and the greater community.

It is not surprising that so few mentor-teachers were willing to participate in the NCATE inquiry project described in this case. Although the inquiry was aligned with the school's professional development goals, teachers felt it went beyond their work agreement for the year. Teachers were not fully included in either the process or the topic of choice, further hindering their interest. The offer of stipends was not a motivating factor, either. In a review of the PDS literature, Teitel (1998) writes:

> Some of the challenges facing PDS inquiry include defining teacher participation in research as something other than scaled-down university faculty research (Kennedy, 1990) and sorting out what appropriate differentiated roles might be, given the differing interests with which school-based and university-based faculty come (Stoddart, 1993). Rafferty (1994) notes that powerful forces make it hard to develop true collaborative research projects. True collaboration is harder because of different perceptions of what is useful as well as different perceptions of status. (p. 48)

Through this experience, teachers were found to relate more readily to "inquiry as teaching and learning" (Berry & Boles, 1998), rather than "inquiry in PDS," such as case studies, action research, and curriculum development. When inquiry as teaching and learning helps to provide technical assistance in a specific area, for example, teachers see its immediate value as it relates to working with students. This could be due, in part, to the skills-driven nature of professional development and the current emphasis on state and national testing. As one teacher in the PDS network stated, "The needs of our children come first, improving their test scores second, and systematic action research projects are lower in priority" (Berkeley, 2003). This prompts the question: What is more important to a school—technical support or research?

Another threat to inquiry is that the small state grants (under the state reform known as Maryland's "Redesign of Teacher Education") in which support was provided for the development and early implementation of the PDS, disappeared with no funding at the state or local level forthcoming (unless there is to be a marked and dramatic change in support through No Child Left Behind). Even the federal Eisenhower program guidelines have been changed. The priority of assisting the support for professional development efforts in populations that have been historically under-represented has acceded to the new, "highly qualified" requirement. Therefore, the preparation of new teachers is precluded to assist development activities for practicing teachers and school staff.

So, what is the incentive to engage in inquiry with these competing demands? Often, university faculty members are told by school staff in the most respectful of ways, "I do not have time to do action research and inquiry. If I do it, it will take additional time." This type of response is understandable in a field in which there is an expectation of having to do more with less. School staffs know that, in other fields, additional time means additional pay. The appearance and disappearance of funding support is an issue. One can talk around professional obligation, a new era with its sense of entitlement, the advancing of the field of education, but somehow, this pales in light of the appearance of new realities and other obligations.

Finally, the school leadership that is guiding PDS efforts has much to do with how far along PDS efforts can move. The role of the principal is important for sustaining the PDS effort on a continuing basis. This also pertains to the impetus for ongoing and collaborative inquiry. In the case of the PDS that participated in the NCATE project, inquiry frequently appeared and disappeared in various manifestations during the partnership's development. The "back-stage story" related by the university research liaison reveals the transformative and personal journey of becoming a PDS insider. Yet collaborative inquiry (inquiry "within" PDS) requires the endorsement and active support of the school's principal. This commitment to collaborative inquiry can be thwarted when a principal's "administrative and teaching skills that have distinguished the principal from other teachers and contributed to his advancement in the school's hierarchical system may prevent the principal from working comfortably and effectively in a collaborative inquiry group" (Dickens, 2000, p. 34).

When all is said and done, however, the personal experience of doing PDS work continues to be a satisfying one. There is a belief that inquiry, regularly accomplished, benefits everyone in a partnership. Can inquiry, then, occur on a regular basis?

The answer from this perspective is, "Perhaps." Respect for the school and university professionals engaged in PDS work needs to be ongoing, and made an important part of the enterprise. There is a need for more resources (as described by the National Commission on Teaching & America's Future), fewer competing priorities, recognized understanding of PDS, and support for PDS by school superintendents. Schools, colleges, and universities need to be seen moving in similar directions toward understanding what occurs at the street level in schools. School personnel need to recognize and support the crucial role that colleges and universities play in the professional preparation of educators.

In the meantime, there will be a delightful struggle in meeting the challenges associated with PDS work. In reality, if there is magic in PDS work, it may be in the constant, continual communications over great amounts of time that demonstrates respect and caring among the partners. Somehow, it seems, this is quite a good place to be.

References

Berkeley, T. (2003, March). *The constancy of changing: Maintaining form when all around us is different.* Paper presented at the Ethnography in Education Research Forum, Philadelphia, PA.

Berry, B. & Boles, K. (1998). Inquiry and professional development schools. In Lauter, N. (Ed.), *Professional development schools: Confronting realities.* New York: The National Center for Restructuring Education, Schools, and Teaching.

Bullough, R., Kaucheak, D., Crow, N., Hobbs, S., & Stokes, D. (1996, April). *Teacher and school change in professional development schools: A cross case analysis of seven elementary and secondary school programs.* Paper presented at the Annual Meeting of the American Educational Research Association, New York, NY.

Dickens, C. (2000). Too valuable to be rejected, too different to be embraced: A critical review of school/university collaboration. In Johnston, Brosnan, Cramer, & Dove (Eds.), *Collaborative reform and other improbable dreams.* Albany, NY: SUNY Press.

Holmes Group (1995). *Tomorrow's schools of education.* East Lansing, MI: Author.

National Commission on Teaching & America's Future (1996). *What matters most: Teaching for America's Future.* New York: Author.

National Council for Accreditation of Teacher Education (2001). *Standards for professional development schools.* Washington, DC: Author.

Teitel, L. (2000). *Assessing the impacts of professional development schools.* Washington, DC: American Association of Colleges of Teacher Education.

Teitel, L. (1998). Professional development schools: A literature review. In Levine, M. (Ed.), *Designing standards that work.* Washington, DC: National Council for Accreditation of Teacher Education.

Trachtman, R. (1997). The stories of insiders. In M. Levine & R. Trachtman (Eds.), *Making professional development schools work: Politics, practice, and policy* (pp. 185-193). New York: Teachers College Press.

Contributors

Terry R. Berkeley is professor and chair of the Department of Early Childhood Education at Towson University, where he has developed numerous partnerships. These partnerships are an outgrowth of his doctoral work at Harvard University, his university teaching, and local service, which all focus on the building of community. He is co-editor of *Ensuring Safe School Environments: Exploring Issues, Seeking Solutions* (2003), and *Traditions, Standards, and Transformations: A Model for Professional Development School Networks* (2004), published by Peter Lang.

Jennifer E. Aldrich is a faculty member in the Department of Curriculum and Instruction at Central Missouri State University. She is a PDS coordinator and professor for the on-site Early Childhood Curriculum course taught to college seniors. In Fall 2002, she collaborated with faculty and administration to begin the first PDS in her department.

Andrew Bennett is professor in the Department of Mathematics at Kansas State University. He earned a Ph.D. in Mathematics from Princeton University in 1985 and has been at Kansas State University since 1988. Over the past 15 years he has been a participant and/or director in five different collaboratives working with Professional Development Schools.

Lisa Bietau is an elementary-level teacher with the Manhattan-Ogden School District. She has taught primary, intermediate, and upper-level elementary including multi-age classes. She has been a mentor-teacher, a clinical instructor, a teacher-in-residence, and an instructor with the Kansas State University PDS Partnership since 1989.

John R. Bing, associate professor of education in the Seidel School of Education and Professional Studies at Salisbury University, is the Title II project director and PDS coordinator at Delmar/North Salisbury Elementary Schools in Salisbury, MD.

James S. Cantor is associate professor in the Teacher Education Department at California State University, Dominguez Hills. He serves as University Coordinator for PDS by coordinating communication with all partners and participants in order to ensure faithful implementation of the teacher-credentialing program.

Mary Gendernalik Cooper, Ph.D., is professor and dean of the School of Education, Georgia Southwestern State University. She has fourteen years of experience leading university-school collaboratives, seven of which have been devoted to designing, implementing, and evaluating standards-based Professional Development School networks.

Diane Davis, associate professor, serves as the PDS coordinator at the College of Notre Dame, Baltimore. Her role is to assist the operations of the various PDSs within the CND PDS partnerships.

Carol Frierson-Campbell, assistant professor of music education, teaches in music education and research at William Paterson University. As the music coordinator for WPU's Professional Development School partnership, she works with music teachers from three urban school districts in northern New Jersey to improve opportunities for professional development, collegiality, and pre-service music education.

Teena R. Gorrow, assistant professor of education in the Seidel School of Education and Professional Studies at Salisbury University, is the former coordinator of the PDS Program and chair of the Regional Professional Development Schools Committee at Salisbury University in Salisbury, MD. She is also a former central office administrator, principal, and teacher in Maryland's public schools.

Melisa Hancock is teacher-in-residence at Kansas State University in Manhattan, Kansas. Her experience is in 5th and 6th grades, and she currently works with teachers in districts throughout Kansas in providing professional development to improve mathematics instruction in grades K–8. She serves on the leadership team for Professional Development Schools and has been involved in action research for many years.

Carl Holmes is an elementary-school physical-education teacher for the Cuba–Rushford School District in Cuba, NY, and is also a clinical faculty member for the St. Bonaventure University's Elementary Physical Education Professional Development School. He has been teaching and coaching for more than 23 years. He holds B.S. and M.Ed. degrees in Physical Education from Houghton College.

Betty Kansler is the College of Notre Dame's PDS liaison for Baltimore Highlands Elementary School in Baltimore County, MD. She taught an action research course for school faculty interested in participating in the inquiry process. Research projects were based on the ASCD/MASCD research project that used Robert Marzano's book, *Classroom Instruction That Works*. Ms. Kansler also teachers courses and supervises interns for the College of Notre Dame.

Dennis R. King, assistant professor of education at the University of Maine, serves as the Penobscot River Educational Partnership/Professional Development Network's University liaison to School Union 90. He teaches undergraduate classes in curriculum, instruction, and foundations, and works with school personnel to prepare teacher candidates to enter the teaching profession as reflective educators who are proficient in the state and national standards for beginning teachers.

Clare Kruft is the former interim director of teacher education at Loyola College in Maryland, where she served as the college coordinator for two elementary professional development schools. She is currently taking two years to return to teaching at the elementary level, to regain the perspective of a daily instructional decision-maker in this time of increased accountability for all.

Marsha Levine is a senior consultant for professional development schools for the National Council for Accreditation of Teacher Education, where she directed a six-year project to design and field test standards for these innovative institutions. The NCATE PDS Standards and assessment process are being used in PDS partnerships throughout the country. She is the author of numerous publications, including *Professional Practice Schools: Linking Teacher Education to School Reform* (1992), and co-editor of *Making Professional Development Schools Work: Politics, Practice, and Policy* (1997).

Marybeth P. Miller, associate professor of Physical Education at St. Bonaventure University, is a university supervisor for the Elementary Physical Education Field Block PDS. Her action research focuses upon early-childhood physical-education service learning as it relates to teacher education preparation and inclusive learning processes involving young children. She holds a Ph.D. in Motor Development from the University of Pittsburgh.

Martha M. Mobley directs the Teaching Performance Center within the College of Education at Kean University, Union, NJ. Her responsibilities include oversight of more than 1,100 field placements each semester and the implementation of 16 standards-based professional development schools, six of which are in Abbott or special-needs districts.

Jane E. Neapolitan is associate professor in the Department of Elementary Education at Towson University. She earned an Ed.D. in Curriculum and Teaching from Teachers College, Columbia University in 1994. She currently serves as director of the Institute for Professional Development School Studies at Towson University and is co-editor of *Traditions, Standards, and Transformations: A Model for Professional Development Schools* (2004), published by Peter Lang.

Nancy Norris-Bauer is director of the Office of Field Experiences at William Paterson University, where she is responsible for 1,200 student placements per year and related professional development for students, clinical instructors, and cooperating teachers. Her role includes working closely with professional development schools that are preferred placement sites and the location of onsite field experience seminars.

Patricia Rawson is an elementary-school physical-education teacher for the Cuba-Rushford School District in Cuba, NY, and is also a clinical faculty member of the St. Bonaventure University Elementary Physical Education Professional Development School. She has more than 35 years of teaching and coaching experience and is currently head coach of the Cuba-Rushford girl's varsity volleyball and softball teams. She holds B.S. and M.Ed. degrees in Physical Education from SUNY Brockport.

Cherie L. Roy, first-grade teacher at the Lewis Libby School in Milford, Maine, serves as a teacher representative for School Union 90 on the Teacher Education Committee of the Penobscot River Educational Partnership/Professional Development Network. She is an experienced mentor-teacher and works with teacher candidates in the College of Education and Human Development at the University of Maine during their field experiences and internships (clinical experiences).

Sue A. Schaar is associate professor of Education at California State University Dominguez Hills with an Ed.D. from Teachers College, Columbia University, in Education of the Gifted. She is also the co-director of a FIPSE grant, a collaborative effort among CSUDH, the California Commission on Teacher Credentialing, Los Angeles Unified School District, and three smaller urban districts. The project identifies emergency permit teachers and provides services that expedite the credentialing process as well as builds a database for providing credentialed teachers for Los Angeles–area classrooms.

Gail Shroyer is professor of education at Kansas State University and a director of the KSU PDS Partnership. She is a science educator and former high-school science teacher who has been involved in PDS work since 1989.

Jo Ellen Smallwood is director of Professional Development Schools for Hood College, MD, which has partnerships with both Frederick County Public Schools and Montgomery County Public Schools.

Roberta Strosnider is professor of special education and director of the Elementary Education and Special Education Integrated Program of Towson University held at Shady Grove, MD. She serves as PDS liaison to four elementary and two middle schools in Montgomery Public Schools. She has served as department chair of the Education Department at Hood College and received a doctorate from Virginia Polytechnic Institute and State University.

Frank Sweeney is associate professor and chair of the Education Department at Hood College in Frederick, MD. He holds a Ph.D. (1985) in Curriculum and Instruction from the University of Maryland, College Park. Prior to his present position as chair, he was director of Professional Development Schools for Hood College, where he provided leadership for initiating and establishing partnerships with local school systems.

Lee Teitel is professor of educational leadership and former associate dean for Community, University, and School Partnerships at the University of Massachusetts at Boston. He has been active in understanding and promoting Professional Development Schools since 1989 and has spoken and written extensively about PDS startup, development, assessment, and leadership issues. His most recent book is *The Professional Development Schools Handbook: Starting, Sustaining, and Assessing Partnerships That Improve Student Learning* (2003).

Roberta Trachtman is president of Allenwood Company, an education consulting firm in the northeast. She and her colleagues work with teachers, schools, districts, and universities to help participants evaluate their teacher preparation programs and practices in order to improve them. Company associates use both qualitative and quantitative methodologies to help people help themselves and improve their programs.

Linda Williams is a teacher-mentor at Kenwood High School PDS and was instrumental in developing a yearlong action research project for interested teachers at Kenwood High School PDS, Baltimore County, MD. Ms. Williams also serves on the PDS Coordinating Council.

RaeAnn T. Wuestman, associate professor at the College of Notre Dame, serves as PDS liaison for Longfellow and Northfield Elementary PDSs in Howard County,

MD. She implemented the action research project and served as the instructor for GEDU 604. She is also a Service Learning Fellow at CND and teaches a variety of graduate courses with the Department of Education.

Sally Yahnke is associate professor in Secondary Education at Kansas State University. She serves as the co-coordinator for the KSU PDS Partnership working with elementary and secondary clinical instructors from five partnership districts across Kansas.

Index

action research, 52, 61–62
    differentiated, 154–64
Adelphi University, 166
Allen, R., 79
American Association for the Advancement of Science, 129
A Nation at Risk, 37
Apprentice Assessment, 133
assessment, 127–29
    analysis and, 138–39
    evaluation, inquiry, and, 139–40
    performance, 129–35
    process, 135–37
    program, 137–38
Association of Childhood Education International, 129
Association of Supervision and Curriculum Development, 56
AT&T Foundation, 98
Auburn University, 58

Baltimore Highlands Elementary School, 158
Berkeley, T., 179
Bing, J., 81
Bolman, L. G., 47, 48, 52
Boreen, J., 87
Bullough, R., 186

California Commission on Teacher Credentialing, 4

California Preliminary Multiple Subject Teaching Credential, 6
California Standards for the Teaching Profession, 13
California State University Dominguez Hills (CSUDH), 3, 5, 9
Carnegie Forum on Education and the Economy, 37, 38
Clark, R., 38
Classroom Instruction That Works, 80, 154, 158
Coalition Music Teachers, 68
collaboration
    K–16 education reform and, 21–23
    learning communities and, 59–60
    Professional Development schools and, 55–56
    public school–university, 39–40, 165
    systematic change through, 56–57
collaborative inquiry, 179
College of Notre Dame of Maryland, 153, 154–62, 163
Conkling, S. W., 69
Connected Mathematics, 32
Core Curriculum Content Standards for the Visual and Performing Arts (NJ), 70, 76
Criterion Reference Competency Test, 135
Cuba Elementary School (New York), 167

Darling-Hammond, L., 37, 84
Deal, T. E., 47, 48, 52
DeCarbo, N. J., 75

Delandshere, G., 140
differentiated action research, 154-62
DuFour, R., 57

Eaker, R., 57
early-childhood education and PDSs, 40-42, 42-43
Eastman School of Music, 69
Educational Leadership, 56
educational reform
  PDS and, 21-23, 28-34
Essential Dimensions of Teaching, 61

Fiese, R. K., 75
Finan, E. C., 43
Freeman, D., 101
Fulghum, R., 64

Gill, H., 85, 86
Going in Circles, 80
Gorrow, T., 81

Harvard University, 129
Henry, W., 69
Holmes Group, 21, 22, 37, 38, 68, 165, 179
  guidelines for PDSs, 57-58
Hood College, 83, 84, 85, 86, 89

impact research, 179
improvement-oriented inquiry, 179
inquiry, 179-80, 186-88
  teacher education, student learning, and, 180-86
INTASC/Conceptual Framework Principles, 132, 133, 138
Interstate New Teacher Assessment and Support Consortium, 61, 129
Investigations in Numbers, Data, and Space, 32

Kansas State University Professional Development School Partnership, 22-23
  continued professional development and, 23
  new teachers and, 23
  organizational impact, 27-28
  practice-based inquiry and, 24
  PDS impact on, 28-34
  research framework of PDS, 26-27
  simultaneous improvement process and, 24
  support of children's learning and, 23-24
Kenwood High School (Maryland), 153, 156, 157

Kochan, F. K., 58, 61
Kunkel, R. C., 58, 61

Learning Coalition, 58
Levine, M., 56
literature circles, 79-80, 80-81
Los Angeles Educational Partnership, 3, 9
Los Angeles Unified School District (LAUSD), 3, 5-6, 9, 17
  admission to PDS program in, 9-10
  difficulties of PDS program in, 7-9
  participants in PDS in, 7
  roles and responsibilities of, 6-7
Loyola College (Maryland), 59, 60, 61, 62-63, 66

Maine's Beginning Teacher Standards, 145
Marshall, C. S., 38, 84
Maryland Association for Supervision and Curriculum Development, 158, 162
Maryland Professional Development Schools Standards, 59
Maryland School Performance Assessment Program, 181
Marzano, R. J., 79, 80, 154, 158
Master Teacher Evaluation, 135
mentoring, 62-63, 83-85, 89-92, 92-93, 185
  training program for interns, 86-89
  training program for mentors, 85-86
Minner, S., 38
Modern Approaches to Understanding and Managing Organizations, 47
Morrison, K. L., 84
music education, 67-68, 68-71, 72-73, 73-74, 75-76, 76-77
Music Education Association, 77

National Association for the Education of Young Children, 129
National Board for Professional Teaching Standards, 25, 145
National Commission on Excellence in Education, 37, 165
National Commission on Teaching and America's Future, 188
National Council for Accreditation of Teacher Education (NCATE), 26, 27, 38, 39, 72, 97, 98, 99, 102, 105, 120, 128, 144, 180
  standards of, 41
National Council for Accreditation of Teacher Education 2000 Standards, 128, 141, 179

Index • 199

National Council for the Social Sciences, 129
National Council of Teachers of English, 129
National Council of Teachers of Mathematics, 129
National Middle School Association, 129
National Science Teachers Association, 129
National Standards for Beginning Physical Education, 173
Neapolitan, J., 180
networking, 57-58, 59, 61-62
New England Accreditation of Schools and Colleges, 145
New Jersey Music Education Association, 71
New Jersey State Teacher Quality Enhancement Consortium, 67, 70
New Jersey Teacher Enhancement Consortium, 77
No Child Left Behind, 60, 154, 187
Norton, P., 80

Odell, S., 85
Ohio State University, 69

Peer Coaching, 33
Peer Consultation process, 25
Penobscot River Educational Partnership/Professional Development Network, 143
    description of, 144
    goals of, 145
    portfolios, 145
performance-based assessment, 181
physical education, 165-66, 166-67, 169-73
Pickering, D. J., 79, 80, 154, 158
Pollock, J. E., 79, 80, 154, 158
practice-based inquiry, 24
Prater, G., 38
PRAXIS II exam, 134
Professional Development Plans, 146
Professional Development School/School-University Partnership model (PDS/SUP), 5
Professional Development Schools (PDS)
    action research and, 52, 61-62
    benefits of, 40
    celebrating accomplishments of, 51
    clinical instructors and, 49-50
    collaboration and, 55-56, 56-57
    early-childhood education and, 40-42, 42-43
    evolution of, 3
    goals of, 13-16, 39, 58
    governance of, 48-49
    guest teachers and, 8
    human resources and, 17

Professional Development Schools *(continued)*
    inclusive collaboration and, 18
    inquiry and, 179-80, 180-86, 186-88
    literature circles and, 79-80, 80-81
    maintenance of, 47-48, 53
    mentoring and, 83-85, 85-86, 86-89, 89-92, 92-93
    music education and, 67-68, 68-71, 72-73, 73-74, 75-76, 76-77
    goals of, 73-74
    networking and, 57-58, 59, 61-62
    non-credentialed teachers and, 4
    Open Court and, 8
    operational structure of, 17
    physical education and, 165-66, 165-66, 169-73
    Professional Development Days, 10-11
    public school-university collaboration and, 39-40
    research and evaluation of, 11-12
    service learning and, 153-54, 154-62
    standards for, 41-42, 97-98, 99-100, 100-102, 104-106, 106-109, 109-110, 110-111, 112-14, 115-18, 119-21, 121-22, 122-24, 124-25
    union concerns and, 50-51
Professional Development School Network, 128, 136, 137
Professional Development School Standards Project, 99, 102
Project Zero, 129

Regents' Principles and Guidelines for Educator Preparation, 129
Robinson, M., 72

Sandholtz, J. H., 43
Scannell, D. P., 139
Senge, P., 56
service learning, 153-54, 154-62
Sharpe, T., 166
simultaneous improvement process, 24-26
Snyder, J., 102
standards, 41, 97-98, 99-100, 100-102, 104-106, 106-109, 112-14, 115-18, 119-21, 121-22, 122-24, 124-25, 127-28
    children's learning and, 111
    field tests for, 105
    research process for, 109-110
    self-study process and, 110-111
    teacher candidates' learning and, 112
St. Bonaventure University, 165, 166
    PDS, 167-68

Stiggins, R. J., 128, 138, 140
Strategic Improvement Plans, 146
Stroble, B., 128, 140
Strosnider, R., 85, 86
SUPPORT-PE, 166
Sweeney, F., 85, 86
Sykes, G., 100, 102

Teitel, L., 100, 187
Tomlinson, C. A., 80
Tomorrow's Schools of Education, 21, 179
Tomorrow's Schools: Principles for the Design of Professional Development Schools, 165
Towson University, 181
Trachtman, R., 101

University of Nebraska-Lincoln, 166

University of Maine, 143, 144
University of North Texas, 69
university-school collaboration, 165
Urban Learning Centers, 5

Varner, M., 38
Vital Research, 13

webquests, 80, 81
Weisenbach, E. L., 128, 140
Western Kentucky University, 166
William Paterson University, 67, 68, 70, 77
Wilson, T. A., 102

Zimpher, N. L., 69